THE ART AND SCIENCE OF TEACHING:

AN INTRODUCTION TO AMERICAN EDUCATION

Timothy Reagan
The University of Maine
The University of the Free State

Terry A. Osborn
The University of South Florida

Kendall Hunt
publishing company

Cover image © Shutterstock.com

www.kendallhunt.com
Send all inquiries to:
4050 Westmark Drive
Dubuque, IA 52004-1840

Published in the United States of America

Table of Contents

Preface

The Art and Science of Teaching: An Introduction to American Education is the product of a long-standing friendship and partnership. We first met when Tim was a faculty member in the Neag School of Education at the University of Connecticut and Terry was a PhD student in Foreign Language Education there. Because of his background in foreign language education, Tim was assigned to serve as Terry's advisor, and we quickly discovered that we shared a number of interests and concerns related to public schooling and education in general, and foreign language education in particular. Tim supervised Terry's doctoral dissertation, and we published several articles together outlining what we believed to be some of the major challenges facing foreign language education in the United States. After graduating, Terry was a faculty member at Queen's College of the City University of New York before returning to join the faculty at the University of Connecticut. Working together for several years at the University of Connecticut allowed us to further explore our shared commitment to critical pedagogy in foreign language education, and this led us to co-author *The Foreign Language Educator in Society: Toward a Critical Pedagogy* in 2002, as well as to found the International Society for Language Studies. Each of us ultimately moved on to other positions. Tim became Dean of the School of Education at Roger Williams University in Bristol, Rhode Island, then the Executive Dean of the Faculty of Humanities at the University of the Witwatersrand in Johannesburg, South Africa, a CSU (Distinguished) Professor at Central Connecticut State University, and the Founding Dean of the Graduate School of Education at Nazarbayev University in Kazakhstan before finally moving to become Dean of the College of Education and Human Development at the University of Maine. Terry moved to Fordham University, where he served as department chair, and then to the University of South Florida Sarasota-Manatee, where he served first as Dean of the College of Education, and then as the Vice Chancellor of Academic and Student Affairs and the Interim Chancellor.

When Tim returned to the faculty of the University of Maine in 2019, he was asked to teach the EHD 101 course ("The Art and Science of Teaching"). He realized that while there were many introductory books for courses of this type, none really met the needs of the students at the University of Maine particularly well. In discussing this, the two of us agreed about what such a book should include and, further, agreed to begin working on a book of this sort. This book is the product of that collaboration.

Timothy Reagan
Terry A. Osborn

Acknowledgments

Over the course of our careers, both as teachers in the public schools and as faculty members at a variety of different universities in the United States and overseas, we have learned a great deal from many colleagues and students. In addition, our perspectives on public education have been further developed and changed as a result of having children ourselves, and, in Tim's case, of serving on a Board of Education. It would be impossible for us to list all of the individuals whom we really ought to thank here, but the experiences, discussions, and debates that we have had with colleagues at all of the institutions where we worked have been invaluable. Finally, Tim was teaching EHD 101 ("The Art and Science of Teaching") during the Fall 2020 semester when much of this book was written. We would especially like to thank the four Graduate Assistants who worked with him during that semester – Camden Bock, Marwa Elkelani, Danielle Gabrielli, and Martha Gladstone – for their feedback and insights about the course content and the material in this book.

In any book, there are bound to be factual errors, mistaken judgments, misleading passages, and so on, and we, of course, take full responsibility for these. In reflecting on the many mistakes that are no doubt present in this book, we remember many years ago when we were both conducting research in Istanbul, and went to the Grand Bazaar. In one of the many shops there where incredibly beautiful oriental carpets were sold, we were told that every carpet contained a deliberate flaw – put there to remind all of us that only God is perfect.

Abbreviations

AAP	American Academy of Pediatrics
AAFP	American Academy of Family Physicians
ACLU	American Civil Liberties Union
ADL	Anti-Defamation League
AYP	Annual Yearly Progress
BCE	Before the Common Era (BC)
CAEP	Council for the Accreditation of Educator Preparation
CAN	Christian Action Network
CDC	Centers for Disease Control and Prevention
CE	Common Era (AD)
CAIR	Council on American-Islamic Relations
CNN	Cable News Network
COVID-19	Coronavirus Disease 2019
ESEA	*Elementary and Secondary Education Act*
ESSA	*Every Student Succeeds Act*
IDEA	*Individuals with Disabilities Education Act*
IEP	Individualized Education Program
LDS	Latter Day Saints
LRE	Least Restrictive Environment
NAACP	National Association for the Advancement of Colored People
NAEP	National Assessment of Educational Progress
NCLB	*No Child Left Behind Act*
NDACAN	The National Data Archive on Child Abuse and Neglect
NDEA	*National Defense Education Act*
NEA	National Education Association
OCR	Office of Civil Rights
OECD	Organisation for Economic Co-operation and Development
PISA	Programme for International Student Assessment
PL	Public Law
SDF	State Defense Forces
SDGs	Sustainable Development Goals
SHAPE	Society of Health and Physical Educators
SMART	Specific, Measurable, Attainable, Realistic, Timely
STEMI	ST-Segment Elevation Myocardial Infarction
TRACON	Terminal Radar Approach Control (New York)
USSR	Union of Soviet Socialist Republics
VPDs	Vaccine-Preventable Diseases
WHO	World Health Organization
ZPD	Zone of Proximal Development

Tables

Chapter 1

The Purposes of Public Schooling

*If we do not pay for children in good schools,
then we are going to pay for them in prisons and
mental hospitals.* (Eleanor Roosevelt)

*The purpose of education ... is to create in a
person the ability to look at the world himself,
to make his own decisions.* (James A. Baldwin)

According to the U.S. Census Bureau, in 2018 total expenditure on K-12 public schooling in the United States was $720.8 billion, or about $12,600 per student (U.S. Census Bureau, 2019b). This amount, substantial though it is, does not include the costs of private schools, nor does it include the billions of dollars devoted to higher education in the country.[1] The amount per pupil also varies considerably from one state, and from one school district, to another: Utah spends $7,628 per student annually, while New York spends $24,040 per student annually (see Table 1.1).

State	Total Expenditure	Per Pupil Expenditure
Alabama	8,155,523	9,696
Alaska	2,539,488	17,726
Arizona	8,656,253	8,239
Arkansas	5,625,843	10,139
California	91,054,455	12,498
Colorado	11,561,312	10,202
Connecticut	10,851,095	20,635
Delaware	2,098,148	15,639
District of Columbia	1,547,292	22,759
Florida	29,838,546	9,346
Georgia	20,988,208	10,810
Hawaii	3,070,859	15,242
Idaho	2,410,373	7,771
Illinois	35,033,057	15,741
Indiana	11,836,660	10,262
Iowa	6,958,710	11,732
Kansas	6,907,549	11,653
Kentucky	8,580,534	11,110
Louisiana	8,079,072	11,452
Maine	2,877,061	14,145

[1] In 2016-2017, expenditures for all degree-granting postsecondary institutions (public, private and for profit, as well as two- and four-year institutions) in the United States was $584 billion (National Center for Educational Statistics, 2018a).

Maryland	14,920,717	14,762
Massachusetts	17,889,700	17,058
Michigan	18,975,838	12,345
Minnesota	13,875,489	12,975
Mississippi	4,773,606	8,935
Missouri	10,864,199	10,810
Montana	2,048,275	11,680
Nebraska	4,684,483	12,491
Nevada	5,045,173	9,417
New Hampshire	3,125,315	16,893
New Jersey	30,480,796	20,021
New Mexico	3,636,084	9,582
New York	73,368,427	24,040
North Carolina	15,153,240	9,377
North Dakota	1,841,875	13,758
Ohio	24,805,833	13,027
Oklahoma	6,267,595	8,239
Oregon	8,661,035	11,920
Pennsylvania	31,531,702	16,395
Rhode Island	2,501,593	16,121
South Carolina	10,027,593	10,856
South Dakota	1,655,222	10,073
Tennessee	10,811,478	9,544
Texas	65,202,332	9,606
Utah	5,556,089	7,628
Vermont	1,570,861	19,340
Virginia	17,367,248	12,216
Washington	18,042,261	12,995
West Virginia	3,345,139	11,334
Wisconsin	12,465,177	12,285
Wyoming	1,727,633	16,224
TOTAL	720,892,046	12,621

Table 1.1 Expenditures by State for K-12 Public Schooling, 2018 (U.S. Census Bureau, 2019a)

This is a huge investment in public education – in fact, the United States spends more per child on public schooling than virtually any other country in the world (see Table 1.2).[2] Given this expenditure, it is only reasonable to ask what we expect the public schools to accomplish. The answer to this question is not only complex and multifaceted but also helps us to understand the central role of schools in our society. In this chapter, we identify and discuss some of the many expectations that schools are called upon to meet in the United States. While many of these expectations are commonly and publicly articulated (see Abowitz, 2008; Barton & Coley, 2011; Lubienski, 2003; McDonnell & Timpane, 2000; Reimers, 2006), others are less so. As we discuss them, you should also keep in mind that the some of these expectations are more important than others, and further, that the different purposes that we expect the public schools to accomplish sometimes overlap (and, occasionally, may also be contradictory).

---

[2] The only countries that often exceed the U.S. annual expenditure on public schooling (on a per-student basis) are Luxembourg, Switzerland, Austria, and Norway.

Country	Spending Per Student (US$)	Percentage of GDP	FY
United States	12,621	5.0	2018
Austria	11,100	5.5	2015
Belgium	12,300	6.6	2015
Finland	10,100	7.1	2015
France	10,000	5.5	2015
Germany	11,000	4.8	2015
Iceland	11,600	7.7	2017
Italy	9,100	4.1	2015
Japan	10,200	3.6	2015
Netherlands	11,000	5.4	2015
Portugal	8,700	4.9	2015
South Korea	12,000	5.3	2015
Sweden	11,400	7.6	2015
United Kingdom	11,400	5.5	2015

Table 1.2 Comparison of National Spending for Public Schooling (DeGeurin, 2019)

Basic Knowledge and Skills

One of the most widely recognized functions of public education is to ensure that every member of the society is able to read, write, and do basic kinds of mathematics. Our society is a literate and numerate one, and we generally assume that all adults are able (or should be able) to function in these areas. Indeed, when we come across a person who cannot read, it is generally a major surprise. Robert Pattison has written about what has been called the "Ann Landers Fallacy" (Pattison, 1982, pp. 118-119). This "Ann Landers" fallacy is based on an account of a woman who wrote to the advice columnist Ann Landers about a terrible discovery that she had just made: her husband of many years, who had a good job and was a good provider, who was a wonderful husband, a great father to their children, and who seemed happy with his life was – *gasp!* – unable to read. Landers, sympathetically, advised the woman to discuss this openly and honestly with her spouse and help him to locate resources and services that could help him learn how to read. Now, we are certainly in favor of everyone being able to read, and we also believe that being able to do so opens many new doors for anyone. However, what is interesting here is that there is an unspoken assumption that – in spite of all of the man's stellar qualities – he is horribly diminished by being illiterate, even though there is actually no suggestion that he himself is bothered by the situation. It is important to remember, we would suggest, that although literacy and numeracy are indeed incredibly important skills in our society, and that they are arguably among the most significant skills that are taught in schools, this is a very recent development in human history. Although human beings have been using language for somewhere between 50,000 and 150,000 years, language has only been reduced to a written form for about the last 5,000 years[3] – and until the

---

[3] The Sumerians were the first civilization to develop a system of writing, using cuneiform markings on clay tablets. In addition to Sumerian, several other languages employed cuneiform as well, most notably Akkadian, Elamite, and Hittite (see Crawford, 2013).

time of the Reformation,[4] literacy in virtually every society on earth was an élite activity reserved to only a tiny percentage of the population.[5]

Although there is an assumption in the United States that all adults are able to read and write, at least at basic levels, this is also a somewhat mistaken belief. In reality, a 2003 study of functional literacy conducted by the U.S. Department of Education and the National Institute of Literacy found that 32 million adults (about 14% of the total population) were functionally illiterate, and 21% of the population read below the 5th grade level. Perhaps most depressing, about 19% of high school graduates – nearly one in five – is not functionally literate (Gaille, 2017). Although functional literacy is more complex than the measures of basic literacy used in international comparisons, and while there is no commonly accepted definition of literacy,[6] the United States nevertheless does not compare particularly well with many other developed nations with respect to its literacy rate (Burton, 2018). There are, not surprisingly, significant differences around the world in terms of national literacy rates as well as in the differences between adult male and female literacy rates, and the expansion of literacy is one of the United Nations' (2020) Sustainable Development Goals – which points out the significance of the underlying challenge (see Table 1.3).[7]

---

[4] One of the key concerns of the Protestant Reformation, which began in the 16th century, was of the importance for individual Christians to read the Scriptures on their own. This belief had two important consequences: First, it let to efforts to translate the Bible into vernacular languages, and second, it meant that *all* people – not just a tiny élite – needed to be educated so that they would be able to read (see Fishman, 2010).

[5] One interesting exception to this general rule is found among Jews, for whom there was a centuries old tradition of religious scholarship among virtually all males that required literacy in both Hebrew and Aramaic, and often in other languages for secular purposes as well (see Botticini & Eckstein, 2012).

[6] Defining literacy as most of us might in everyday conversation as "being able to read" actually begs the question: "Is that all it takes for a person to be regarded as 'literate'?" Clearly, reading is a far more complex process. The reading skills needed to complete an employment application or pass a driver's test are very different from those required to read the *New York Times*, or even this book.

[7] The 17 Sustainable Development Goals (SDGs) were adopted by the United Nations in 2015. The fourth sustainable development goal was the expansion of quality education. As the United Nations noted in 2020, "Over the past decade, major progress was made towards increasing access to education and school enrollment rates at all levels, particularly for girls. Nevertheless, *about 260 million children were still out of school* in 2018 — nearly one fifth of the global population in that age group. And more than half of all children and adolescents worldwide are *not meeting minimum proficiency standards* in reading and mathematics" (United Nations, 2020).

Country	Literacy Rate (Percentage)	Male Literacy Rate (Percentage)	Female Literacy Rate (Percentage)	Year
Afghanistan	43	55	30	2018
Argentina	99	99	99	2018
Bangladesh	74	77	71	2018
Brazil	93	93	93	2018
Chile	96	96	96	2017
China (PRC)	97	98	95	2018
Cuba	100	100	100	2012
Egypt	71	76	66	2017
Estonia	100	100	100	2011
Greece	98	99	97	2018
Haiti	62	65	58	2016
Hungary	99	99	99	2014
India	74	97	66	2018
Iran	86	90	81	2016
Iraq	86	91	80	2017
Israel	92	95	89	1983
Italy	99	99	99	2018
Latvia	100	100	100	2018
Lithuania	100	100	100	2011
Mexico	95	96	95	2018
Nigeria	62	71	53	2018
Pakistan	59	71	46	2017
Poland	99	99	98	2008
Portugal	96	97	95	2018
Russia	100	100	100	2018
South Africa	87	88	86	2017
Spain	98	99	98	2018
Turkey	96	99	93	2017
Ukraine	100	100	100	2012
WORLD	86	90	83	2018

Table 1.3 Comparative National Literacy Rates[8] (World Bank, 2018a, 2018b, 2018c)

In short, whatever else public schooling is expected to accomplish, teaching children to read, write, and do basic mathematics is clearly fundamental, not only in the United States but also around the world.

---

[8] Countries for whom data were not reported by UNESCO included Australia, Austria, Canada, Denmark, Finland, France, Germany, Iceland, Ireland, Japan, Netherlands, New Zealand, Norway, Sweden, the United Kingdom, and the United States.

As important as the basic skills of literacy and numeracy are, they are really only the foundation upon which most of an individual's education rests. In addition to acquiring basic skills, the child must also be introduced to a whole variety of different content and disciplinary knowledge. As we will discuss further in Chapter 4, when we talk about the process by which a person becomes an "educated person" (as well as what it means to be an "educated person"), we need to focus on the knowledge and skills that must be acquired by the student. There must be a breadth of knowledge that guarantees that each person is familiar with the different branches of human knowledge – that is, we all need to know some of the basics of mathematics, literature, science, history, art and music, and so on. We do not expect students in K-12 settings to become experts in any of these disciplines, of course. Such expertise only comes from intensive and in-depth study over many years. We do, though, expect all students to have a general, basic familiarity with all of the major content areas of the curriculum.

We will explore the details of the process by which students can become "educated persons," as well as the specifics of the curriculum, later in this book, but for our purposes here it is worth noting that the broad outlines of the curricula that we expect most if not all students in K-12 schools to master include such subjects as:

- English Language Arts
- Mathematics
- Health and Physical Education
- Physical and Natural Sciences
- Social Studies
- Visual and Performing Arts
- World Languages
- Career and Technical Education
- Computer Science

This list is not a randomly selected one by any means. It is drawn from an examination and comparison of a number of different state curricular guidelines and regulations, and of high school graduation requirements, from several states.[9] We do not necessarily support all of the curricular guidelines that one might discover in documents from different state departments of education, nor would we expect you to do so. Indeed, we would very much hope and expect that you can offer reasons for including or excluding not only some of the subjects on this list, but others as well. We would also point out that these subjects are intended to provide a general framework within which most schools should operate, but there may always be exceptional cases.

---

[9] Among the states whose state-mandated curricula we examined in compiling this list were Connecticut, Florida, Illinois, Maine, New York, and Ohio. The list provided in the text is broadly reflective of the curricula in most of these states generally, but not every state matches the list perfectly.

Life Skills

We recently came across a poster that said,

> Things I never learned in high school:
>
> - how to do taxes.
> - what taxes are.
> - how to vote.
> - how to write a resume/cover letter.
> - anything to do with banking.
> - how to apply for loans for college.
> - how to buy a car or house …
>
> … but thank my lucky stars, I can tell you all about Pythagorean theorems.

Although intended to be humorous, this poster makes a valuable point: One important outcome of schooling *ought* to be to provide students with the different life skills that they will need to function in society as adults. The typical example of this is that everyone should know how to balance a checkbook, but in fact (as the above poster suggests) there are many other things that we need to know about and understand to function effectively as well. To be fair, most of the things identified on this poster require skills and knowledge that actually *are* taught in the schools, but perhaps not as explicitly as some might prefer. In any case, it is clear that there is a great deal of knowledge that one needs to acquire in order to survive as an adult in *any* society, as well as a substantial skill set and a collection of appropriate dispositions, attitudes and beliefs, that will help the individual to fit into their particular society – and an important function of the school is to ensure that this knowledge and these skills are mastered.

Vocational and Career Preparation

In addition to the broad, generic life skills that everyone needs, each of us must also be prepared to earn a living. This has been true throughout human history, of course. Historically, when our society was an overwhelmingly rural and agricultural one, most Americans learned what they needed to know from their parents – boys learned the many different aspects of farming and husbandry from their fathers, and girls learned from their mothers the domestic skills that they needed to be wives and mothers and to successfully run and maintain households. In addition, small numbers of children (primarily, but not exclusively, boys) learned more specialized occupations, becoming craftsmen in carpentry, shoemaking (cordwaining), barrel making (coopering), blacksmithing, printing, and so on, largely through apprenticeships. Only a very tiny number of boys received preparation for élite professions through higher education. To be sure, a number of universities were established in colonial America quite early: Harvard in 1636, William and Mary in 1693, and Yale in 1701. While these institutions (and especially Harvard and Yale) were originally founded primarily to train religious leaders, they also provided the classical education required for young men who would go on to serve as state and national leaders in a variety of ways.

As the United States became increasingly urban and industrialized following the Civil War, the necessary skills and knowledge required of workers changed. In addition, the rising tensions between organized labor and capital created additional challenges related to the preparation of youth for jobs in industry as well as in more traditional occupations. As early as 1881, the public sector began to take more and more control of the training of future workers. In 1917, motivated to a significant extent by World War I, Congress passed the *Smith-Hughes Act*, which provided federal support for vocational education (see Hillison, 1995). By the 1920s, many urban school systems had established "apprenticeship extension courses" (which required prior work experience) and other kinds of vocational education (Wirth, 1972). The creation of vocational education programs was intended to provide an educational response to such problems as the lack of a skilled workforce, the shortage of well-trained and prepared workers in a number of significant vocations, overcrowded classrooms, and so on – but they also disproportionately targeted poor and working-class children, children from rural parts of the country, and the children of immigrants – all populations who were marginalized in one way or another (see Benavot, 1983; Violas, 1978, 1981). Thus, although vocational education of this period did provide employable skills for many students, it also functioned to reproduce social class divisions in American society by making a liberal arts education, and the possibility of a college education, difficult if not impossible for most students who were not from middle-class or upper-class backgrounds.

The *Perkins Act*, first passed by Congress in 1984, was an effort to address many of the weaknesses that were believed to exist in vocational education, and specifically to improve the overall quality of technical education in the United States. The *Perkins Act* led to the replacement of the phrase "vocational education" (which had developed negative connotations for some students) with "career and technical education," but it constituted far more than a change in nomenclature. Providing more than $1.2 billion in federal support to public schools, the *Perkins Act* was concerned with helping to prepare students to compete more effectively in the increasingly globalized economy, and focused not only on preparing students for the workplace but also for postsecondary schooling options.

The Transition to Adulthood and Entry into the Labor Market

In addition to providing future workers with both the basic and vocational skills, knowledge and dispositions that they would need to survive in the economic marketplace, the public schools serve an additional purpose related to the entry of students into the workforce. Since the early 20th century, the average student in the United States has spent longer and longer periods of time in school, beginning schooling earlier and remaining in schooling institutions longer (both secondary schools and post-secondary institutions). As Pallas (1993) has explained:

> American children throughout this century thus have spent more of their early lives in school, both through starting school at earlier ages and by extending the time spent in school. Decennial census data indicate that the median age of entering school dropped from 7.0 years in 1900 to 4.6 years in 1980 for males,

and 6.8 years in 1900 to 4.7 years in 1980 for females ... Simultaneously, the median age at leaving school of 16.7 years for males and 17.0 years for females in 1900 increased monotonically to 19.6 years for males and 19.2 years for females in 1960 and appears to have leveled off slightly since then ... This increase in the median school-leaving age reflects rapid expansion in the rates of both secondary and postsecondary enrollment through most of this century. (p. 415)

This trend reflects several important social and economic changes in our society: the relative importance of the family in preparing young people for adulthood, the increasing and changing requirements of the workforce, and the need to be able to predict and control the entry of new workers into the workforce more effectively (see Pallas, 1993; Violas, 1978).

Political Socialization

All schooling is profoundly political and ideological in nature. This is not only the case in the United States but is also true for every other country. To say that schooling is political is not necessarily a bad thing; many aspects of political socialization are not only essential in a society but, in fact, are highly desirable. The South African liberation leader and first democratically elected President Nelson Mandela once argued, "Education is the most powerful weapon which you can use to change the world." Schooling can function to promote democracy, social justice, tolerance, and equity, and these are all positive outcomes of an educational system. At the same time, though, schools can (and often do) accomplish just the opposite – they can be profoundly anti-democratic, oppressive, racist, and reactionary institutions that perpetuate social injustices of all sorts. Schools – often very efficient schools – operated in Nazi Germany, Stalinist Russia, and apartheid South Africa, after all.

In contemporary society, children are prepared for their future lives as citizens in public schools. Schools in the United States engage in political socialization in many different ways. Perhaps most obviously, children and young people study American history and government, so that they learn about the "official" version of our history and the formal structures and organization of our government.[10] In addition, they are not only exposed to, but are immersed in, belief systems supported by values, attitudes, and claims that present our society in a particular light. They also learn what kinds of information and beliefs should be accepted as credible, and which sorts should be rejected. All of these things are taught and reinforced not only in formal, direct teaching, but also indirectly in textbooks, songs, stories, poems, folk

---

[10] History is never a completely objective and neutral recounting of the past. By its very nature, it involves making judgments about what (and who) is important and significant, how particular events and individuals should be understood, and so on. The way we view and understand history also changes over time. Examples of this would include the way in which we now understand the colonization of the Americas, the enslavement of millions of people in the United States, the internment of Japanese Americans during the Second World War, and so on. For the implications of these changes on public schooling in general, and for the teaching of American history in particular, see Bigelow (2008). For specific historical debates about national standards in the teaching of history and social studies, see Nash, Crabtree and Dunn (2000).

stories and legends, and in many other common school practices, such as reciting the "Pledge of Allegiance."[11] They are also, of course, reinforced outside of the school – in the media, in religious institutions, and at home.

Social Control

One important outcome of political socialization is for students to learn to accept the political, and economic structures of their society as legitimate. When such acceptance is absent or missing, the social, political and economic structures of the society are resting on a very weak foundation – and in such cases, revolutions and other kinds of political, economic and social upheavals often occur that can result in profound changes in the institutional structures of the society. The French Revolution, which witnessed the collapse of the *ancient régime*, was one such example, as were the Russian Revolution in 1917, the collapse of the Soviet Union in 1991, and the end of apartheid in South Africa in the early 1990s.

Preventing the delegitimation of the institutions and structures of a society is, understandably, one of the more important functions of public education. It has long been recognized that schools are profoundly conservative places that are dedicated in many ways to the maintenance of the status quo. This was one of the explicit justifications for the development of the Common Schools in the United States in the 19th century. As Horace Mann, the "father" of the Common School Movement, argued:

> Finally, in regard to those who possess the largest shares in the stock of worldly goods, could there, in your opinion, be any police so vigilant and effective, for the protections of all the rights of person, property and character, as such a sound and comprehensive education and training, as our system of Common Schools could be made to impart; and would not the payment of a sufficient tax to make such education and training universal, be the cheapest means of self-protection and insurance?

Teaching students to accept the legitimacy of the political and ideological order in which they live remains one of the key functions of the public school, although perhaps neither as publicly recognized nor as openly confessed as by Horace Mann.

Socialization and Acculturation

Human beings live in societies, and are social creatures. With very few (extreme) exceptions, we live with, interact, and rely upon other human beings in almost every part of our lives. Socialization refers to the process by which the individual internalizes the norms of their society. It is a lifelong process and takes place in virtually every sphere and domain of the person's life, and the school plays a key role in this process. Socialization requires social

---

[11] Sometimes songs, texts, slogans, and so on are reinterpreted to convey quite different messages from those that they were originally created to convey. One excellent example of this phenomenon is the song "This Land is Your Land," written by Woody Guthrie in 1940, which was originally a very powerful protest song.

experiences (i.e., interactions with other human beings), and is essential to the development and even survival of the person. Learning how to interact with others – learning what is normal and appropriate, and what is not -- is a necessary part of child development (see Horgan, Taylor, Bloom, & Winter, 2017; Xiao, 1999; Kochanska, Boldt, & Goffin, 2019; Roopnarine & Carter, 1992).

Each of us is socialized into our own culture and society. Some of us, however, must also learn to live and work in a different culture and society than the one in which we initially belonged. This process, called acculturation, can refer to members of a minority group adapting to function in the dominant culture and society or can refer to someone moving from one society to another. Acculturation involves not only cultural changes, but also social, psychological, and often linguistic ones (see Berry, 2003, 2008; Phinney, 2003). Included in acculturation may be tensions with respect to attitudes and responses to different social institutions, beliefs and attitudes about health and health care, ideas about foods and nutrition, religious beliefs and practices, practices relating to clothing and attire, and many other things, which we will discuss in detail in Chapter 7. In the context of public schools, while socialization impacts every child, acculturation is important primarily for some students – but often these students are among the most marginalized ones in the school.

In recent years, immigration, which has always been an issue of tension in American history, has again become a point of considerable controversy in the United States. It is worth noting, we would suggest, that resistance to immigration, as well as the openness to immigration, is nothing new, and has always been a characteristic of the American ambivalence about the arrival of outsiders. Often, this ambivalence has been motivated by racism,[12] fears of being overwhelmed by groups who are "different" from the self-image of the dominant majority of Americans, and concerns about the economic impact of immigration. One powerful example of how these different concerns sometimes come together can be seen in the case of the growing *latinx* population in the United States. Today, Spanish is the second most commonly language spoken in the United States, and there are over 50 million native speakers of Spanish in the country. What is less recognized is that the United States is also the second largest Spanish-speaking country in the world, following only Mexico in terms of the total number of Spanish speakers. More to the point, in many parts of the United States, the presence of Spanish speakers predates the arrival of English speakers by a considerable period of time. Although there are large numbers of Spanish-speaking immigrants arriving in the United States, there are also substantial numbers of citizens born in the United States who are native speakers of Spanish – not to mention the fact that Puerto Rico, a legal part of the United States, is Spanish-speaking. However, concerns about the presence of the Spanish language (and the threat that it is sometimes suggested that it poses to English) are overstated, at the very least. In fact, in the Spanish-speaking population we see for the most part the same shift to monolingual English dominance in about three generations that we have seen historically within other groups. The idea that the English language is somehow in danger in the United States is, to put it mildly, almost certainly ludicrous. This does not mean that there are not

---

[12] One clear example of such racism is the *Chinese Exclusion Act* of 1882, the first effort to legally restrict immigration to the United States, which suspended Chinese immigration for a decade and declared Chinese immigrants ineligible for naturalization.

substantial, and in some parts of the country growing, numbers of students in the public schools who arrive at school unable to speak English. For these students, the public schools offer various kinds of English as a Second Language (ESL) programs and bilingual education programs. It is important to note that while there are dual language programs that seek to develop the child's bilingual abilities (in their native language and in English), bilingual education programs in the United States are for the most part transitional in nature, which means that their primary goal is to assist the student to reach the point where they can fully function in a "regular," English-medium classroom.[13]

Religious Socialization

In the First Amendment to the U.S. *Constitution*, there is a clear, unequivocal guarantee of freedom of religion. This commitment to the freedom of religion was inspired by the experiences and knowledge of the nation's founders with respect to religious oppression and domination in Europe, and was intended to ensure that no person in this country would be persecuted because of their religious faith. The First Amendment actually has two clauses: the Establishment Clause and the Free Exercise Clause. The former, basically, forbids the government from establishing an official religion for the country, while the latter guarantees that any person may practice their religion as they wish.[14] Although the phrase "a wall of separation between Church and State" does not actually appear in the First Amendment, this was how Thomas Jefferson summarized its meaning with respect to religious freedom, and it is how this part of the First Amendment is commonly described.

Regardless of the constitutional status of religion in the United States, however, *normatively* the society remains very much a (nominally) Christian one, and children from non-Christian religious backgrounds are all too often placed in positions of being seen as "outsiders" or even as somehow "un-American." As Dhaya Ramarajan and Marcella Runell (2007) have argued,

> Despite the significance of religion in public life in the USA, American school curricula generally fail to address religious pluralism. This omission is creating problems that are compounded by increasing Islamophobia … Taken together, these trends call out for a response -- educational programming that effectively promotes interreligious respect and inclusion, notwithstanding the complicated and difficult history of religion in public schools. (p. 87)

---

[13] There is an especially odd use of the term "bilingual" in U.S. public schools much of the time. When a child comes to school unable to speak English, they are considered a "bilingual student" and may be placed in a "bilingual education program." Once the child is able to function in English and is truly bilingual, however, they are no longer labelled "bilingual" and are considered to be ready for placement in a monolingual, "regular" English language classroom.

[14] There are, of course, some limits on religious freedom. One may, for example, *believe* that the gods wish for you to sacrifice newborn children (there have been societies and religions in which such beliefs were accepted, after all). However, in our society you are not free to *act* upon such beliefs; the Supreme Court has ruled that the federal government may limit religious freedom when it has a "compelling interest" to do so in order to protect the common good and limit people's ability to harm others.

The "complicated and difficult history of religion in public schools" to which Ramarajan and Runell refer is indeed complex, and the targets of discrimination have shifted throughout the nation's history. The formula for understanding what is legitimate with respect to educational efforts concerned with religion is typically presented as "teaching *about* religion" is acceptable, while "teaching religion" is not. Public schools, basically, are not to engage in proselytizing on behalf of any religion, but may legitimately teach students about the history of different religions, the beliefs and practices associated with different religions, and to engage in the study of religious texts as literary texts. As Supreme Court Justice Tom Clark wrote in the 1963 opinion in *Abington vs. Schempp*,

> It might well be said that one's education is not complete without a study of comparative religion or the history of religion and its relationship to the advancement of civilization. It certainly may be said that the Bible is worthy of study for its literary and historic qualities. Nothing we have said here indicates that such study of the Bible or of religion, when presented objectively as part of a secular program of education, may not be affected consistently with the First Amendment.

The place of religion in public schools in the United States remains both a complex and controversial one that has been the subject of numerous Supreme Court decisions, and there continue to be requests for judicial involvement and clarification to resolve conflicts (see DelFattore, 2004; Douglass, 2002; Passe & Willox, 2009).

Health Care

The idea that among the functions of the public schools is the provision of health care to children and young adults may strike one as somewhat strange, but providing for issues of health and wellness is an important aspect of contemporary schooling. Historically, both the addition of homeroom periods and the employment of school nurses were part of the recognition of the need for the public schools to concern themselves to some degree with issues of health. Today, this is accomplished in a number of different ways, some directly and some indirectly. For example, in order to be admitted to a public school, states routinely require proof that a child has been vaccinated. The Centers for Disease Control and Prevention (CDC) recommends that all children between the ages of four and six receive five vaccinations, including those for:

- Smallpox.
- Diphtheria, tetanus, and pertussis.
- Measles, mumps, and rubella.
- Polio.
- Flu.

All of these illnesses – which are known as vaccine-preventable diseases (VPDs) -- are extremely serious for children, and indeed all are potentially fatal. Each state has its own specific requirements for vaccinations for day care and school entry, and for the most part these requirements apply to both public and non-public facilities. All states allow medical exemptions, and many also allow exemptions for religious and/or philosophical reasons.

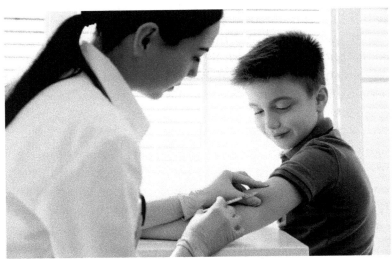

Boy Being Inoculated
© New Africa/Shutterstock.com

It is worth noting here that in recent years there has been an increase in both the numbers and percentages of parents electing to not have their children vaccinated. A recent Gallup Survey compared support for parents vaccinating their children in 2001 and 2019. In 2001, about 94% said that it was extremely important or very important for children to be vaccinated; by 2019, that percentage was only 84% (Reinhart, 2020). This is true in spite of the overwhelming medical evidence supporting the value of vaccinations – and the evidence *is* overwhelming. To be sure, there are also risks involved in vaccinations, as there are risks in any medical treatment or procedure, but these risks are extremely rare. In addition, there has been a great deal of misinformation spread through alternative and social media, and even by some individuals with legitimate credentials, suggesting that the risks are greater than they actually are. One common theme of such misinformation campaigns has been the claim that vaccinations increase the risk of autism. Although anything is possible, we would stress here that the near-universal medical view is that this is simply not the case – a perspective promulgated not only by the CDC but also by the American Academy of Family Physicians (AAFP) and the American Academy of Pediatrics (AAP). The reason that such resistance matters is that the objective of a vaccination program, including how and why it is effective, lies in the fact that it creates what is called "herd immunity." In order for vaccinations to prevent a major spread of an infectious disease, it is not necessary for every single person in the community to get vaccinated. It is, rather, only necessary that a certain percentage of the population be immune to the disease. That percentage is typically estimated to be between 85% and 95% of the total population (which constitutes the "herd immunity"). However, once "herd immunity" is lost, then all of the individuals not vaccinated become vulnerable to the illness, and there is the very real risk of a major outbreak of the disease.

Another way in which the health care needs of students in public schools are addressed is in the requirement that every child have a medical examination at selected points in their school career. Although such examinations sometimes take place under the auspices of the school, they are often simply required as prerequisites for entry to public schools. Depending on the state, the medical provider is required to complete appropriate documentation on the child's physical condition. In some states, dental and vision examinations are also required or provided.

The public schools also provide direct instruction addressing issues of health and healthy lifestyles. The *National Health Education Standards*, which were developed by the Joint Committee on National Health Education Standards, were first promulgated in 1995 and have been revised and updated since then. The Joint Committee, supported by the American Cancer Society, included representatives from the American Public Health Association, the American School Health Association, and SHAPE America (the Society of Health and Physical Educators). The *National Health Education Standards* provide indications of what all students should know at different grade levels (grades 2, 5, 8, and 12) to promote personal, family, and community health (CDC, 2019a). There are eight standards:

Standard 1	Students will comprehend concepts related to health promotion and disease prevention to enhance health.
Standard 2	Students will analyze the influence of family, peers, culture, media, technology, and other factors on health behaviors.
Standard 3	Students will demonstrate the ability to access valid information, products, and services to enhance health.
Standard 4	Students will demonstrate the ability to use interpersonal communication skills to enhance health and avoid or reduce health risks.
Standard 5	Students will demonstrate the ability to use decision-making skills to enhance health.
Standard 6	Students will demonstrate the ability to use goal-setting skills to enhance health.
Standard 7	Students will demonstrate the ability to practice health-enhancing behaviors and avoid or reduce health risks.
Standard 8	Students will demonstrate the ability to advocate for personal, family, and community health. (Joint Committee on National Health Standards, 2007)

The specific content of the health education curriculum, as recommended by the CDC, should include the following topics:

- Promoting an alcohol and other drug-free lifestyle (preventing alcohol and other drug use).
- Promoting healthy eating and nutrition.
- Promoting mental and emotional health.
- Promoting personal health and wellness.
- Promoting safety and injury prevention.
- Promoting sexual health.
- Promoting a tobacco-free lifestyle (preventing tobacco use).
- Preventing violence and intentional injury.

Most of these topics are relatively uncontroversial; there are not too many parents or other adults in our society who would advocate encouraging children to smoke, drink alcohol, or use drugs. The exception, of course, occurs when we talk about "promoting sexual health." To be sure, virtually everyone is in favor of "promoting sexual health" – but what this actually means in terms of the curriculum is highly debatable and contentious. There are significant policy debates about the relative roles and responsibilities of the schools and the parents in teaching children about sexual matters. Among the more controversial aspects of education about sexual health are appropriate and inappropriate behaviors, sexual orientation and identity, recognizing and addressing abusive relationships, and so on – all matters that can be extremely difficult to discuss. What is certain, however, is that whatever the role of the school is in teaching about sexual health, it cannot be the only source of such information for students. As the Mayo Clinic staff have stressed in their advice to parents, "Sex education is offered in many schools, but don't count on classroom instruction alone. Sex education needs to happen at home, too" (Mayo Clinic Staff, 2017).

Associated with the goal of promoting a healthy lifestyle generally, in almost every state in the United States physical education classes in the public schools are required. As the CDC (2020) notes,

> Physical education is the foundation of a Comprehensive School Physical Activity Program. It is an academic subject characterized by a planned, sequential K–12 curriculum … that is based on the national standards for physical education. Physical education provides cognitive content and instruction designed to develop motor skills, knowledge, and behaviors for physical activity and physical fitness. Supporting schools to establish physical education daily can provide students with the ability and confidence to be physically active for a lifetime.
>
> There are many benefits of physical education in schools. When students get physical education, they can:
>
> - Increase their level of physical activity.
> - Improve their grades and standardized test scores.
> - Stay on-task in the classroom.
>
> Increased time spent in physical education does not negatively affect students' academic achievement.

In fact, physical education has been shown to positively impact student learning.

Finally, one of the greatest health challenges faced by children in the United States (and, indeed, around the world) is the dramatic increase in the rate of childhood obesity, which the World Health Organization (WHO) has called "one of the most serious public health challenges of the 21st century" (World Health Organization, 2016). Although there are somewhat different definitions of what constitutes "overweight" and "obesity" in children, regardless of the definition that one uses, the rate of childhood obesity has been rising significantly over the past three decades. The rate of childhood obesity in the United States has tripled during this period, and at present roughly one out of six children is obese, and one out of three children is overweight or obese (Ogden, Carroll, Kit, & Flegal, 2012). This is profoundly important – as the Harvard T. H. Chan School of Public Health (2012) has noted:

> Obesity can harm nearly every system in a child's body -- heart and lungs, muscles and bones, kidneys and digestive tract, as well as the hormones that control blood sugar and puberty -- and can also take a heavy social and emotional toll. What's worse, youth who are overweight or obese have substantially higher odds of remaining overweight or obese into adulthood, increasing their risk of disease and disability later in life.

Although not a *purpose* of public schooling, it is important to note here the related issues of bullying and school violence. These are significant problems – every child has a right to learn in a physically and psychologically safe environment. School violence includes such behaviors as bullying, fighting, weapons use, cyberbullying, and gang violence. The CDC's 2019 *Youth Risk Behavior Survey* (YRBS) (2019c) found the following:

- Nearly 9% of high school students had been in a physical fight on school property one or more times during the 12 months before the survey.
- About 6% of students had been threatened or injured with a weapon (for example, a gun, knife, or club) on school property one or more times during the 12 months before the survey.
- About 7% of students had not gone to school at least one day during the 30 days before the survey because they felt they would be unsafe at school or on their way to or from school.

Stop Bullying
© Suzanne Tucker/Shutterstock.com

School violence in general, and bullying in particular, actually involves a triad of participants: the bully, the victim, and onlookers. Onlookers play a key role in making bullying possible, and are a central feature in preventing such behavior and ensuring safe school environments. Bullying, and school violence, can be prevented, and there is an extensive body of research about how to go about doing so (see Olweus, 1988, 2003; Orpinas & Horne, 2006; Smokowski & Kopasz, 2005). It is important to understand that bullying and related behaviors are not simply individual or singular phenomena – they are part of the ecology of a school.

The most extreme instances of school violence are school shootings. Because there are different definitions of what counts as a "school shooting," it is not always easy to provide completely accurate comparisons of the situation in the United States and that found in other countries. However, even taking this challenge into account, a CNN study in 2018 painted a frightening picture. During the period January 1, 2009 to May 21, 2018, there were a total of 288 school shootings in the United States, although not all of these resulted in fatalities. This number was compared with the number of school shooting incidents in several other countries in the CNN study (see Figure 1.4).

Country	School Shooting Incidents
United States	288
Mexico	8
South Africa	6
India	5
Pakistan	4
Nigeria	3
Afghanistan	2
France	2
Canada	2
Brazil	1
Greece	1
China	1
Kenya	1
Azerbaijan	1
Germany	1
Russia	1
Estonia	1
Turkey	1
Hungary	1

Figure 1.4 Number of School Shootings, 2009-2018. (Grabow & Rose, 2018).

The CNN study was flawed in a number of ways; it did not take the relative size of the populations of different countries into account, for instance; nor did it include some Central American countries that have extremely high rates of firearms-related homicides. Nevertheless, the overall picture is a devastating one. There is not a simple set of causes for this situation; the U.S. Department of Homeland Security notes, "There is not a 'profile' of a school shooter --

instead the students who carried out the attacks differed from one another in numerous ways" (U.S. Department of Homeland Security, n.d.). The students who carry out school shootings do so for many reasons, and in fact more than half have multiple reasons. Among the more common reasons identified have been:

- 75% felt bullied, persecuted or threatened by others.
- 61% were motived by a desire for revenge.
- 34% were motivated by an attempt to solve a problem.
- 27% were motivated by suicide or desperation.
- 24% were motivated by desire for attention or recognition (U.S. Department of Homeland Security, n.d.)

If there is not a "profile" of school shooters, though, there are some common characteristics that describe most of them. In a very thorough study of school shooters, the U.S. Secret Service found that while there is definitely not a single profile of such students, they are more likely to be:

- Male.
- Caucasian.
- Withdrawn.
- Isolated from or rejected by peers.
- Living in a rural community.
- Have easy access to weapons.
- Have been bullied (or have become a bully).
- From a troubled home.

School Resource Officer
© Kate Way/Shutterstock.com

Although informative, this list does not either explain or help us to predict when and where school shootings might occur, though it does suggest some things that a school can do to help reduce the risk of a school shooting.

Mandated Reporting

Indirectly connected to health care concerns is the requirement that teachers and others in public schools serve as "mandated reporters" for suspected physical or sexual abuse. Being a mandated reporter means that one is *required by law* to report any cases or suspected cases of abuse or neglect to legal authorities. Educators are not the only mandatory reporters in society; others with the same legal obligations include physicians, nurses, pharmacists, dentists, therapists and other mental health professionals, police officers, clergy, social workers, and so on – basically, anyone in a profession in which they are likely to come into contact with children are likely required to report abuse and neglect. As Vicki Polin (2007) has argued, "When one suspects a child is at risk of being abused or neglected, morally we are all mandated reporters." It is important to understand several points with respect to one's obligations as a mandated reporter. First, you have no legal choice about making a report if you know about or suspect child abuse or neglect – if you do not do so, you are in violation of the law. Second, your obligation is to report the case to the legal authorities for further investigation and action. It is *not* your job as a teacher to attempt to investigate such a matter, nor should you attempt to do so. Finally, firm or definitive knowledge of abuse is not required for making a report, only reasonable suspicion. Many states even shield mandated reporters who make a report in good faith from civil or criminal penalties.

Child abuse is a real and very serious problem. The National Data Archive on Child Abuse and Neglect (NDACAN) documented about 678,000 victims of child abuse and neglect in the United States in 2018, roughly 9.2 victims per 1,000 children in the general population; furthermore, the victimization rate was higher for girls than for boys (with a victimization rate of 9.6 per 1,000 for girls, and 8.7 per 1,000 for boys; U.S. Department of Health and Human Services, 2018). There are several different types of abuse that need to be reported: physical abuse, neglect, sexual abuse, and some forms of emotional or psychological abuse. Examples of situations in which you should report suspected abuse include the following:

- If a child tells you that they have been harmed by someone.
- If you see marks that do not appear to be from developmentally appropriate behavior.
- If a child has not received appropriate medical care for an injury.
- If a child appears to be undernourished, is dressed inappropriately for the weather, or is young and has been left alone.

Educators, incidentally, play a key role in identifying cases of child abuse and neglect: Educational professionals are responsible for 20.5% of the referrals, while legal and law enforcement personnel are responsible for 18.7% and social services personnel for 10.7% (U.S. Department of Health and Human Services, 2018).

Providing Nutrition

We have already mentioned that teaching children about nutrition is an important component of our broader efforts to promote healthy lifestyles. Issues of nutrition in the public schools are also addressed in a more direct manner: We provide free or reduced cost meals to millions of children. Through the U.S. Department of Agriculture's Food and Nutrition Service, the United States supports not only the National School Lunch Program, but also the School Breakfast Program, School Milk Program, Child and Adult Care Food Program, Summer Food Service Program, Team Nutrition, and Community Food Systems. The importance of these programs can be seen in the numbers of children served: The National School Lunch Program alone provided meals for 30.4 million children in 2016, while the School Breakfast Program served 14.6 million children in the same year. The CDC has pointed out that the research suggests that "students who participate in the school meal programs consume more milk, fruits, and vegetables during mealtimes and have better intake of certain nutrients, such as calcium and fiber" than do students who do not participate in school meal programs (CDC, 2019b). It is also important to note that for many children in the public schools, the breakfast program is a key factor in their academic success – having eaten breakfast is positively correlated with better school attendance rates, fewer missed days of school, and better test scores (CDC, 2019b).

Children in School Cafeteria
© Monkey Business Images/Shuterstock.com

Childcare

The COVID-19 crisis, which arrived in the United States in December 2019, resulted in changes to virtually every aspect of American's daily lives. In addition to the millions of people who had the virus, and the hundreds of thousands of deaths associated with COVID-19, all but essential businesses and workplaces closed, travel was restricted, and quarantines and curfews were imposed. Across the country, public schools and universities switched from face-to-face approaches to instruction to different kinds of remote, online and hybrid teaching and learning. As the country began to open up once again, and as Americans moved to restart the economy, a common challenge around the nation was that of deciding whether the schools would open in the fall as parents needed to return to work. There was never any real debate about *whether* the public schools should reopen; the debate – and it was a vociferous one – was about *when*, *how*, and *under what conditions* they should do so. We do not want to address this particular policy issue here; hopefully, by the time that you are reading this, our responses to COVID-19 will be of primarily historical interest. What we believe is important for our purposes here is for you to understand the argument that was commonly employed in favor of reopening the schools as quickly as possible. This argument was summarized by Rep. Kevin McCarthy, the Minority Leader in the U.S. House of Representatives, who asserted that "We now see a looming crisis for schools and childcare. If it's left unaddressed, *it will exacerbate the economic crisis caused by the pandemic by preventing parents across the country from returning to work*, and continue to widen the socioeconomic gap" (2020, emphasis added). Rep. McCarthy's point – and a position shared by many, many others across the political spectrum -- reminds us of one of the arguably most important purposes of public schooling in the United States. Although as teachers we may resent being compared to babysitters and "just" day care providers, we *do* need to recognize that the public schools provide millions of children with safe, secure, and healthy places to spend large amounts of time each and every weekday for most of the year – leaving their parents free to work and engage in other activities.

The Creation of Employment Opportunities

Schools serve a number of different constituencies: students, parents, and the society as a whole. They also serve the needs of those whom they employ, either directly or indirectly. We began this chapter by noting that in 2018, the United States spent some $720.8 billion to support K-12 schooling. This money is a huge contribution to the local, state, and national economies. A large percentage of school funding is devoted to salaries and benefits for teachers, administrators, and other staff, but it also goes to cover transportation costs, physical plant operations and maintenance, instructional technology equipment and services, the cost of textbooks and other instructional materials, food services, and so on. We would be remiss if we did not pay attention to such significant social spending, and the impact such expenditures inevitably have on the local, state, and national economies.

One common criticism of public schooling in many places has been its cost, and, most specifically, teacher salaries. Putting aside the adage, attributed to Derek Bok, that "if you think education is expensive, try ignorance," it is worth considering such objections and taking them seriously. During the 2017-2018 school year, there were about 3.3 million full- and part-time teachers employed in K-12 schools, earning an average salary of $59,700. Almost 97% of these teachers had bachelor's degrees, and almost 60% had either master's degrees or post-master's degrees (National Center for Educational Statistics, 2018b). Teacher salaries vary both based on number of years of experience, as indicated in Table 1.5, and by state, as indicated in Table 1.6. The average salary in the United States for a person with a bachelor's degree is $59,124, while it is $69,732 for those with master's degrees (Josephson, 2018).

Years of Experience	Average Salary
1	40,540
2-4	41,480
5-9	47,300
10-14	54,860
15-19	58,880
20-24	60,930
25-29	63,780
30+	64,820

Table 1.5 U.S. Teacher Salaries by Years of Experience (Caffee, 2019)

Teachers Protesting
© SoupAhDopeVisuals/Shutterstock.com

State	Average Starting Salary	Average Salary
Alabama	38,477	48,868
Alaska	46,785	68,138
Arizona	34,068	47,403
Arkansas	33,973	48,616
California	44,782	78,711
Colorado	32,980	46,506
Connecticut	45,280	72,561
Delaware	41,415	60,214
District of Columbia	51,359	76,131
Florida	37,405	49,407
Georgia	34,872	54,602
Hawaii	45,963	57,674
Idaho	33,743	47,504

Illinois	38,820	61,602
Indiana	35,241	50,554
Iowa	35,766	55,443
Kansas	34,883	47,984
Kentucky	36,494	52,339
Louisiana	40,128	50,000
Maine	33,875	51,077
Maryland	44,675	66,961
Massachusetts	44,726	77,804
Michigan	36,234	62,200
Minnesota	37,644	57,346
Mississippi	34,780	42,925
Missouri	31,842	48,293
Montana	30,036	51,422
Nebraska	33,854	52,338
Nevada	37,973	57,376
New Hampshire	36,845	57,253
New Jersey	51,179	69,623
New Mexico	34,544	47,500
New York	44,935	79,637
North Carolina	37,514	49,837
North Dakota	38,032	51,618
Ohio	35,249	57,000
Oklahoma	31,919	45,245
Oregon	35,534	61,631
Pennsylvania	44,144	65,863
Rhode Island	41,481	66,477
South Carolina	33,057	48,598
South Dakota	37,419	42,668
Tennessee	36,402	48,456
Texas	40,725	52,575
Utah	35,722	47,244
Vermont	38,483	60,187
Virginia	39,398	51,049
Washington	40,426	54,147
West Virginia	33,684	45,701
Wisconsin	36,983	54,998
Wyoming	45,207	58,650

Table 1.6 Average Teacher Salaries by State (Caffee, 2019)

There are, we would suggest, two conclusions that can be drawn from this data: First, one very important outcome of public schooling in our society is the amount of money put back into the economy, primarily but not exclusively through salaries (and especially teacher salaries). This is not an *educational* benefit of schooling, of course, but it is an extremely important social and economic benefit that nevertheless needs to be taken into account.[15] Second, in spite of the frequent claims that teachers and other educators are overpaid, the evidence does not appear to support such a conclusion. Indeed, we are reminded here of an anonymously authored commentary written in response to the claim that teachers are overpaid precisely because they are little more than babysitters. Although obviously written tongue-in-cheek, there is an element of truth in this commentary:

> Teachers' hefty salaries are driving up taxes, and they only work 9 or 10 months a year. It's time we put things in perspective and pay them for what they do – babysit. We can get that for less than minimum wage.
>
> That's right. Let's give them $3 an hour and only the hours they worked; not any of that silly planning time, or any time they spend before or after school. That would be $19.50 a day (7:45 am to 3:00 pm with 45 minutes off for lunch and planning – that equals 6½ hours).
>
> Each parent should pay $19.50 a day for these teachers to baby-sit their children. Now how many students do they teach in a day … maybe 30? So that's $19.50 x 30 = $585.00 a day.
>
> However, remember they only work 180 days a year. I am not going to pay them for any vacations.
>
> Let's see …that's $585 x 180 = $105,300 per year …
>
> What about those special education teachers and the ones with master's degrees? Well, we could pay them minimum wage ($7.75), and just to be fair, round it off to $8.00 an hour. That would be $8 x 6½ hours x 30 children x 180 days = $280,800 per year.
>
> Wait a minute — there's something wrong here. There sure is. The average teacher's salary (nationwide) is $50,000. $50,000/180 days = $277.77/per day/30 students = $9.25/6.5 hours = $1.42 per hour per student – a very inexpensive baby-sitter and they even *educate* your kids!)
>
> *What a deal!*

In this chapter, we have identified and discussed a number of important purposes that are served by the public schools in American society. The list is by no means exhaustive, nor are all of the purposes listed here of equal importance. Furthermore, it is clear that many of these purposes overlap, while some may even contradict others. Finally, perhaps among the most significant questions that needs to be asked is, what does the U.S. population as a whole

---

[15] School professionals are, however, typically required to engage in continuing education, often at their own expense. This continuing education often leads to an advanced degree, but is widely seen, as in the case of other licensed professionals, as key in keeping the individual's skills up to date.

believe the key purposes of public schooling should be? In response to this question, there is actually a fairly clear response. In its 48th annual poll, conducted in 2016, the *Phi Delta Kappan* found that:

> Americans don't agree on the most basic question about the very purpose of a public school education. Is it to prepare students for work? To prepare them for citizenship? Or to prepare them academically? Less than half (45%) of adult Americans say preparing students academically is the main goal of a public school education, and just one-third feel that way strongly. Other Americans split between saying the main purpose of public schools is to prepare students for work (25%) and for citizenship (26%).

As a future citizen, and perhaps as a future educator, it is important for you to determine for yourself for what you believe the actual purposes served by public schools in our society are, and what purposes the public schools ought to serve. We hope that this chapter has provided you with some of the necessary background and understanding to begin to answer these questions.

Questions for Reflection and Discussion

1. In this chapter, a number of purposes that public schooling serves in our society are identified. Are there any additional purposes that you can think of? Once you have a fairly complete list of the purposes of schooling, try to rank them in order of importance, from the most essential to the least important. What can you learn from this activity?

2. Some writers have suggested that the purpose of the public schools is to reproduce the social, economic and political status quo in society, while others believe that it is essential for the schools to serve as agents of social change. Which do you believe? Why?

3. What kinds of "general knowledge" do you believe that the schools ought to provide for all students? Are there some subjects that should be included as "general knowledge" that some but not all students should study? If you believe so, what are these subjects? What reasons would you offer for this?

4. To what extent do the public schools mirror or reflect the existing society? To what extent do they attempt to promote an image and model of a different (presumably preferred) society? What examples can you provide of each?

5. Is there a difference between "political socialization" and "indoctrination"? If so, how would explain this difference? In American public schools, do you believe that we engage in "political socialization," in "indoctrination," or in both?

References

Abowitz, K. (2008). On the public and civic purposes of education. *Educational Theory, 58*(3), 357-376.

Barton, P., & Coley, R. (2011). *The mission of the high school: A new consensus of the purposes of public education?* Princeton, NJ: Policy Information Center, Educational Testing Service.

Benavot, A. (1983). The rise and decline of vocational education. *Sociology of Education, 56*(2), 63-76.

Berry, J. (2003). *Conceptual approaches to acculturation.* In K. Chun, P. Organista, & G. Marín (Eds.), *Acculturation: Advances in theory, measurement, and applied research* (pp. 17–37). Washington, DC: American Psychological Association.

Berry, J. (2008). Globalisation and acculturation. *International Journal of Intercultural Relations, 32*(4), 328-336.

Bigelow, B. (2008). *A people's history for the classroom.* Milwaukee, WI: Rethinking Schools.

Botticini, M., & Eckstein, Z. (2012). *The chosen few: How education shaped Jewish history, 70-1492.* Princeton, NJ: Princeton University Press.

Burton, J. (2018, September 14). List of countries by literacy rate. *Society.* Retrieved from https://www.worldatlas.com/articles/the-highest-literacy-rates-in-the-world.html.

Caffee, A. (2019, May 8). Teacher salaries in America. *Niche.* Retrieved from https://www.niche.com/blog/teacher-salaries-in-america/.

Centers for Disease Control and Prevention (CDC). (2019a). *CDC Healthy Schools: National Health Education Standards.* Retrieved from https://www.cdc.gov/healthyschools/sher/standards/index.htm.

Centers for Disease Control and Prevention (CDC). (2019b). *CDC Healthy Schools: School meals.* Retrieved from https://www.cdc.gov/healthyschools/npao/schoolmeals.htm.

Centers for Disease Control and Prevention (CDC). (2019c). Preventing school violence. Retrieved from https://www.cdc.gov/violenceprevention/youthviolence/schoolviolence/fastfact.html.

Centers for Disease Control and Prevention (CDC). (2020, April 21). *CDC Healthy Schools: Physical education.* Retrieved from https://www.cdc.gov/healthyschools/physicalactivity/physical-education.htm.

Crawford, H. (Ed.). (2013). *The Sumerian world.* New York, NY: Routledge.

DeGeurin, M. (2019, August 22). The U.S. spends more on education than any other country, but students lag behind academically. Here's how much other countries spend and how well their students perform. *Insider*. Retrieved from https://www.insider.com/how-much-countries-around-the-world-spend-on-education-2019-8.

DelFattore, J. (2004). *The fourth R: Conflicts over religion in America's public schools*. New Haven, CT: Yale University Press.

Douglass, S. (2002). Teaching about religion. *Educational Leadership, 60*(2), 32-36.

Fishman, J. (2010). *European vernacular literacy: A sociolinguistic and historical introduction*. Bristol, UK: Multilingual Matters.

Gaille, N. (2017, May 22). US Literacy Rate and Illiteracy Statistics. *BrandonGaille Small Business & Marketing Advice*. Retrieved from https://brandongaille.com/us-literacy-rate-and-illiteracy-statistics/.

Grabow, C., & Rose, L. (2018, May 21). The US has had 57 times as many school shootings as the other major industrialized nations combined. Retrieved from https://www.cnn.com/2018/05/21/us/school-shooting-us-versus-world-trnd/index.html.

Harvard T. H. Chan School of Public Health. (2012). Obesity prevention source: Child obesity. Retrieved from https://www.hsph.harvard.edu/obesity-prevention-source/obesity-trends/global-obesity-trends-in-children/#References.

Hillison, J. (1995). The coalition that supported the Smith-Hughes Act, or a case for strange bedfellows. *Journal of Vocational and Technical Education, 11*(2), 4-11.

Horgan, J., Taylor, M., Bloom, M., & Winter, C. (2017). From cubs to lions: A six stage model of child socialization in the Islamic State. *Studies in Conflict and Terrorism, 7*, 645-664.

Joint Committee on National Health Standards. (2007). *National health education standards: Achieving excellence* (2nd ed). Atlanta, GA: American Cancer Society.

Josephson, A. (2018, May 15). The average salary by education level. *SmartAsset*. Retrieved from https://smartasset.com/retirement/the-average-salary-by-education-level .

Kochanska, G., Boldt, L., & Goffin, K. (2019). Early relationship experience: A foundation for the unfolding dynamics of parent-child socialization. *Child Development Perspectives, 13*(1), 41-47.

Lubienski, C. (2003). Instrumentalist perspectives on the "public" in public education: Incentives and purposes. *Educational Policy, 17*(4), 478-502.

Mayo Clinic Staff. (2017, August 2). *Healthy lifestyle: Sexual health*. Retrieved from https://www.mayoclinic.org/healthy-lifestyle/sexual-health/in-depth/sex-education/art-20044034.

McCarthy, K. (2020, July 7). Prioritize COVID aid for childcare and schools to help parents and the economy. *USA Today*. Retrieved from https://www.usatoday.com/story/opinion/2020/07/07/economic-recovery-schools-child-care-must-reopen-column/5383471002/.

McDonnell, L., & Timpane, M. (Eds.). (2000). *Rediscovering the democratic purposes of education: Studies in government and public policy*. Lawrence: University of Kansas Press.

Nash, G., Crabtree, C., & Dunn, R. (2000). *History on trial: Culture wars and the teaching of the past*. New York, NY: Vintage.

National Center for Educational Statistics. (2018a). Digest of educational statistics. Retrieved from https://nces.ed.gov/programs/digest/d18/tables/dt18_334.10.asp.

National Center for Educational Statistics. (2018b). *Teacher characteristics and trends*. Retrieved from https://nces.ed.gov/fastfacts/display.asp?id=28.

Ogden, C., Carroll, M., Kit, B., & Flegal, K. (2012). Prevalence of obesity and trends in body mass index among US children and adolescents, 1999-2010. *Journal of the American Medical Association, 307*, 483-490.

Olweus, D. (1988). Bullying in the schools: How educators can help. *The Education Digest, 53*(7), 30.

Olweus, D. (2003). A profile of bullying at school. *Educational Leadership, 60*(6), 12-17.

Orpinas, P., & Horne, A. (2006). *Bullying prevention: Creating a positive school climate and developing social competence*. Washington, DC: American Psychological Association.

Pallas, A. (1993). Schooling in the course of human lives: The social context of education and the transition to adulthood in industrial society. *Review of Educational Research, 63*(4), 409-447.

Passe, J., & Willox, L. (2009). Teaching religion in America's public schools: A necessary disruption. *The Social Studies, 100*(3), 102-106.

Pattison, R. (1982). *On literacy: The politics of the word from Homer to the Age of Rock*. New York, NY: Oxford University Press.

Phi Delta Kappan. (2016, September). *The 48ᵗʰ annual PDK poll of the public's attitudes towards the public schools.* Retrieved from https://www.heartland.org/_template-assets/documents/publications/PDKpollofpublicopinion2016.pdf.

Phinney, J. (2003). *Ethic identity and acculturation.* In K. Chun, P. Organista, & G. Marín (Eds.), *Acculturation: Advances in theory, measurement, and applied research* (pp. 63–81). Washington, DC: American Psychological Association.

Polin, V. (2007, October 9). *On mandated reporting.* Retrieved from http://theawarenesscenter.blogspot.com/2012_04_01_archive.html.

Ramarajan, D., & Runell, M. (2007). Confronting Islamophobia in education. *Intercultural Education, 18*(2), 87-97.

Reimers, F. (2006). Citizenship, identity and education: Examining the public purposes of schools in an age of globalization. *Prospects, 36*, 272-294.

Reinhart, R. (2020, January 19). Fewer in U.S. continue to see vaccines as important. *Gallup.* Retrieved from https://news.gallup.com/poll/276929/fewer-continue-vaccines-important.aspx.

Roopnarine, J., & Carter, D. (1992). *Parent-child socialization in diversity cultures.* Norwood, NJ: Greenwood.

Smokowski, P., & Kopasz, K. (2005). Bullying in school: An overview of types, effects, family characteristics, and intervention strategies. *Children and Schools, 27*(2), 101-110.

United Nations. (2020). *Sustainable development goals: Quality education.* Retrieved from https://www.un.org/sustainabledevelopment/education/.

U.S. Census Bureau. (2019a). *2018 Public Elementary-Secondary Education Finance Data.* Retrieved from https://www.census.gov/data/tables/2018/econ/school-finances/secondary-education-finance.html.

U.S. Census Bureau. (2019b, May 21). U.S. school spending per pupil increased for fifth consecutive year, U.S. Census Bureau reports. Retrieved from https://www.census.gov/newsroom/press-releases/2019/school-spending.html.

U.S. Department of Health and Human Services. (2018). Child maltreatment, 2018. Retrieved from https://www.acf.hhs.gov/sites/default/files/cb/cm2018.pdf#page=10.

U.S. Department of Homeland Security. (N.d.). School shooter: A quick reference guide. Retrieved from https://www.hsdl.org/?abstract&did=727626.

Violas, P. (1978). *The training of the urban working class: A history of 20ᵗʰ century American education.* Chicago, IL: Rand McNally.

Violas, P. (1981). Reflections on theories of human capital, skills training and vocational education. *Educational Theory, 31*(2), 137-151.

Wirth, A. (1972). Charles A. Prosser and the Smith-Hughes Act. *The Educational Forum, 36*(3), 365-371.

The World Bank. (2018a). *UNESCO Institute for Statistics: Literacy rate, adult total (% of people ages 15 and above)*. Retrieved from https://data.worldbank.org/indicator/SE.ADT.LITR.MA. ZS?view=chart.

The World Bank. (2018b). *UNESCO Institute for Statistics: Literacy rate, adult female (% of females ages 15 and above)*. Retrieved from https://data.worldbank.org/indicator/SE.ADT. LITR.MA.ZS?view=chart.

The World Bank. (2018c). *UNESCO Institute for Statistics: Literacy rate, adult male (% of males ages 15 and above)*. Retrieved from https://data.worldbank.org/indicator/SE.ADT.LITR. MA.ZS?view=chart.

World Health Organization. (2016). Global strategy on diet, physical activity, and health: Childhood overweight and obesity. Retrieved from https://www.who.int/ dietphysicalactivity/childhood/en/.

Xiao, H. (1999). Independence and obedience: An analysis of child socialization values in the United States and China. *Journal of Comparative Family Studies, 30*(4), 641-657.

Chapter 2

The Legal and Organizational Foundations of Public Schooling

Certain other societies may respect the rule of force – we respect the rule of law. (John F. Kennedy)

Privatizing our public schools makes as much sense as privatizing the first department or the police department. (Diane Ravitch)

The public education system in the United States is in many ways unique when compared to the educational systems in virtually all other countries in the world (see Arnove, Torres, & Franz, 2013; Bray, Adamson, & Mason, 2014). Internationally, the norm with respect to government educational systems is that there is a single, national ministry or department of education, which is responsible for establishing the curricula used in schools, deciding how students are assessed and evaluated, employing teachers, administrators and other school staff, determining licensure requirements for educators, constructing and maintaining buildings and other facilities, and so on, as well as for funding public education. Depending on the size and complexity of the particular country, there are also often regional departments of education. The central point here, though, is that there is a *single* national educational system, and public education is seen as the responsibility of the national government.

In the United States, although there is a federal Department of Education and while the national government does provide a small percentage of the overall funding necessary for public education, education is *primarily* the responsibility of the states.[1] Thus, there are 50 different state departments of education, each of which is responsible for curricula, assessment, licensure of educational professionals, the construction and maintenance of educational facilities, and so on. With the notable exception of Hawai'i, in each state there are local school districts that then implement state policies and procedures, while adding their own as well. There are between 14,000 and 15,000 school districts in the United States today, each a separate legal and political entity.[2] Furthermore, every school district has its own curricula, policies, contracts with educational professionals, and so on – all of which must be in compliance with those of the state, but among which there are also significant local differences. Within individual school districts are the schools themselves -- in 2017-2018, there were a total of slightly more than 130,000 public schools in the country – each of which is also somewhat

---

[1] Our focus in this chapter is on the formal organization of public schooling in the United States, but it is important to bear in mind that there are many other factors that influence educational policy and practice – such as lobbying and coalition efforts, both research and philanthropic foundations, political parties, and so on (see Lugg & Robinson, 2009; Posey-Maddox, 2016; Reckhow, 2013).

[2] Although this may seem like a very large number, in 1930 there were about 130,000 school districts in the United States, with an average student population of around 500 students. Today, the average school district serves about 5,000 students.

unique (National Center for Educational Statistics, 2018). We tend to take this all for granted, but for those from other countries the system appears to be unorganized, inefficient, and even chaotic. In this chapter, we will discuss how and why our educational system exists as it does by examining the U.S. *Constitution*, federal legislation, state constitutions and laws, and judicial decisions. We will also examine the institutions with which parents, teachers, and citizens are likely to have the most contact and involvement.

The Branches of Government: The Federal Level

A core feature of the structure of government in the United States is that at both the federal and state levels, there are three branches of government: the legislative branch, the executive branch, and the judicial branch. This division of power and responsibility is intended to ensure that each branch of government is co-equal with the other two branches – that is, no branch of government is more important than the other two branches. Furthermore, although each branch of government has unique responsibilities and obligations, these responsibilities and obligations also overlap those of the other branches of government (see Morone, 1998; Stein, 2001; Yarwood, 1993). Broadly speaking, the legislative branch of government is concerned with making laws, the executive branch with administering and enforcing the laws, and the judicial branch with interpreting the laws. This system is often described in terms of the three branches of government functioning to ensure a system of "checks and balances."

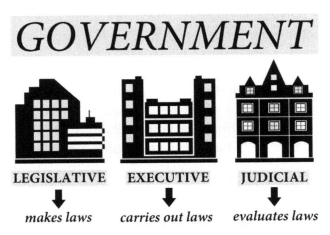

Branches of Government
© desdemona72/Shutterstock.com

The Legislative Branch

The U.S. *Constitution* established the Legislative Branch of the federal government in Article I, Section 1: "All legislative Powers herein granted shall be vested in a Congress of the United States, which shall consist of a Senate and a House of Representatives." Thus, the U.S. Congress is a *bicameral* legislative body. The House of Representations consists of 435 elected Representatives,[3] based on the population of each state.[4] The Senate consists of 100 members,

---

[3] There are additional non-voting delegates in the House of Representatives representing the District of Colombia, Puerto Rico, Guam, American Samoa, the Northern Mariana Islands, and the U.S. Virgin Islands.

with each state having two senators. Representatives serve terms of two years, while senators serve terms of six years.[5]

U.S. Capitol Building
© lunamarina/Shutterstock.com

Congress is responsible, first and foremost, for introducing and passing legislation. It is the only branch of the government that can make new laws or change existing laws, although the Executive Branch may issue regulations to enforce the laws passed by Congress and the judiciary may declare particular laws unconstitutional (Quirk & Binder, 2005). Anyone may propose a piece of legislation, but only a member of Congress may officially introduce it for consideration. In addition, Congress is responsible for establishing the annual budget of the federal government (as well as for matters of taxation), regulating commerce with other nations, and declaring war. The Senate is responsible for confirming Presidential appointments to the cabinet and the judiciary and ratifying treaties (which it does with a two-thirds "super-majority"). Finally, Congress has the responsibility to maintain oversight of the Executive Branch of government.

The Executive Branch

The Executive Branch, created by Article II of the *Constitution*, is headed by the President, and includes not only the President but also the Vice President, the Cabinet, and the huge federal bureaucracy – in fact, the Executive Branch currently employs more than 4 million

---

[4] The organization of the Legislative Branch of the U.S. government established in the *Constitution* was a compromise between two competing models of how membership in Congress should be determined. The "Virginal Plan," advocated by Thomas Jefferson, argued that representation in a legislature should be based on the relative size of the population of different states, while the "New Jersey Plan" argued that each state should have the same representation. By creating the House of Representatives and the Senate – one based on relative population and one on equality of representation by state – both models were accepted. This compromise at the Constitutional Convention was called the "Connecticut Compromise."

[5] Prior to the ratification of the Seventeenth Amendment in 1913, senators were not elected by the popular election; rather, they were chosen by state legislatures.

people. The President and Vice President are elected in national elections every four years,[6] while members of the Cabinet are nominated by the President and confirmed by the Senate (by a simple majority vote) and serve at the pleasure of the President. The constitutional duties of the President are extensive. In addition to being responsible for the execution and enforcement of the laws passed by Congress (which is accomplished through the 15 executive departments headed by the members of the President's Cabinet, in conjunction with more than 50 other federal agencies and bodies), the President also conducts diplomacy with other countries, negotiates and signs treaties, issues executive orders to clarify and further existing legislation, grants pardons and clemencies for federal crimes, and so on. The President of the United States serves as the Head of State (i.e., the ceremonial head of government), the chief executive and administrative office of the country, and the Commander-in-Chief of the armed forces.

The President's Cabinet includes the Secretaries of the 15 cabinet-level departments in the Executive Branch, which include the following:

Department of Agriculture
Department of Commerce
Department of Defense
Department of Education
Department of Energy
Department of Health and Human Services
Department of Homeland Security
Department of Housing and Urban Development
Department of Interior
Department of Justice
Department of Labor
Department of State
Department of Transportation
Department of Treasury
Department of Veteran Affairs

One of the most important aspects of the Executive Branch that should be taken into account is how it has changed over time and, specifically, how its power relative to the other branches of government (and especially vis-à-vis Congress) has increased (see Bertelli & Grose, 2011). This phenomenon, which had begun far earlier, was labelled the "imperial Presidency" in the 1960s and 1970s (see Schlesinger, 1973). As William Marshall has commented,

---

[6] This is not quite true – although there are indeed elections for the presidency every four years, as we know the outcome is not determined by the popular vote, but rather, by the vote of the Electoral College. This means that there are occasions when the candidate with the largest number of popular votes is not the winner of the election – a situation that took place in two of the six presidential elections held between 2000 and in 2020 (in 2000, when Al Gore won the popular vote but George W. Bush was elected President, and 2016, when Hilary Clinton won the popular vote but Donald Trump was elected President; see Mahler & Eder, 2016).

The notion that presidential power has expanded exponentially since the time of the framing is, of course, uncontestable ... The extent of that growth, however, is not always fully appreciated. At the time of the framing, for example, Madison, among others, believed the legislature was the most powerful branch ... and for that reason he supported the creation of a bicameral legislature ... Congress needed to be divided into two branches so that it would not overwhelm the other branches ... Correspondingly, the executive needed to be unitary so that it would not be weakened in its battles with the legislature ... Two hundred years later, any suggestion that Congress is twice as powerful as the executive would be deemed ludicrous ... Particularly in the areas of national security and foreign affairs ... the Presidency has become the far more powerful branch ... In 2006, for example, a new Congress was elected based in large part on the desire of the American people to get out of an unpopular war ... Yet, the President was able to use his authority to continually out-maneuver the newly-elected Congress and pursue a war that even many of those in his own party opposed ... (2008, pp. 507-508)

U.S. Department of Education
© Mark Van Scyoc/Shutterstock.com

Regardless of how one might feel about this growth of presidential power, it is clear that this is a development in our constitutional system that is likely to continue in the years ahead. One important point to keep in mind is that the growth of presidential power takes place *regardless* of who the President is at any given point in time: *Every* U.S. President in recent times has used his authority in ways that caused political opponents to object.

Article III of the *Constitution* created the Judicial Branch of the federal government, but in doing so it allowed Congress considerable freedom to determine many of the key details of this third branch of government. This is clear in Section 1, which reads: "The judicial Power of the United States, shall be vested in one supreme Court, and in such inferior Courts as the Congress may from time to time ordain and establish." The *Constitution*, interestingly enough, does not even specify the number of Supreme Court Justices. Although the number today is set at nine (with one Chief Justice, and eight Associate Justices), this has been true only since 1869. The *Judiciary Act* of 1789 first established a Supreme Court with six members, and that was the norm until 1807 (when Congress increased the number to seven), and it was again increased by Congress to nine in 1837 and to ten in 1863.[7] As for the "inferior Courts," Congress has established a system of district courts and circuit courts. Thus, the federal judicial system has three levels: districts courts, which are basically trial courts; circuit courts, which are the first level of appeal; and the Supreme Court, which is the final court of appeal. There are currently 94 district courts and 13 circuit courts in the United States. All judges (i.e., "justices") are appointed by the President and confirmed by the Senate, and all serve life terms.[8]

U.S. Supreme Court
© Rob Crandall/Shutterstock.com

The Supreme Court is unique in a number of important ways. It can decide appeals brought from any federal court and can also decide cases from state courts that deal with matters of federal law (including issues that are related to constitutional protections, such as freedom of speech, freedom of religion, etc.). Unlike other courts, the Supreme Court is not

---

[7] In 1937, President Franklin D. Roosevelt attempted to increase the number of justices up to a maximum of 15 – an effort that was widely seen as an attempt to "pack" the Supreme Court, which Roosevelt saw as hostile to his "New Deal." This move was blocked by Congress. Recent events surrounding the nomination of Justice Amy Comey Barrett to the Supreme Court led once again to discussions of the possible expansion of the number of justices on the Supreme Court.

[8] That is, a judge serves until they retire, die, or (extremely rarely) are impeached by the House of Representatives and convicted by the Senate.

obligated to hear any particular case; the members of the Court themselves select the cases that they will hear. This makes a great deal of sense, when one considers that the Court receives about 7,000 petitions a year to hear cases, while it can only hear about 100 (see Provine, 1980). In deciding which cases to hear, the Court only grants petitions for "compelling reasons," which include:

- Resolving a conflict in the interpretation of a federal law or a provision of the *Constitution*.
- Correcting an egregious departure from the accepted and normal course of judicial proceedings.
- Resolving an important question of federal law, or reviewing a decision of a lower court that conflicts directly with a previous decision of the Court.

The Branches of Government: The State Level

The separation of powers that characterizes the federal government in the United States is also present at the level of state government, although each state has its own constitution and unique institutions and structures to some extent. Each state possesses legislative, executive, and judicial authority over its own geographical area except where federal authority supersedes state authority.[9] The relationship between the powers of the federal government and the powers of the individual states in the United States was laid out in the Tenth Amendment to the *Constitution*, which states that "The powers not delegated to the United States by the *Constitution*, nor prohibited to it to the states, are reserved to the States respectively, or to the people."[10] This might appear to suggest that the federal and state governments are to a considerable degree independent in many matters, and while this may have been the case early in the history of the United States, it is no longer the case -- rather, it is far more accurate to think about the relationship between the federal and state governments as one characterized by interdependence (see Grodzins, 1984). At the time of the writing of the *Constitution*, the United States consisted of the 13 original colonies; as permitted under Article IV, Section 3 of the *Constitution*, 37 additional states have been added since that time – and additional states could be added by Congress in the future. Two possible additions that are often mentioned in this regard are Puerto Rico and the District of Columbia.

---

[9] The states hold legal jurisdiction over their respective territories but do not possess international sovereignty.

[10] The relationship between the federal government and the state governments – and disagreements about how that relationship should be best understood – were reflected in debates leading up to the Civil War. The earlier *Articles of Confederation* had strictly limited the powers of Congress, using the term "expressly" to identify the powers of the national government. The Tenth Amendment, however, also recognizes "implied powers" of the federal government.

The Legislative Branch

The Legislative Branch of government in each state parallels that of the federal government, with each state having a bicameral legislature consisting of an upper house and a lower house.[11] The name given to the legislature differs from state to state: In most states, the state legislature is just called the "Legislature," but in 19 states it is called the "General Assembly," while in Oregon and North Dakota it is called the "Legislative Assembly" and in Massachusetts and New Hampshire it is called the "General Court." The upper house of the legislature is called the Senate in all of the bicameral state legislatures (and is the name of the unicameral legislative body in Nebraska as well), while the precise name of the lower houses varies from state to state. The "House of Representatives" is by far the most common name of the lower house, but in Maryland, Virginia and West Virginia the lower house is called the "House of Delegates," while in California and Wisconsin the lower house is known as the "General Assembly." Unlike at the federal level, both the upper and lower houses of the state legislatures are elected based on relative population.[12]

The Executive Branch

The Executive Branch in each state is headed by the Governor, who serves as both Head of State and Head of Government.[13] Because each state has its own constitution, there is considerable diversity in terms of the relative powers of the Governor and the legislature, the structure and organization of the state government, and so on. Basically, the state governors are responsible for implementing and enforcing state laws and overseeing the operation of the Executive Branch of the state government. Most states have what is called a "plural executive," which means that in addition to the Governor there are a number of other members of the Executive Branch who are elected rather than appointed. Examples of these additional elected positions often include the Lieutenant Governor (all states except Arizona, Maine, New Hampshire, Oregon, and Wyoming have Lieutenant Governors), the Attorney General, the Secretary of State, the Treasurer, and so on.

---

[11] There is a single exception to the practice of using a bicameral model for the legislative branch: Nebraska has a unicameral legislature.

[12] Prior to the 1964 *Reynolds vs. Sims* decision of the Supreme Court, it was the practice in some states to elect state Senators by county – a practice that inevitably gave greater power to rural parts of the state (just as the membership of the U.S. Senate gives disproportionate power to states with small populations). In *Reynolds vs. Sims*, the Court ruled that state Senates must be elected from districts of approximately equal population, unlike the case with the U.S. Senate.

[13] The Governor also serves as the Commander-in-Chief of the state's National Guard, unless the National Guard is federalized, and of the state's defense forces (SDF). The SDF typically operate with emergency management and homeland security missions. Unlike the National Guard, the SDF may not be federalized.

The Judicial Branch

At the state level, both the structure of the judicial system and the manner by which judges are selected are determined by the individual state constitutions. Most states have a Supreme Court (sometimes called the "Court of Appeals"), which serves as the court of last resort on all matters of state law, and which can be overruled on matters of federal law only by the U.S. Supreme Court. It is worth noting here at especially at the state level – the level with which most school districts are likely to interact with the Judicial Branch of the government -- the role of school law has become increasingly specialized in recent decades (Goldstein, Daniel, & Gee, 1995; Kern & Alexander, 2000; McCarthy, Cambron-McCabe, & Thomas, 1997; Reutter, 1998; Stephenson, 2004).

The Branches of Government and Public Schooling

All three of the branches of government, at both the federal and state levels, play important roles with respect to public schooling in the United States, and it is important to bear in mind that there is considerable overlap in the roles that each plays vis-à-vis the others. In this section of the chapter, we will examine the role of each of the branches of the federal government in public education in the United States.

The Legislative Branch and Public Schooling

As we have seen, the primary responsibility for public education in the United States rests at the state and local levels, but that does not mean that the federal government does not play an important role with respect to public schooling. However, the role of the federal government in education is a relatively new one in our history – it was only in the 20th century that the federal government really began to play a role in public education, and that role dramatically increased in the second half of the 20th century. Congress has passed a number of important pieces of legislation concerned with public schooling in the past 60 years. This is significant, and indicates important changes in the relative power of the federal and state governments in some ways, but it is also the case that virtually all of the federal legislation that deals with education does so by approving funding for different kinds of programs (or in some instances, by denying federal funding if states and local school districts do not agree to do what the federal government wishes). Thus, the federal role in public schooling in the United States remains, even today, largely indirect rather than direct in nature.

We have already mentioned the *Smith-Hughes Act* of 1917 and the *Perkins Act*, both of which dealt with vocational and career education, but there are many other examples of important Congressional action related to public schooling. Five extremely important pieces of federal legislation that have had, and continue to have, major significance for public schools are the *National Defense Education Act*, the *Elementary and Secondary Education Act*, the *Education for All Handicapped Children Act*, the *No Child Left Behind Act*, and the *Race to the Top Act*.

On October 4, 1957, the Soviet Union successfully launched *Sputnik*,[14] the first artificial satellite to be placed in an elliptical, low Earth orbit, marking the beginning of the Space Age. One of the outcomes of the launch of Sputnik in the United States was a great deal of soul-searching – it was, for many Americans, almost inconceivable that the USSR had demonstrated its technological and scientific superiority over the United States in such a powerful and visible manner. There were concerns about the quality of public education in the United States, especially in the areas of mathematics and the sciences, as well as about the fact that the country was not producing sufficient numbers of skilled professionals in a number of areas, including mathematics, engineering, computer science, and so on. In response to all of these factors, Congress passed the *National Defense Education Act* (NDEA), and it was signed into law by President Eisenhower on September 2, 1958.

The NDEA provided over $1 billion in federal funding to support the teaching of mathematics, the sciences, modern foreign languages, and area studies at both the secondary school and university levels. It was the first comprehensive federal education legislation and marked the first major expansion of the role of the federal government in public education (U.S. House of Representatives, n.d.).

Sputnik (Stamp)
© rook76/Shutterstock.com

The *Elementary and Secondary Education Act* (ESEA), passed by Congress and signed into law by President Lyndon Johnson in 1965, was part of Johnson's "War on Poverty." In many ways, the ESEA has been the most important and enduring piece of federal legislation addressing public education. The ESEA provides funding to public schools for a wide variety of purposes, and these purposes have changed and evolved since its original passage in 1965. When it was reauthorized by Congress in 2015, the ESEA was renamed the *Every Student Succeeds Act* (ESSA) As of 2019, the Titles identified in ESSA include:

---

[14] Although almost universally referred to as simply Sputnik, the technical name of the satellite was Простейший Спутник-1 ("Elementary Satellite-1").

Title I	Programs for disadvantaged students, student assessment, migratory students, and neglected and delinquent students.
Title II	Programs for teachers, principals, and school leaders; literacy; and American history and civics education.
Title III	Programs to support English language acquisition for English learners.
Title IV	Programs to support a well-rounded education, safe and healthy students, and technology; after-school instruction and care; charter schools; magnet schools; family engagement in education; and various national activities.
Title V	Programs to support rural education.
Title VI	Programs for Indian education, Native Hawaiian education, and Alaska Native education.
Title VII	Impact Aid programs.
Title VIII	General provisions.

Although there have been major changes since it was first passed in 1965, the central purpose of the ESSA has remained fundamentally the same across time: to improve the educational opportunities and student achievement for children from lower-income families.

The *Education for All Handicapped Children Act*, originally passed by Congress in 1975, is probably best known as simply Public Law (PL) 94-142.[15] This important piece of legislation expanded the government's concern with ensuring the provision of equal access to education for all children to include those with special needs. Specifically, the *Education for All Handicapped Children Act* required all public schools that accepted federal funding to assess and evaluate the educational needs of children with disabilities[16] and, based on the results of such evaluations, work collaboratively with parents to design individualized education programs (IEPs) that would provide such students with educational experiences as close as possible to those received by non-disabled students. In essence, then, each child's IEP is created by a team of professional educators and the student's parents who meet annually to identify the child's unique educational needs, identify appropriate annual goals for the child, and determine the placement, modifications, testing accommodations, and other services that must be provided to the student. Ideally, the goals of every IEP are that it should be specific, measurable, attainable, realistic, and timely (hence, known by the acronym SMART).

---

[15] PL 94-142 did not actually appear in a vacuum; it was in fact an Amendment to Part B of the *Education of the Handicapped Act* that had been enacted in 1966.

[16] In the years since the passage of the *Education for All Handicapped Children Act*, there has been a growing concern among many educators and others, as well as in the field of Disability Studies, about the language and terminology used to describe the individuals who are the focus of this legislation. The term "handicapped" is now generally seen as profoundly problematic; in addition, it is now general practice to describe such persons as "people with intellectual impairments," and so on – and even the term "impairment" has become controversial (see Davis, 2006; Goodley, 2017; Linton, 1998).

The *Education for All Handicapped Children Act* specifies quite clearly what conditions are eligible for inclusion under its requirements. There are 13 "eligibility categories" identified in PL 94-142, including:

- Autism.
- Deaf-blindness.
- Deafness.
- Emotional disturbance.
- Hearing impairment.
- Intellectual disability.
- Multiple disabilities.
- Orthopedic impairment.
- Other health impairment.
- Specific learning disability.
- Speech or language impairment.
- Traumatic brain injury.
- Visual impairment, including blindness.

Philosophically underpinning the *Education for All Handicapped Children Act* was a commitment to placing children in the "least restrictive environment" (LRE) in which they could be educated – and it was this commitment that has been manifested in educational practice in mainstreaming and inclusive education. The *Education for All Handicapped Children Act* was, in short, concerned with accomplishing four goals:

- Ensuring that special education services would be available to all children who require them.
- Ensuring that decisions about the services to be provided to children with disabilities would be both fair and appropriate.
- Establishing common management and auditing requirements for special education programs.
- Providing federal funding to states to assist them in providing the necessary services to meet the needs of handicapped children.

The *Education for All Handicapped Children Act* was renamed the *Individuals with Disabilities Education Act* (IDEA) in 1990.

When the *Elementary and Secondary Education Act* was reauthorized by Congress in 2002, it was significantly changed in a number of important ways. The legislation was renamed the *No Child Left Behind Act*, or NCLB, and was passed with overwhelming bipartisan support in Congress – it was passed in the House of Representatives 381 to 41, and in the Senate by a margin of 87 to 10. President George W. Bush signed it into law on January 8, 2002. The *No Child Left Behind Act* focused heavily on new requirements for accountability, created new options for increased school choice for parents and students, mandated "scientifically based research" and data to be used in educational evaluation and decision-making, and attempted to address a number of issues related to the quality of the teaching force.

The major shift represented by the *No Child Left Behind Act* (NCLB) from earlier versions of the *Elementary and Secondary Education Act* was the move to a dramatically increased concern with accountability in a number of **areas. At the heart of this new focus on accountability** was the requirement that all public schools receiving federal education funding had to administer standardized academic evaluations annually.[17] Schools were thus required to demonstrate "Adequate Yearly Progress" (AYP) as measured by test scores, particularly in reading and mathematics – in other words, the 5th graders this year must perform better than those 5th graders performed when they were in 4th grade the previous year. **If this did not take place, a system of mandatory responses was triggered.** Schools that failed to show AYP for two consecutive years were labelled "In Need of Improvement." If a school did not demonstrate AYP for a third year, it was required to offer tutoring and other supplemental services for students. Failure in the fourth year resulted in a school being labelled as needing "Corrective Action," which could involve changes in staff, curriculum, an extension of classroom time, and so on. Finally, if a school failed to demonstrate AYP for five years in a row, it was subject to plans for a complete restructuring, which might then take effect in year six. "Complete restructuring" could mean that the state Department of Education would take over running the school, a private company might take over the school, or the school might be converted to a charter school. The basic goal of this process was to ensure that all students – including those from economically disadvantaged backgrounds, students with disabilities, and students with limited English proficiency – would be able to demonstrate proficiency in several key academic areas. To ensure that this would really happen, schools were required to ensure that 95% of the students in each group of learners participated in the mandatory assessments.

The *No Child Left Behind Act* has proven to be quite controversial. Although there is some evidence that student achievement did improve, the evidence is subject to question. Results from the 2005 National Assessment of Educational Progress (NAEP), for instance, suggested that:

- For America's nine-year-olds in reading, more progress was made in five years than in the previous 28 combined.
- America's nine-year-olds posted the best scores in reading (since 1971) and math (since 1973) in the history of the report. America's 13-year-olds earned the highest math scores the test ever recorded.
- Reading and math scores for African American and Hispanic nine-year-olds reached an all-time high.
- Math scores for African American and Hispanic 13-year-olds reached an all-time high.
- Achievement gaps in reading and math between white and African American nine-year-olds and between white and Hispanic nine-year-olds are at an all-time low. (U.S. Department of Education, 2006)

At the same time, critics have pointed out that *No Child Left Behind* never received the funding that was originally intended to support its implementation, that the resources that

---

[17] The determination of the particular testing regimen was left to each state to determine.

were dedicated to *No Child Left Behind* might have been more effectively utilized in alternative ways that focused less on testing and more on directly on teaching and learning, that the result of the legislation has been an overly narrow focus on testing and "teaching to the test," that the positive results claimed for *No Child Left Behind* were selectively identified and not actually representative of the overall consequences of the legislation, that one important consequence of the implementation of *No Child Left Behind* has been to devalue subjects such as art, music, science, and world languages, that are not subject to the testing requirements, and a host of other concerns. Typical of many of the criticisms of *No Child Left Behind* was the comment by the noted educationist Alfie Kohn, who described it as "unredeemable" and argued that it should be scrapped altogether. Kohn's principal criticism of *No Child Left Behind* is that,

> *No Child Left Behind* (NCLB) is an appalling and unredeemable experiment that has done incalculable damage to our schools — particularly those serving poor, minority and limited-English-proficiency students .... NCLB didn't invent the scourge of high-stakes testing, nor is it responsible for the egregious disparity between the education received by America's haves and have-nots. But by intensifying the former, it exacerbates the latter .... This law cannot be fixed by sanding its rough edges. It must be replaced with a policy that honors local autonomy, employs better assessments, addresses the root causes of inequity and supports a rich curriculum. The question isn't how to save NCLB; it's how to save our schools — and kids — *from* NCLB. (Kohn, 2007, emphasis in original)

Kohn was not alone in his lack of faith in the merits of *No Child Left Behind*; in a 2007, 50-state survey, only 3% of teachers indicated that they felt that *No Child Left Behind* helped them to teach more effectively (Kohn, 2007). Recognizing the challenges associated with *No Child Left Behind*, the Obama administration proposed a number of modifications to the legislation, and in 2012, granted a number of states waivers from specific NCLB requirements – including waivers in Arkansas, Colorado, Connecticut, Delaware, Florida, Georgia, Indiana, Kentucky, Louisiana, Maryland, Massachusetts, Minnesota, Missouri, New Jersey, New Mexico, New York, North Carolina, Ohio, Oklahoma, Rhode Island, South Dakota, Tennessee, Utah, Virginia, Washington, and Wisconsin.[18] The *Race to the Top* initiative, announced by President Barack Obama and Secretary of Education Arne Duncan on July 24, 2009, also provided almost $4.5 billion to fund innovation and reform in public education in the United States as a way of providing additional financial support for *No Child Left Behind*.

The Executive Branch and Public Schooling

The job of the Executive Branch of the federal government with respect to the provision of public education in the United States to a significant extent *sounds* as if it would be relatively trivial: It is responsible for implementing the legislation related to education that has been passed by Congress. We have emphasized the word "sounds" here because while that may at first appear to entail little more than putting bureaucratic procedures in place, it actually

---

[18] The fact that more than half of the states needed to request such waivers, we would argue, suggests that there were some fundamental problems in either the assumptions and design of *No Child Left Behind* or in its implementation.

involves a great deal more than this – and, in fact, the Executive Branch plays a very important role in terms of public education in the United States (Aberbach & Peterson, 2005). This is the case for a number of reasons.

The primary agency in the Executive Branch that deals with educational matters is the Department of Education. The Department of Education was created in 1979, and began operating in 1980, as a result of the division of the Department of Health, Education, and Welfare into the Department of Education and the Department of Health and Human Services. It is a cabinet-level department, headed by the U.S. Secretary of Education. It has about 4,000 employees, an annual budget of approximately $70 billion, and administers an additional $139 billion in various kinds of postsecondary loans, grants, work study assistance, and so on, which benefit more than 11 million students. The major tasks of the Department of Education are to establish related policies, administer, and coordinate different kinds of federal assistance to public schooling, to collect, analyze, and maintain data on education in the United States, and to enforce federal laws dealing with matters of privacy and civil rights in the educational domain. The power of the Department of Education over public education, like that of Congress, is largely indirect, through the funding of educational programs (or through decisions not to provide funding).

An additional way in which the Department of Education influences public schooling at both the state and local levels is in the development of regulations designed to implement federal legislation. The Supreme Court's 1974 *Lau vs. Nichols* decision is generally seen as one concerned with the educational rights of minority language students, and this was true to a degree. *Lau*, which we will discuss in more detail later in this chapter, was brought to the Court as an example of the violation of students' Fourteenth Amendment Equal Protection rights. However, it was not on this basis that the Supreme Court found in favor of the plaintiffs. Rather, the court found that the school district was in violation of Section 601 of the *Civil Rights Act* and, further, that the district's actions were not in compliance with the guidelines promulgated by the Office for Civil Rights (OCR) and the Department of Health, Education and Welfare. In other words, in the absence of legislation to the contrary, the rules and regulations developed by the Department of Education that are intended to implement federal law basically have the same force as the legislation itself. This is an incredible power, with serious implications not only for public schooling but also for many other aspects of society.

The Judicial Branch and Public Schooling

As we have seen, the Judicial Branch of government is concerned with interpreting the *Constitution*, legislation, and the interplay between the two. Historically, public education was not a significant concern of the federal judiciary, since schooling was clearly the responsibility of the states. As Stephen Sugarman (2020) noted,

Prior to the 20th century, the United States Supreme Court issued few important decisions concerning education, and virtually none dealing with schooling at the elementary and secondary levels. Schooling has always been considered primarily a state and local government function in America, and it was not until well into the 20th century that the Court seriously imposed on the states provisions of the U.S. *Constitution* that have turned out to be importantly relevant to education.

As the federal government's role in public education has increased, however, there has been a concomitant increase in judicial action related to constitutional and legal reviews (U.S. Department of Justice, n.d.; Yudorf, Kirp, Levin, & Moran, 2001). Another aspect of the increase in judicial review of educational issues has been the Court's recognition of the implications of parts of the *Constitution* – especially the Free Speech and Free Exercise of Religion clauses of the First Amendment, the Equal Protection and Due Process clauses of the Fourteenth Amendment, and the Fourth Amendment's protections against unreasonable searches and seizures – for public schooling. As a result, beginning in the second half of the 20th century, there were a number of extremely significant decisions of the Supreme Court that have had profound impacts on and implications for the public schools.

Meyer vs. Nebraska (1923). Shortly after the end of the First World War, in 1919 the state of Nebraska passed the *Siman Act.* The *Siman Act* was largely a reflection of the strong anti-German xenophobia that had swept the United States as a result of our involvement in the First World War. Early in the 20th century, there were still significant numbers of German Americans who continued to speak German at home and at church, in particular. There were even many bilingual education programs in the schools that worked to maintain the German language while ensuring that German-speaking students learned English (see Kloss, 1998; see also Freese, 1998). The war led to popular beliefs that the Germans were not only sympathetic to the goals of Germany in Europe but also that they were actively working to subvert the American war effort. One result of this anti-German bias, which was to be repeated during the Second World War (Holian, 1998), was a kind of linguistic hysteria targeting the German language. There were public burnings of German books in many parts of the country (Gilbert, 1971; Salmons, 1993), bans on the performance of German music, and by the early 1920s over 30 states had passed legislation requiring English-only instruction in the schools. In addition, in 1918 South Dakota had passed legislation prohibiting the use of German over the telephone and banning its use in public gatherings of more than three persons. The *Espionage Act,* which prohibited the mailing of any materials "advocating or urging treason, insurrection, or forcible resistance to any law of the United States" was passed by the U.S. Congress in 1918, as was the infamous *Sedition Act*, which made it illegal to speak, write, or publish any "disloyal, profane, scurrilous, or abusive language" about the U.S. government, the *Constitution*, the military, or the flag. Nebraska's legislation banning the German language in its schools, in short, was far from uncommon at the time. The *Meyer vs. Nebraska* case had its origins in Hampton, Nebraska, when Robert Meyer, the teacher at Zion Lutheran School, made the decision to teach one of his students, ten-year-old Raymond Parpart, who was then a fourth grader, to read in German. When the Hamilton Country attorney came to the school and witnessed the boy reading the Bible in German, Meyer was charged with violating the *Siman Act*, and fined $25.

On appeal, the Nebraska Supreme Court upheld the conviction, by a vote of 4 to 2. The case was then appealed to the Supreme Court of the United States, which in 1923 ruled that the *Siman Act* was a violation of the Due Process Clause of the Fourteenth Amendment.

Brown vs. Board of Education of Topeka, Kansas (1954). The *Brown vs. Board of Education* decision is arguably the single most important decision ever handed down by the Supreme Court. In 1896, the Supreme Court, in its *Plessy vs. Ferguson* decision, had ruled that racial segregation was legal and constitutional so long as the facilities provided to blacks and whites were equal. In spite of the fact that the facilities provided for blacks through the segregated parts of the United States were obliviously not equal, throughout the "Jim Crow" era the *Plessy* decision legitimized racial discrimination throughout the American South. In the early 1950s, the National Association for the Advancement of Colored People (NAACP) began challenging racial segregation in the public schools and had filed lawsuits in Delaware, South Carolina, and Virginia. In 1951, Oliver Brown filed a class-action lawsuit against the Board of Education in Topeka, Kansas, on behalf of his daughter Linda, who had been denied entrance to Topeka's all-white elementary schools. Brown argued that the segregated schools provided for African American students were not in fact equal to the schools provided for white students and that this therefore constituted a violation of the Equal Protection Clause of the Fourteenth Amendment. The case was initially decided by the U.S. District Court in Kansas, which, although granting that segregated schooling had a detrimental effect upon black children and that it did create a sense of inferiority in the children, nevertheless upheld the doctrine of "separate but equal."

Desegregation (Stamp)
©catwalker/Shutterstock.com

The case was appealed to the Supreme Court, where it was combined with four related cases concerning challenges to the segregation of public schools. The NAACP legal team that argued the case before the Supreme Court was headed by Thurgood Marshall, who was later the first African American to be appointed to the Supreme Court. In its decision, which was issued on May 17, 1954, the Supreme Court unanimously found that "in the field of public education the doctrine of 'separate but equal' has no place" and, further, that segregated schools were "inherently unequal" and that the plaintiffs had indeed been "deprived of the equal protection of the laws guaranteed by the Fourteenth Amendment." The original *Brown* decision was followed by a second decision in May 1955, which remanded future desegregation cases to lower courts and ordered that the courts and school districts proceed to desegregate the schools "with all deliberate speed."

To say that there was a powerful backlash to the *Brown* decision would be a huge understatement:

> Though well intentioned, the Court's actions effectively opened the door to local judicial and political evasion of desegregation. While Kansas and some other states acted in accordance with the verdict, many school and local officials in the South defied it … In one major example, Governor Orval Faubus of Arkansas called out the state National Guard to prevent black students from attending high school in Little Rock in 1957. After a tense standoff, President Eisenhower deployed federal troops, and nine students — known as the "Little Rock Nine" – were able to enter Central High School under armed guard. (History.Com editors, 2020)

At the same time, the *Brown* decision provided a significant boost for the Civil Rights Movement and at least indirectly laid the foundation for the *Civil Rights Act* of 1964, the *Voting Rights Act* of 1965, and the *Fair Housing Act* of 1968. In 1976, the Supreme Court issued another landmark decision in *Runyon vs. McCrary,* in which it found that even private, nonsectarian schools that sought to deny admissions to students on the basis of race were in violation of federal civil rights laws. The legacy of *Brown* is incredibly significant, but the battle that civil rights advocates were fighting in *Brown* is far from finished. As the History.Com editors (2020) noted,

> By overturning the "separate but equal" doctrine, the Court's decision in *Brown vs. Board of Education* had set the legal precedent that would be used to overturn laws enforcing segregation in other public facilities. But despite its undoubted impact, the historic verdict fell short of achieving its primary mission of integrating the nation's public schools …Today, more than 60 years after *Brown vs. Board of Education,* the debate continues over how to combat racial inequalities in the nation's school system, largely based on residential patterns and differences in resources between schools in wealthier and economically disadvantaged districts across the country.

Engel vs. Vitale (1962). Although by far the most important educational decision decided by the Supreme Court in the 20th century, *Brown* was not the only decision with important implications for public schools. In several cases in the 1960s and 1970s, the Supreme Court issued rulings that deal with both the Establishment and Free Exercise clauses of the First Amendment. These decisions, addressing issues of religion in the public schools have, not surprisingly, also been controversial. The first of these decisions was *Engel vs. Vitale,* in which the court ruled that public schools could not mandate Bible reading and the recitation of the *Lord's Prayer.* Although retrospectively it might seem obvious that what were essentially denominational Christian mandates in public schools would violate the *Constitution*, such practices had been part and parcel of public education throughout the United States from the very beginnings of public schooling.

Lemon vs. Kurtzman (1971). *Lemon vs. Kurtzman* was another decision related to the Establishment clause. In this case, the issue at hand was the financial support provided to parochial schools to fund teacher salaries and textbooks. In the *Lemon* decision, the Supreme Court unanimously ruled that such funding violated the Establishment clause of the First Amendment. In what has come to be known as the "Lemon test," the Court provided clear guidance for when public monies might be used to support private religious schools. In order for such funding to be constitutional, the relevant statutes (i) must have a secular legislative purpose, (ii) must have primary effects that neither inhibit nor advance religion, and (iii) cannot foster an "excessive government entanglement with religion."

Wisconsin vs. Yoder (1972). The state of Wisconsin mandated that children attend school until the age of 16, either in a public or private school. On religious grounds, three Amish fathers,[19] Jonas Yoder, Wallace Miller, and Adin Yutzy, who had children aged 14 and 15, refused to enroll their children in school after they had completed eighth grade, arguing that schooling beyond eighth grade was not necessary for their children. The fathers were initially found guilty of violating the law, and each was fined. The conviction was upheld on appeal to a circuit court, which held that the state law was a "reasonable and constitutional" use of state power. The Wisconsin Supreme Court, however, reversed this decision, finding that the law violated the First Amendment's Free Exercise clause. The decision was ultimately referred to the U.S. Supreme Court.

The Supreme Court's decision in *Yoder* was based in large part on the unique characteristics of the Amish community. The Court, in a detailed review and analysis of the Amish community, faith, and lifestyle, determined that the religious beliefs and way of life of the Amish were "inseparable and interdependent," and that they had not changed "in fundamentals for centuries." Furthermore, the Court argued that secondary schooling – public or private – would entail exposing the children to values, attitudes, and beliefs that ran counter to those of the Amish community and which could potentially lead to harm to both their religious development and their future integration into the Amish community. The Court went on to assert that by compelling the children to attend school past the eighth grade, they would be forced to "either abandon belief and be *assimilated* into society at large or be forced to migrate to some other and more tolerant region." In rejecting the state's claim that it had a compelling interest in mandating compulsory schooling, the Court also noted that during the time when the Amish children were not to be in school, they were nevertheless engaged in an "alternative mode of continuing informal vocational education" and, therefore, that there was no reason to believe that the children would become burdens of society or that there would be any threat to their health or safety. Thus, the Supreme Court in *Yoder* ruled that the state of Wisconsin had violated the Free Exercise clause of the First Amendment.

---

[19] The Amish do not constitute a monolithic group. The families involved in this particular case were members of the Old Order Amish Mennonite Church.

Tinker vs. Des Moines (1969). The *Tinker vs. Des Moines Independent Community School District* case dealt with the Free Speech clause of the First Amendment. The Tinker family, which included John (age 15), Mary Beth (age 13), Hope (age 11), and Paul (age 8), had been active in both the Civil Rights Movement and in protests against the war in Vietnam. In 1965, to show their support for the protests against the war in Vietnam and for the "Christmas Truce" that had been called for by Senator Robert F. Kennedy, the children, together with their friend Christopher Eckhardt (age 16), decided to wear black armbands to school on December 16. Prior to December 16, the administration of the Des Moines schools found out about their intentions, and created a policy that forbade the wearing of armbands and that required students doing so to remove them immediately when asked by school personnel. Any student in violation of this policy would be suspended, and further, would only be allowed to return to school after agreeing to comply with the policy. In spite of the new policy, the Tinker children and Christopher Eckhardt decided to wear their armbands, which they did. John, Beth, and Christopher Eckhardt were all suspended for violating the policy.[20] In a 7 to 2 decision, the Supreme Court argued that the First Amendment Free Speech protections applied to public schools and that in order to regulate speech in the classroom the school district must provide constitutionally valid reasons for doing so. As the majority on the Court wrote, "It can hardly be argued that either students or teachers shed their constitutional rights to freedom of speech or expression at the schoolhouse gate." Determining that the children's wearing of armbands did not significantly disrupt the schooling process, the Court decided that their wearing the armbands did constitute constitutionally protected symbolic speech.[21]

San Antonio Independent School District vs. Rodriguez (1974). The public schools in San Antonio, Texas, are funded in large part by local property taxes, as is true throughout most of the United States. Property taxes in San Antonio generated significantly less income for the support of public schools than was the case in many surrounding school districts. The San Antonio Independent School District sued the state on behalf of the district's students, arguing that the differences in property taxes and the assessed values of property meant that their students were being underserved due to the lack of funding comparable to that found in the wealthier surrounding school districts. In its lawsuit, the District asserted that the situation violated the Equal Protection clause of the Fourteenth Amendment, which appeared to mandate equal funding among school districts. Although not an unreasonable position, the Supreme Court ruled against the School District, arguing that since the U. S. *Constitution* does not grant a fundamental right to public education and, further, that the Equal Protection clause in any event does not require exact equality, or even "precisely equal advantages" among school districts., the case was rejected by the Supreme Court.

---

[20] Although they also wore black armbands, Hope and Paul Tinker were not suspended because the policy did not apply in elementary schools.

[21] In two later decisions, *Bethel School District vs. Fraser* and *Hazelwood vs. Kuhlmeier*, the Supreme Court modified this, limiting the freedoms granted to students in public schools (see Ingelhart, 1993; Siegel, 1987).

Lau vs. Nichols (1974). Congress passed the *Bilingual Education Act* (Title VII of the *Elementary and Secondary Education Act Amendments*) in 1968 to provide for competitive grants for states to create innovative educational programs for limited-English speaking students. Participation in the programs and efforts that it funded were voluntary. By 1972, although around 5,000,000 students in the United States would have been eligible for participation in Title VII programs, only about 100,000 were actually enrolled in such programs. In 1971, the San Francisco Unified School District, as a result of the Supreme Court decision in *Lee vs. Johnson*, began the process of desegregation. At that time, there were almost 3,000 Chinese students enrolled in the San Francisco schools who were not fluent in English, of whom fewer than one-third were provided with some kind of supplemental English language instruction. In other words, two-thirds of these students were simply mainstreamed into English medium classrooms in which they were unable to adequately follow or benefit from the instruction provided. Some of these students were placed in special education classes only because of their linguistic situation, while others were required to remain in the same grade for several years while they tried to acquire better proficiency in English. A class action lawsuit was filed, challenging the educational practices of the San Francisco Unified School District, arguing that because of their limited English proficiency, these students were entitled to special help under both the Equal Protection clause of the Fourteenth Amendment and the ban on educational discrimination in the *Civil Rights Act* of 1964. The District Court for the Northern District of California ruled against the students, arguing that since a uniform policy was used for all students in the school district, and since the district did not intentionally discriminate against students with limited English proficiency, equal protection was provided and the Fourteenth Amendment was not violated. This decision was affirmed by the Court of Appeals, which ruled that because the district provided the same treatment to all students, even though this same treatment disadvantaged some students as a result of their lack of fluency in English, the district had no obligation to provide additional services to make up for the different language backgrounds of the students. The case was then appealed to the U.S. Supreme Court.

The Supreme Court unanimously voted to overturn the lower court decisions. In its July 1974 decision, the Court found that since the San Francisco Unified School District received federal funding, it was legally obligated to ensure the provision of equal educational opportunities and access to all students. While granting that the same treatment had been provided to all students in the district, the Court asserted that the district nevertheless imposed a policy with a disparate impact on non-English-speaking students, since the result of its policy was that the students could not understand what was taught in the classroom and were therefore deprived of receiving a "meaningful" education. Perhaps as important as the outcome of the *Lau* decision, though, was the reasoning of the Court. *Lau* was not decided based on the claims that students' Fourteenth Amendment Equal Protection rights had been violated. Rather, the Supreme Court argued that the district was in violation of Section 601 of the *Civil Rights Act* and, further, that the district's actions were not in compliance with the guidelines promulgated by the Office for Civil Rights (OCR) and the Department of Health, Education and Welfare[22] in 1970, which had determined that language could function as a

---

[22] The Department of Health, Education and Welfare was a cabinet-level part of the Executive Branch of the federal government from its creation in 1953 until 1979, when it was divided into two separate departments -- the Department of Health and Human Services and the Department of Education.

"proxy" for discrimination based on national origin, and that districts needed to take affirmative action to make appropriate and necessary changes to ensure that non-English-speaking students were provided with equal educational opportunities.[23]

New Jersey vs. TLO (1985). This case concerned the Fourth Amendment's protections against unreasonable searches and seizures and, specifically, the degree to which these protections applied to students in the public schools. The case began at Piscataway High School in Piscataway, New Jersey, when a teacher discovered two students smoking in a school restroom, in violation of established school rules. The teacher brought the girls to the Principal's Office, where they were questioned by Assistance Vice Principal Choplick. TLO[24] denied that she had been smoking and, further, claimed that she did not smoke at all. The Assistant Vice Principal then searched her purse, in which he found not only a pack of cigarettes, but also, in plain view, rolling papers. He then continued his search, finding a small amount of marijuana, a pipe, an empty plastic bag, a large number of $1 bills, an index card that seemed to list students who owed TLO money and two letters that appeared to implicate TLO in selling marijuana. At this point, the police and TLO's mother were contacted. TLO's mother drove her daughter to the police station, where she was booked for both dealing and using illicit drugs. She was also expelled from school.

Because TLO was a minor, her initial court appearance was before the Juvenile and Domestic Relations Court of Middlesex County, New Jersey. The Court found that although the Fourth Amendment does apply to searches carried out by school personnel, a school official may search a student if they have reasonable suspicion that a crime has been, or is in the process of being, committed. Applying this standard, the Court ruled that TLO's Fourth Amendment rights had not been violated, and she was found delinquent and sentenced to probation for one year. This decision was appealed to the Appellate Division of the New Jersey State Court System, which affirmed that there was no Fourth Amendment violation.[25] On appeal to the U.S. Supreme Court, the Court found that the search of TLO's purse did not constitute a violation of her Fourth Amendment rights. Further, the Court argued that school officials do not require a search warrant or have probable cause to believe that a crime has been committed before engaging in a search. It is, rather, the "reasonableness" of the search that determines its legality. In order to constitute a legal search in such a context, two conditions must be met: The search must (i) be justified at its inception, and (ii) be conducted in a manner reasonably related in scope to the circumstances that justified it in the first place.

These landmark cases of the Supreme Court provide you with a broad overview of the types of cases that the Court is likely to hear and the kinds of reasoning that it has historically employed in making its decisions. It is important, however, to keep in mind that while there is a very strong tradition of following the doctrine of *stare decisis* – that is, of granting considerable

---

[23] The Court did not identify any particular remedies for the district to follow, however, and thus did not actually mandate that such students be provided with bilingual education programs.

[24] Because she was a legal minor, the student was only identified by her initials (TLO).

[25] The Appellate Court did, however, remand the decision to the Juvenile Court to decide if TLO had knowingly and voluntarily waited her Fifth Amendment right against self-incrimination before confessing.

respect to past legal precedents – the Supreme Court can and sometimes does introduce decisions that overturn prior Supreme Court decisions, as it did in the *Brown* case when it overturned the *Plessy* decision.

Education at the State Level

Education, as we have seen, is constitutionally and historically primarily the responsibility of the states (see Kelleher & Wolak, 2007). Given this fact, one of the more remarkable aspects of public schooling in the United States is the extent to which public schools and the domain of public education more generally – curricula, assessment, teacher preparation, school organization, even school architecture – are similar if not the same across the nation. This is, of course, understandable in countries in which there is a single, centralized educational system, but in the United States we have never had such a system. It is fairly easy to explain many similarities in the contemporary context – many students move from one state to another, and a relatively common curriculum and organizational structure facilitates this, as fairly common teacher preparation and licensure makes the movement of teachers from one state to another easier. The approval system for textbooks in some large enrollment states, such as Texas, also functions to reduce curricular diversity, and the increasing reliance on accountability through standardized testing called for at the federal level also works to encourage similarities in public education across the nation. These, however, are all relatively recent developments in our society – for most of American educational history, these factors either did not exist or were of far less significance than they now are.

The explanation for the similarity in public education in most parts of the United States does not relate to centralized control or mandates. It is largely the result of historical factors that took place nationally, although in different regions of the country and different states at somewhat different times and often for somewhat different reasons. Although there are exceptions – typically dealing with more controversial topics – much of the education legislation passed into law at the state level has been drafted by the state's Department of Education or by some lobbying group. This is understandable, of course, since most legislators are not professional educators and generally prefer to give a fair degree of freedom to the state Department of Education, which in turn is supposed to work collaboratively with groups of administrators (especially superintendents), professional teacher organizations, parents, and other special interest groups (Ferguson, 2006; Garnett, 2019). For educational legislation at the state level, there are normally public hearings held first by the Department of Education and then, once legislation has been drafted, in the legislature itself. Thus, the legislative and executive branches generally work closely together at the state level, with considerable input from the local level (Little & Ogle, 2006). In addition, there is a state Board of Education and a state Commissioner of Education, each with a special role to play in the legal and constitutional processes related to public education in each state.

The role of the state is a substantial one. It is the state that ultimately mandates curricular guidelines for the public schools, decides on graduation requirements, makes decisions about statewide evaluation and assessment practices and procedures, determines certification requirements for teachers and other educators (and thus impacts teacher education program curricula), and determines the length of the school year. The state also typically provides part of the funding for public schools, especially in terms of the construction of new schools.

Public Schooling at the Local Level

At the local level, the two institutions that are most relevant for understanding public education are the board of education[26] and the school district administration.[27] Of these two institutions, by far the more important legally and constitutionally[28] is the Board of Education. This is an extremely important point, because it often appears to be the case that it is the administration that "runs" the school district and the Board of Education merely "rubber stamps" the decisions of the administration. While it is true that the school district administration does make virtually all of the day-to-day decisions to keep a school district operating, it is the Board of Education that is ultimately responsible for what takes place in the school district. Even the Superintendent in a school district is an employee of the Board of Education. The Board of Education is responsible for approving employment and other contracts, negotiating with the teachers' union, making important policy decisions about all aspects of education in the school district, and proposing a budget and determining how funds are allocated.

Questions for Reflection and Discussion

1. Of the three branches of government, which do you believe has had the greatest impact on the daily lives of teachers and students? Why? Do you believe that this is changing?

2. How does the fact that schools are largely funded on the local level impact equality of education within states, and across the nation? To what extent do you believe that school funding should be a local matter? A state matter? A federal matter?

3. Has the increased emphasis on testing in the schools improved education? Has it improved student achievement? What are the other benefits and limitations of the widescale use of standardized testing in the United States?

4. How would you describe the fundamental place of religion in public schools in the United States? In what ways has the role of religion in the public schools been limited? In what ways has it been protected?

---

[26] There are actually a number of different names for the bodies that we are referring to here. Most are called Boards of Education, but the terms School Committee and School Board are also used.

[27] The organizational structures of school districts vary considerably from one part of the country to another and even within particular states.

[28] As we have seen, education is not directly addressed in the U.S. *Constitution*. It is, however, addressed in state constitutions.

5. How are schools expected to serve students with differing abilities? Do you believe that the public schools really provide equitable educational experiences for all students? Provide examples to support your answer.

References

Aberbach, J., & Peterson, M. (Eds.). (2005). *The executive branch*. Oxford, UK: Oxford University Press.

Arnove, R., Torres, C., & Franz, S. (2013). *Comparative education: The dialectic of global and local* (4th ed.). Lanham, MD: Rowman & Littlefield.

Bertelli, A., & Grose, C. (2011). The lengthened shadow of another institution? Ideal point estimates for the Executive branch and Congress. *American Journal of Political Science, 55*(4), 767-781.

Bray, M., Adamson, B., & Mason, M. (2014). *Comparative education research: Approaches and methods* (2nd ed.). Heidelberg, Germany: Springer.

Davis, L. (Ed.). (2006). *The disability studies reader* (2nd ed.). New York, NY: Routledge.

Ferguson, M. (Ed.). (2006). *The executive branch of state government: People, process, and politics*. Santa Barbara, CA: ABC-Clio.

Freese, J. (1998). Language, symbols, and the Nebraska Councils of Defense. *The Social Science Journal, 35*(3), 423-433.

Garnett, J. (2019). *Reorganizing state government: The executive branch*. New York, NY: Routledge.

Gilbert, G. (Ed.). (1971). *The German language in America*. Austin: The University of Texas Press.

Goldstein, S., Daniel, P., & Gee, G. (1995). *Law and public education: Cases and materials* (3rd ed.). Charlottesville, VA: Michie.

Goodley, D. (2017). *Disability studies: An interdisciplinary introduction* (2nd ed.). Los Angeles, CA: Sage.

Grodzins, M. (1984). *The American system: A new view of government in the United States*. New Brunswick, NJ: Transaction.

History.com Editors. (2020, April 8). Brown *vs.* Board of Education. Retrieved from https://www.history.com/topics/black-history/brown-v-board-of-education-of-topeka.

Holian, T. (1998). *The German-Americans and World War II: An ethnic experience*. New York, NY: Peter Lang.

Ingelhart, L. (1993). The "Hazelwood" decision. *Communication: Journalism Education Today, 27*(2), 16-19.

Kelleher, C., & Wolak, J. (2007). Explaining public confidence in the branches of state government. *Political Research Quarterly, 60*(4), 707-721.

Kern, A., & Alexander, D. (2000). *American public school law* (5th ed.). Belmont, CA: West/Thomson Learning.

Kloss, H. (1998). *The American bilingual tradition*. Washington, DC: Center for Applied Linguistics.

Kohn, A. (2007, May 31). NCLB: Too destructive to salvage. *USA Today*. Retrieved from https://www.commondreams.org/views/2007/05/31/nclb-too-destructive-salvage.

Linton, S. (1998). Disability studies/not disability studies. *Disability and Society, 13*(4), 525-539.

Little, T., & Ogle, D. (2006). *The legislative branch of state government: People, process, and politics*. Santa Barbara, CA: ABC-Clio.

Lugg, C., & Robinson, M. (2009). Religion, advocacy coalitions, and the politics of U.S. public schooling. *Educational Policy, 23*(1), 242-266.

Mahler, J., & Eder, S. (2016, November 10). The Electoral College is hated by many. So why does it endure? *The New York Times*. Retrieved from https://www.nytimes.com/2016/11/11/us/politics/the-electoral-college-is-hated-by-many-so-why-does-it-endure.html.

Marshall, W. (2008). Eleven reasons why presidential power inevitably expands and why it matters. *Boston University Law Review, 88*, 505-522.

McCarthy, M., Cambron-McCabe, N., & Thomas, S. (1997). *Public school law: Teachers' and students' rights* (4th ed.). Boston, MA: Allyn & Bacon.

Morone, J. (1998). *The democratic wish: Popular participation and the limits of American government*. New Haven, CT: Yale University Press.

National Center for Educational Statistics. (2018). *Digest of educational statistics: 2018*. Retrieved from https://nces.ed.gov/programs/digest/d19/tables/dt19_105.50.asp.

Posey-Maddox, L. (2016). Beyond the consumer: Parents, privatization, and fundraising in U.S. urban public schools. *Journal of Educational Policy, 31*(2), 178-197.

Provine, D. (1980). *Case selection in the United States Supreme Court*. Chicago, IL: University of Chicago Press.

Quirk, P., & Binder, S. (Eds.). (2005). *The legislative branch*. Oxford, UK: Oxford University Press.

Reutter, E. (1998). *The law of public education* (4th ed.). Westbury, NY: Foundation.

Reckhow, S. (2013). *Follow the money: How foundation dollars change public school politics*. New York, NY: Oxford University Press.

Salmons, J. (Ed.). (1993). *The German language in American, 1683-1991*. Madison, WI: Max Kade Institute.

Schlesinger, A. (1973). *The imperial presidency*. Boston, MA: Houghton Mifflin.

Siegel, P. (1987). When is a student's political communication not political? Bethel School District *vs.* Fraser. *Communication Education, 36*(4), 347-355.

Stein, T. (2001). *Social policy and policymaking by the branches of government and the public-at-large*. New York, NY: Columbia University Press.

Stephenson, M. (2004). Court of public opinion: Government accountability and judicial independence. *The Journal of Law, Economics, and Organization, 20*(2), 379-399.

Sugarman, S. (2020). Supreme Court of the United States and the education: Religion, race, individual rights of students. *The StateUniversity.com education encyclopedia*. Retrieved from https://education.stateuniversity.com/pages/2473/Supreme-Court-United-States-Education.html.

U.S. Department of Education. (2006, December). *No Child Left Behind Act* is working. Retrieved from https://www2.ed.gov/nclb/overview/importance/nclbworking.html.

U.S. Department of Justice. (N.d.). Introduction to the federal court system. Retrieved from https://www.justice.gov/usao/justice-101/federal-courts#:~:text=Introduction%20To%20The%20Federal%20Court%20System%201%20District,3%20Supreme%20Court%20of%20the%20United%20States.%20.

U.S. House of Representatives. (N.d.). *National Defense Education Act*. Retrieved from
https://history.house.gov/HouseRecord/Detail/15032436195.

Yarwood, D. (1993). The Federalist authors and the problem of equality between the branches
of government: A study in institutional development. *Social Science Quarterly, 74*(3),
645-663.

Yudorf, M., Kirp, D., Levin, B., & Moran, R. (2001). *Educational policy and the law*. Belmont, CA:
West/Thomson Learning.

Chapter 3

The Epistemology of Education and Learning Theories

Expecting all children the same age to learn from the same materials is like expecting all children the same age to wear the same size clothing. (Madeline Hunter)

Everybody is a genius. But if you judge a fish by its ability to climb a tree, it will live its whole life believing that it is stupid. (Albert Einstein)

Epistemology is at the heart of education (see Scott, 2010; Siegel, 2010; Slezak, 2010). In essence, epistemology refers to the branch of philosophy that addresses questions of knowledge, belief, the justification of beliefs (including the nature of justified belief), and what it means when we say that one "knows" something. As Peter Paul and Donald Moores (2012) have explained,

> As a branch of philosophy, epistemology entails the study of a construct labeled *knowledge* … Traditionally, the foci have been on the conditions, sources, and limits of knowledge. Debate has centered on perspectives involving the relationship between the knower and what is known – between subject/agent and object, or between the observer and the object of observation … Pertinent questions include the following: Is there a separation of the two entities such that what is known can be shared with and agreed upon by others regardless of conditions (or qualifications) such as location or time? Are these two entities so intertwined that insights can only be personally or socially constructed, influenced by time and context? Is the framing of this issue erroneous, limited, or simply meaningless with no true or specific response or resolution? (p. 5)

At its core, epistemology can be understood to be the attempt to address the questions surrounding the relationship between the knower and the known; the term itself is sometimes even used synonymously with "a way of knowing" or a "worldview." Historically, in the Western intellectual tradition, there has been an assumption that there is a single, universal epistemological stance that would describe and explain all aspects of knowledge. More recently, many have questioned the idea that there is only one way for something to be known. There have been powerful and compelling arguments that only a model that takes into account the possibility of *multiple* ways of knowing (such as feminist epistemologies, black epistemologies, *latinx* epistemologies, queer epistemologies, and indigenous epistemologies) can be appropriate. Such arguments have important implications for understanding learning and learning theories as well as for what it means to "know" something, as we shall see. A good way to come to grips with these developments in epistemological theory is by examining the relationship between epistemology and the philosophy of science, and it is to this relationship that we now turn.

Epistemology and the Philosophy of Science

During much of the modern era, positivistic approaches to epistemology dominated the philosophy of science, as well as educational discourse.[1] Positivism, in a simple way, suggests that truth never changes and that it can be divided into smaller units of truth, that can then be understood and manipulated. For example, if we understand the principles of aerodynamics, we can use that knowledge to build aircraft.

By the 1960s, though, the dominance of positivism came under attack in the work of such individuals as Thomas Kuhn, Michel Foucault, and Paul Feyerabend, among others, each of whom presented distinct challenges to positivistic epistemology. Kuhn's (1970) *The Structure of Scientific Revolutions* introduced the related concepts of "paradigms," "paradigm shifts", and "normal science," which allowed for the distinction between periods of normal science during which a dominant paradigm exists in a particular discipline and times of paradigm shifts during which major scientific revolutions take place (Kuhn, 1970, 1977).[2] In essence, Kuhn's work reflected a shift in the way we think of truth, and explained how such shifts happen.

Foucault focused on the ways in which societies discount, delegitimize, and marginalize the knowledges of various groups (1975, 1976, 2000, 2008). As Philip Stokoes (2004) noted,

> The theme that underlies all Foucault's work is the relationship between power and knowledge, and how the former is used to control and define the latter. What authorities claim as "scientific knowledge" are really just means of social control. Foucault shows how, for instance, in the 18th century "madness" was used to categorise and stigmatise not just the mentally ill but the poor, the sick, the homeless and, indeed, anyone whose expressions of individuality were unwelcome. (p. 187)

In this vein, what is known is tied inextricably to social relationships between groups in society. Conceptualizing "power" dynamically, and focusing on the relationship between power and discourse, especially vis-à-vis the role of academic subjects or disciplines in the determination of what constitutes "legitimate" understandings, Foucault (2001) sought to stress the notion that "philosophy today is entirely political" (p. 266, our translation).

---

[1] This is in fact an oversimplification. There are a number of different kinds of positivism (logical positivism, logical empiricism, etc.), many different scholars associated with different sorts of positivism (e.g., Karl Popper, Quine, Durkheim, Wittgenstein, etc.), and positivism in different academic disciplines also varies to a considerable extent. However, there are core ideas that hold positivism together as a distinctive paradigm, albeit one in which various theories and perspectives compete.

[2] The example of a "paradigm shift" best associated with Thomas Kuhn is the case of the transition in cosmology from a Ptolemaic system to a Copernican one, but others would include the replacement of Galen's miasma theory with the germ theory of disease in medicine, the transition from Aristotelian mechanics to classical mechanics and then the subsequent transition to quantum mechanics, and so on. See, for example, Bird (2000), Brush (2000), and Nickles (2003).

Finally, the philosopher of science Feyerabend sought to take Kuhn's work to what he considered its logical conclusion: not merely epistemological relativism (of which Kuhn was misleadingly accused by many), but rather epistemological *anarchy* – the idea, in Feyerabend's own words, that in science "anything goes" (Feyerabend, 1970, 1981a, 1981b, 1983, 1991, 1995, 2002a, 2002b, 2006, 2010; see also Wolfmeyer, 2017). As Feyerabend (2010) argued in his book *Against Method*, "*Science is an essentially anarchic enterprise: theoretical anarchism is more humanitarian and more likely to encourage progress than its law-and-order alternatives …. anarchism*, while perhaps not the most attractive *political* philosophy, is certainly excellent medicine for *epistemology*, and for the *philosophy of science*" (p. 1, emphasis in original).

By the last quarter of the 20th century, the epistemological debates in the philosophy of science had spread to the social sciences as well as to the field of education, and by 1987 they had become widespread, leading to the appearance of what came to be termed "social epistemology." In essence, social epistemology can be understood to be a:

> field of intellectual inquiry or discipline in which the epistemic agents like traditional epistemology [are] still individual, but, the fundamental attempt stresses the multiple dimensions of knowledge with the fact that the acquisition and justification of our beliefs and knowledge is determined by various forms of social interaction or the translation of knowledge or justification from one person to another. (Jha & Devi, 2014, pp. 12-13)

In other words, what we think we know is actually influenced by our social position rather than being neutral and natural.

Ethnoepistemology

The recognition that knowledge is both individually and socially constructed has extremely significant implications for education, and this is especially true for historically marginalized groups. In the 1970s and early 1980s, challenges to traditional approaches to epistemology arose from two directions: First, feminist scholars raised a number of powerful critiques of academe, not only with respect to existing organizational, structural and personal biases, but also about the actual *content* of disciplinary knowledge: which questions were asked (and which were *not* asked), what methods were used (and which were *not* used) to answer them, what criteria should be (and which should *not* be) used to evaluate research results, and so on (see Alcoff & Potter, 1993; Anderson, 1995; Duncan, 2005; García, 2013; Lennon & Whitford, 1994). In their landmark work *Women's Ways of Knowing* Mary Belenky, Blythe Clinchy, Nancy Goldberger, and Jill Tarule (1997) argued that "gender is a major social, historical, and political category that affects the life choices of all women in all communities and cultures" (p. 13). Furthermore, they identified five epistemological perspectives that are essential in reconceptualizing epistemology to take women's perspectives into account:

Silence
> A position of not knowing in which the person feels voiceless, powerless, and mindless.

Received Knowing
> A position at which knowledge and authority are construed as outside the self and invested in powerful and knowing others from whom one is expected to learn.

Subjective Knowing
> A position in which knowing is personal, private, and based on intuition and/or feeling states rather than on thought and articulated ideas that are defended with evidence.

Procedural Knowing
> A position at which techniques and procedures for acquiring, validating, and evaluating knowledge claims are developed and honored. There are two distinct kinds of procedural knowledge: *separate knowing* and *connected knowing*.

Constructed Knowing
> A position at which truth is understood to be contextual – knowledge is recognized as tentative rather than as absolute, and it is believed that the knower is part of (constructs) the known. (Goldberger, Tarule, Clinchy, & Belenky, 1996, pp. 4-5)

We would suggest that these epistemological perspectives are also not just relevant to, but are essential for, taking into account the epistemological perspectives of other marginalized and oppressed groups as well. As educators, understanding how differing perspectives of knowledge influence what happens in schools is critical.

At the same time that feminist critiques of traditional epistemology were coming to the fore, non-Western scholars began to argue that what had been taken to be epistemology was in fact only *Western* epistemology – a single, particular "folk epistemology" that ought to be taken to be equivalent to, but not necessarily superior to, other folk epistemologies (see Abu-Saad & Champagne, 2006; Christie, 2006; Gélinas & Bouchard, 2014; Laughlin, 2013; Mazzocchi, 2018; Vanier, 2011). As James Maffie (2013) has explained, such *ethnoepistemology* requires us to view "Western epistemology as one among many possible, contingent epistemological undertakings pursued by human beings … [an] approach [which] decenters and provincializes the aims, norms, problems, intuitions, and conclusions of Western epistemology since it no longer regards these as inevitable, universal, or definitive of the epistemology standpoint *per se*" (p. 278). Such an approach to epistemology, which is based on the idea that "different ethnic groups have their own implicit, informal theories of knowledge and that these ethnotheories form the assumptions on which the explicit formal theories are based" (see Zambrano & Greenfield, 2004, p. 251), has profound implications for education as well as other disciplines. As Michelle Salazar Pérez and Cinthya Saavedra (2017) have suggested,

Epistemology refers to what can be known, and the relationship between the knower and the known … however … "epistemology is more than a 'way of knowing'"; rather it encompasses a "system of knowing" that has historically privileged Euro-American perspectives as if they are "the only legitimate way to view the world." This epistemological dominance has had devastating consequences for marginalized children both in their educational experiences and everyday encounters with the world. (p. 3)

Furthermore, it is not merely the case that dominated and marginalized groups have their own distinctive epistemologies, but that there are also multiple, overlapping epistemologies. For example, it is not the case that there is a single "feminist epistemology"; rather,

Most feminists of color recognize that gender, race, class, and sexual orientation – *not* gender alone – determine the allocation of power and the nature of any individual's identity, status, and consequence … Therefore, "endarkened" feminist epistemologies are crucial, as they speak to the failures of traditional patriarchal and liberal educational scholarship and examine the intersection of race, class, gender and sexuality. (Bernal, 1998, p. 556, emphasis added)

The debate about the relationship between the knower and the known that underlies these epistemological concerns is based, in part, on differences of opinion related to the notions of objectivity and relativism (Paul & Moores, 2012, p. 5), and we now turn to a brief discussion of these matters.

The Nature of Knowledge

In an introduction to the art and science of teaching, there are a number of significant epistemological distinctions that should be noted. One useful concept in this regard is the idea of tacit knowledge. Michael Polyani first wrote about tacit knowledge in his 1958 book *Personal Knowledge*, and later in *The Tacit Dimension* in 1966. Tacit knowledge, which can be contrasted with explicit knowledge, has been defined as the skills, ideas, concepts, and experiences that we possess, but which are not "written in stone" or codified, and which may not be easily expressed – indeed, we may not even be aware of our tacit knowledge. What is especially interesting and valuable is that it is in a community of practice – such as a community of classroom teachers – where such tacit knowledge can often be most clear, and also where it can be most effectively passed from one person to another.

A second way of conceptualizing knowledge that is of special relevance in a critical context is by borrowing the anthropological distinction between emic and etic knowledge. In essence, *emic* knowledge refers to knowledge, understanding, and interpretations that come from *within* a particular cultural community, while *etic* knowledge refers to knowledge, understanding and interpretations that are proposed by those *outside* of the community. Finally, Jürgen Habermas and others have noted that knowledge can take three distinct forms: technical knowledge, practical knowledge, and emancipatory knowledge (Habermas, 1972; see also Holub, 1991; McLaren, 2003, p. 197; Outhwaite, 2009). Technical knowledge is the sort that can be measured and quantified and comes principally from the natural sciences. Practical knowledge is concerned with describing and analyzing social situations, and comes mainly from the social sciences. Emancipatory knowledge is knowledge that seeks to understand social relationships and especially seeks to understand how such relationships are distorted by power and inequitable power relations in society.

Metaphors in Educational Discourse

Metaphors are widely used in education and in other kinds of public discourse, and often play key roles in discussion and debates.[3] Thomas Green (1971) has suggested that, "it may be that metaphors are necessary if we are to think about important matters at all. No major philosopher in the history of the subject has escaped their use and no major field of knowledge in the modern world can do without them" (p. 56). Metaphors, at root, are basically unstated analogies, involving the implicit comparison of two different kinds of things, one of which is intended by the speaker to be taken literally, the other figuratively. Examples of common educational metaphors would include the claims that "education is growth," "critical thinking is a tool," and "teachers mold and shape children." Taken literally, each of these claims is clearly not only false but also absurd (see Scheffler, 1960, pp. 49-59; see also Scheffler, 1979). However, it is nevertheless true that we do in fact understand each of these statements quite clearly in the non-literal way in which each is intended. Metaphors, in short, are used because they have value to us. As Green (1971) noted, "The main virtue of the metaphor is that it calls our attention to certain similarities between two things. It carries the mind over from one thing to another by calling attention to resemblances. In other words, a metaphor is a way of establishing 'thought-full' relations between [and among] things" (p. 57).

We commonly use metaphors and metaphorical language to describe such concepts as teaching, learning and knowing, and such metaphors are extremely important. By their very nature, metaphors are intended to be non-literal (see Lakoff & Johnson, 1980), and yet, they reflect underlying beliefs and attitudes and, even more, themselves take on significant pedagogical power. There is a wealth of metaphorical language in the discourse of classroom teachers that relates directly and indirectly to pedagogy and pedagogical issues. As Steven Miller and Marcel Fredericks have argued, the use of metaphors is a worthwhile topic for our attention since, "Metaphorical expressions are so pervasive in ordinary and academic life ... they must reflect a 'fundamental core' of shared meaning. By using these expressions, people must assign meaning. Metaphors are not simply random events but are ways of 'structuring' and extending experience" (1988, pp. 263-264).

Metaphors and metaphorical language function in part to structure the individual's construction of reality, as well as to mediate their experiences with underlying, and often

---

[3] It is important to emphasize that our concern here, and the focus in the literature on metaphors in discourse, is on *metaphorical language* rather than simply on metaphors. Thus, included in this discussion are not only pure metaphors, but also similes and other forms of metaphorical language. For an extended discussion and explanation of this matter, see Lakoff and Johnson (1980); also of interest are Ortony (1980), Smith (1981), and Taylor (1984).

implicit, assumptions, values, and beliefs. As George Lakoff and Mark Johnson have suggested, "Metaphors may create realities for us, especially social realities. A metaphor may thus be a guide for future action. Such actions will, of course, fit the metaphor. This will, in turn, reinforce the power of the metaphor to make experience coherent. In this sense metaphors can be self-fulfilling prophecies" (1980, p. 156).

If it is indeed the case that metaphors not only play a role in the way in which individuals construct their realities but also serve as guides for practice, then it would seem to be evident that the study of the *kinds* of metaphors and metaphorical language employed by teachers and other educators about teaching and learning ought to be of considerable concern to anyone interested in understanding and improving educational practice (see Nattinger, 1993). Siegelman (1990), for instance, believes that metaphors have the potential to generate new ideas and meanings between listener and speaker. Thus, if the goal is to help people better communicate their personal realities, metaphors can provide an infrastructure for supporting shared cultures (see Nuessel, 2000).

The analysis of metaphors in educational discourse can provide us with useful insights, and the use of metaphors can help us to develop clearer understandings and appreciations of complex issues and concepts. Consider, for instance, the kinds of metaphors that are often used by teachers to describe the concept of "teaching." In a fascinating study of classroom teacher discourse, Miller and Fredericks (1988) found that four broad "families" of metaphors were commonly used:

- Teaching as a conduit (the "transfer of knowledge").
- Teaching as a biological process (the "growth of students").
- Teaching as a process of building (the "construction of knowledge and understanding").
- Teaching as war ("working in the trenches" or "teachers are in the front lines"). (pp. 263-272)

Trench Warfare
© Everett Collection/Shutterstock.com

The metaphor chosen to describe teaching tells us a great deal about the teacher. The frequent use of war or military metaphors, for instance, suggests that the teacher perceives the classroom as something of a battleground. Insofar as this is the case, we would expect (and indeed would be likely to find) that concerns of classroom management and control are at the top of such a teacher's worries. This, in turn, will be reflected in the approach to students, teaching methods, assessment, and so on taken by the teacher.

Theories of Learning

Since at least the time of Plato in the 4th and 5th centuries BCE, philosophers have sought to understand how human beings learn. Most of the discussion that took place in this "on-going human conversation" before the 19th century, though, was basically limited to what might be called "armchair theorizing" – that is, it consisted of hypotheses for which there was really no empirical evidence. As the National Research Council (2000) argued in its *How people learn*:

> The essence of matter, the origins of the universe, the nature of the human mind – these are the profound questions that have engaged thinkers through the centuries. Unit quite recently, understanding the mind – and the thinking and learning that the mind makes possible – has remained an elusive quest, in part because of the lack of powerful research tools. (p. 3)

Toward the end of the 19th century, this began to change as the new science of psychology emerged, and throughout the 20th and now early 21st centuries a number of interesting models of human learning – each with its own implications for classroom practice -- have been suggested by psychologists, based on experimental, empirical and increasingly neurological evidence (see, for example, National Research Council, 2000). Entire books have been written about particular learning theories, and whole courses in teacher education programs are devoted to the subjects of educational psychology and learning theories, and it is neither possible nor appropriate for us to cover all of the different learning theories and their implications for educators here. However, it is nonetheless true, as Marion Williams and Robert Burden (1999) noted, that:

> The educational process is one of the most important and complex human undertakings … There exists a common idea that teaching is carried out by a person, the teacher, who is standing in front of the classroom in front of a group of students and transmitting information to these students who are attempting to absorb it … this vision simplifies a very complex process that involves a complicated interaction among the learning process itself, the goals and actions of the teacher, the personality, culture and background of the learner, the learning environment, and many other variables. The effective educator ought to be one who understands the complexities of the teaching-learning process and who can use this knowledge to empower … [their] students both in and beyond the classroom. (p. 15, our translation)

There are three major learning theories that are commonly employed in contemporary education: behaviorism, cognitivism, and constructivism. Each is significant, and each has important implications for understanding learning, as well as for conceptualizing the teaching process. It is important to note that our comments here are necessarily overly simplified, and that not only is each of these theories far more complex than suggested here, but that within each of these theories are actually multiple (and often competing) theories.

Children Doing Science Experiment
© Rawpixel.com/Shutterstock.com

Behaviorism

Behaviorism is the oldest of the different learning theories that we will discuss, and it has had a huge impact on both psychology and education (see Baum, 2017; O'Neil, 1995; Slavin, 2018). Behaviorism first developed in the late-19th century, and was really the first approach to understanding learning that was based on experimental hypotheses and tests. In essence, behaviorism is grounded in the idea that all behaviors – whether human or animal – are in some manner responses to stimuli that the individual is exposed to (in its simplest version, called Stimulus-Response Theory). Among the earliest of the modern psychologists interested in understanding the nature of learning was the Russian physician and physiologist Ivan Pavlov, who is credited with first identifying what is called classical conditioning, which serves in many ways as the foundation for contemporary behavioral learning theories. Pavlov is best known for an important, but also fairly simple, set of experimental results that originated from informal observations that he made while conducting studies on the digestive processes of dogs. When given food, dogs salivate. This is a natural (and necessary) part of the eating process. What Pavlov noticed, though, was that his test animals salivated whenever they saw the laboratory technician who fed them – whether or not they were actually being fed. This was an *unconditioned* stimulus which led to an *unconditioned* response. Pavlov further discovered, however, that he could produce a *conditioned* response in the dogs in a deliberate fashion, and that there were certain things that increased the speed at which the conditioned response would develop. The conditioned response here is basically learning, and it takes place not only in dogs and other animals, but can also be used with people in a variety of ways and for a number of different purposes.

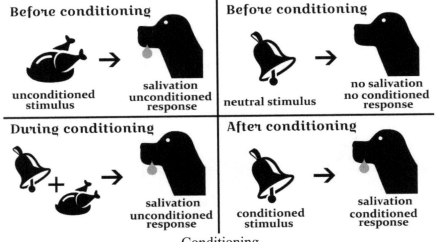

Conditioning
© desdemona72/Shutterstock.com

The American psychologist Edward Thorndike added to the concept of classical conditioning by demonstrating that responses to stimuli that produced pleasant consequences tended to be repeated, while those produced unpleasant consequences were less likely to be repeated – which is called the "Law of Effect" (see Beatty, 1998; O'Neil, 1995; Thorndike, 2000). John Watson, in the early decades of the 20th century, sought to develop "methodological behaviorism" by focusing only on behaviors, events and outcomes that could actually be measured, thus effectively eliminating thoughts and feelings from an understanding of learning (see Watson, 1970). Beginning in the 1930s, another American psychologist, B. F. Skinner, critiqued both the idea that classical conditioning could adequately explain much of human behavior and elements of Thorndike's work (especially Thorndike's references to mental states that could not be observed), and expanded the application of the "Law of Effect" into what came to be known as operant conditioning. For Skinner, operant conditioning refers to how learning can be strengthened or weakened as a result of either positive reinforcement or negative reinforcement (see Skinner, 1971, 1974); Skinner's approach to behaviorism is commonly called "radical behaviorism" (Chiesa, 1992, 1994; Johnson, 2014).

There are a number of very direct implications for educational practice that emerge from behaviorist learning theory, including:

- An emphasis on producing observable and measurable outcomes in students (including the use of behavioral objectives, task analysis, and criterion-referenced assessments).
- Pre-assessment of students to determine where instruction should begin.
- Emphasis on mastering early steps before progressing to more complex levels of performance (sequencing of instruction, mastery learning).
- Use of reinforcement to impact performance.

- Use of cues, shaping and practice to ensure a strong stimulus-response association. (Ertmer & Newby, 2013, pp. 49-50)

It has become fairly common in some educational circles to view behaviorism very critically, but it is important to understand that behaviorist approaches in many areas have proven to be extremely effective. This is especially true in terms of the application of behaviorism in applied behavioral analysis, including not only in the field of special education (where it is widely utilized), but also in different cognitive-behavioral therapies, including in the treatment of mood disorders, phobias, and post-traumatic stress disorder. Basically, behaviorism is most useful in "facilitating learning that involves discriminations (recalling facts), generalizations (defining and illustrating concepts), associations (applying explanations), and chaining (automatically performing a specified procedure) … however, it is generally agreed that behavior principles cannot adequately explain the acquisition of higher level skills or those that require a greater depth of processing (e.g., language development, problem solving, inference generating, critical thinking" (Ertmer & Newby, 2013, p. 49).

Cognitivism

Beginning in the 1960s, there was a move away from behaviorism, toward what has come to be called "cognitivism," although this transition actually began far earlier and was in some ways embedded in some of the major limitations of behaviorism (see Mandler, 2002). As George Mandler (2002) noted,

> The well-documented cognitive "revolution" was, to a large extent, an evolving return to attitudes and trends that were present prior to the advent of behaviorism and that were alive and well outside of the United States, where behaviorism had not developed any coherent support. The behaviorism of the 1920 to 1950 period was replaced because it was unable to address central issues in human psychology, a failure that was inherent in part in J. B. Watson's founding manifesto with its insistence on the seamless continuity of human and nonhuman animal behavior. The "revolution" was often slow and piecemeal … With the realization that different approaches and concepts were needed to address a psychology of the human, developments in German, British, and Francophone psychology provided some of the fuel of the "revolution." (p. 339)

Perhaps the single most important distinction between behaviorist approaches and cognitivist approaches to understanding learning is how "thinking" is conceptualized. For behaviorists, thinking is a *behavior*, while for cognitivists it is far more than merely a behavior – it is foundational, and is therefore far more than merely a behavior (see Lilienfeld et al., 2015, pp. 31-32). In other words, "according to cognitivists, predictions of behavior based solely on rewards and punishments from the environment will never be adequate, because our interpretation of rewards and punishments is a crucial determinant of our behaviour … Without understanding how people evaluate information, cognitivists maintain, we will never fully grasp the causes of their behaviour" (Lilienfeld et al., 2015, p. 31).

Cognitivism focuses on such concepts as memory, perceptions, thinking, knowing and problem-solving, and defines learning as changes in the learner's mental schemata. It is often suggested that cognitivism views the mind as a "black box" – a "black box" that we wish to open and understand. Prior to learning, we are in a state of equilibrium, and learning is, on Jean Piaget's account, basically the process of "adaptation." Adaptation involves the state of equilibrium being challenged by a new situation that challenges our existing schemata, leading to disequilibrium. Disequilibrium leads, in turn, to accommodation and ultimately assimilation (see Piaget, 1928, 1932, 1948a, 1948b, 1976, 1979, 1993, 1996, 2012; Sinclair, Berthoud, Gerard, & Venesiano, 1985). Essentially, what this means, as Peggy Ertmer and Timothy Newby (2013) have explained, is that "the real focus of the cognitive approach is on *changing the learning by encouraging … [students] to use appropriate learning strategies*" (p. 52, emphasis in original).

Cognitivism, like behaviorism, has a number of implications for educational practice, including:

- An emphasis on the active involvement of the learning in the learning process.
- The use of hierarchical analyses to identify and illustrate prerequisite relationships.
- An emphasis on structuring, organizing, and sequencing information to facilitate optimal processing.
- The creation of learning environments that allow and encourage students to make connections with previously learned material. (Etmer & Newby, 2013, p. 53)

To a very considerable extent, cognitivism can be best thought of as analogous to the way that a computer operates – and, indeed, cognitivists often use the metaphor of "mind as a computer" to explain the core assumptions of cognitivism.

Constructivism

In recent years, a number of academic disciplines, not the least of which are mathematics and science, have undergone significant changes in the epistemology that underlies their pedagogical practice, moving increasingly toward constructivist approaches to learning theory (see Boudourides, 2003; Jones & Brader-Araje, 2002; Matthews, 2002; Mintzes, Wandersee, & Novak, 1997; Nola, 1997; Oxford, 1997; Spivey, 1997; Steffe & Kieren, 1994; Tobin, 1993; Von Glasersfeld, 2002; Wood, Cobb, & Yackel, 1995). This change in learning theory has, in essence, involved a change in the *metaphors* that we use to conceptualize knowledge, teaching, learning, and knowing (see Tarsitani, 1996). Although to some extent arguably implicit in many contemporary discussions about teaching, and often fairly clearly embodied in actual teaching practice, constructivist approaches to epistemology and learning theory have only recently, and relatively rarely, been explicitly examined in terms of their implications for teaching and learning (see Kaufman & Grennon Brooks, 1996).

Girl Studying
© Iakov Filimonov/Shutterstock.com

Although constructivism has gained considerable attention in the educational literature, there is no clear definition or consensus of what is meant by the term (see Fosnot, 1996a; Kafai & Resnick, 1996; Merrill, 1992; Nicaise & Barnes, 1996; Schwandt, 1994; Steffe & Gale, 1995). As Virginia Richardson (1997b) has noted, "One cannot think of constructivist teaching … as a monolithic, agreed-upon concept …. There are fundamental theoretical differences in the various constructivist approaches" (p. 3). Indeed, there is even debate about whether constructivism is best understood as an epistemology, an educational philosophy, a pedagogical approach, a theory of teaching, or a theory of learning (see Kaufman & Grennon Brooks, 1996, p. 234). Arguably the best articulation of the nature of constructivism in the educational literature remains that of Catherine Fosnot (1993), who compellingly suggests that, "Constructivism is not a theory about teaching. It's a theory about knowledge and learning" (p. vii). However, "some general principles of learning derived from constructivism may be helpful to keep in mind … as we rethink and reform our educational practices" (Fosnot, 1996b, p. 29). Such a view of constructivism essentially confirms its status as an epistemology — a theory of *knowledge and learning*, rather than a theory of *teaching* (see Von Glasersfeld, 1993, pp. 23-24). As an epistemology, constructivism entails the rejection of traditional transmission-oriented views of learning, as well as behaviorist models of learning. Instead, emphasis is placed on the individual learner's construction of their knowledge. Beyond this, though, constructivism assumes not only that learning is constructed, but also that the learning process is a personal and individual one, that learning is an active undertaking, that learning is collaborative in nature, and that all learning is situated (see Merrill, 1992, p. 102). In other words, what constructivism offers is a radically different view of the nature of the learning process — a view that is grounded in a rejection of what Von Glasersfeld (1995) has called the "domination of a mindless behaviorism" (p. 4). This view includes, as Fosnot (1996b) notes, a number of general principles of learning, including:

- Learning is not the result of development; learning *is* development. It requires invention and self-organization on the part of the learner.
- Disequilibrium facilitates learning. "Errors" need to be perceived as a result of learners' conceptions and therefore not minimized or avoided … Contradictions, in particular, need to be illuminated, explored, and discussed.

- Reflective abstraction is the driving force of learning. As meaning-makers, humans seek to organize and generalize across experiences in a representational form.
- Dialogue within a community engenders further thinking. The classroom needs to be seen as a "community of discourse engaged in activity, reflection, and conversation."
- Learning proceeds toward the development of structures. As learners struggle to make meaning, progressive structural shifts in perspective are constructed — in a sense, "big ideas" ... These "big ideas" are learner-constructed, central organizing principles that can be generalized across experiences and that often require the undoing or reorganizing of earlier conceptions. This process continues throughout development. (pp. 29-30)

It is important to stress here that constructivist epistemology is more than simply an alternative to other approaches to epistemology; rather, it entails a rejection of some of the core assumptions that have been shared by Western epistemology for some two and a half millennia (see Gergen, 1982, 1995). As Von Glasersfeld (1995) has argued, "the crucial fact [in understanding constructivism is] that the constructivist theory of knowing breaks with the epistemological tradition in philosophy" (p. 6), which is why it has been labeled not merely postmodernist but *postepistemological* by some writers (see Noddings, 1990).

While it is obviously important to keep in mind that constructivism is not, and could not be, a pedagogical theory or approach *per se,* it is also true that certain characteristics of the constructivist-based classroom can be identified. For example, Jacqueline Grennon Brooks and Martin Brooks (1993) and Dorit Kaufman and Jacqueline Grennon Brooks (1996) have identified eight characteristics that have been observed in constructivist classrooms:

- Use raw data and primary sources, along with manipulative, interactive, and physical materials.
- When framing tasks, use cognitive terminology, such as *classify, analyze, predict, create,* and so on.
- Allow student thinking to drive lessons. Shift instructional strategies or alter content based on student responses.
- Inquire about students' understandings of concepts before sharing your own understandings of those concepts.
- Ask open-ended questions of students and encourage students to ask questions of others.
- Seek elaboration of students' initial responses.
- Engage students in experiences that might engender contradictions to students' initial hypotheses and then encourage a discussion.
- Provide time for students to construct relationships and create metaphors. (Kaufman & Grennon Brooks, 1996, p. 235)

What these characteristics, taken together, are all about really focuses on what could be called "guided discovery" or, more accurately, "structured induction" both in and as the learning process. These characteristics function both as descriptive and normative attributes in that they have not only been observed in practice but have also been used for evaluation purposes. It is important to note here, incidentally, that "Many of these attributes are not unique to constructivist teaching but are representative of good teaching in general" (Kaufman & Grennon Brooks, 1996, p. 235) — a point that would seem to confirm Von Glasersfeld's claim that, "Constructivism does not claim to have made earth-shaking inventions in the area of education; it merely claims to provide a solid conceptual basis for some of the things that, until now, inspired teachers had to do without theoretical foundation" (Von Glaserfeld, 1995, p. 15). Furthermore, while it is the case that "constructivist principles of learning do not automatically engender principles of teaching … [since] learners construct meaning on their own terms no matter what teachers do" (Winitzky & Kauchak, 1997, p. 62), it is also true that:

> Constructivist theorists would maintain … that learning is better or more effective when teachers use constructivist teaching methods, like culturing … bacteria as opposed to lecturing about bacteria. Constructivist teaching typically involves more student-centered, active learning experiences, more student-student and student-teacher interaction, and more work with concrete materials and in solving realistic problems … Nevertheless, students still create their own meanings based on the interaction of their prior knowledge with instruction, and the meanings they make may not be the ones the teacher had in mind, no matter how constructivist the instruction … Teachers create constructivist learning experiences for students based necessarily on what they, the teachers, find salient. But what is salient to the teacher is not necessarily so to the learner. (Winitzky & Kauchak, 1997, pp. 62-63)

Constructivist epistemology has clear implications for classroom practice, the curricula, student evaluation and assessment, and, indeed, virtually all aspects of the teaching/learning process (see Henning, 1995; Zietsman, 1996). It also has the potential to impact in significant ways the preparation of educators (see Condon, Clyde, Kyle, & Hovda, 1993; Rainer & Guyton, 1994; Richardson, 1997a) and the challenge of preparing such educators to engage in reflective and analytic classroom practice (see Parker, 1997; Reagan, Case, & Brubacher, 2000; Richards & Lockhart, 1994; Zeichner & Liston, 1987, 1996). The ultimate purpose of taking constructivist epistemology seriously, though, is its potential for helping teachers empower students to learn more effectively. An additional point that needs to be stressed here is that constructivist epistemology, while certainly having clear implications for classroom practice, is concerned first and foremost with helping us to understand the learning process itself, rather than with dictating pedagogical practice. Much of the common pedagogical practice of classroom teachers is fully compatible with constructivist learning theory; the power of constructivist epistemology for education may well be more in its explanatory, legitimating and justificatory power than in terms of any specific implications that it may have for classroom practice.

Lev Vygotsky and the Zone of Proximal Development (ZPD)

One of the more widely cited psychologists in recent years in educational circles has been the Soviet psychologist Lev Vygotsky, who is perhaps best known for his concept of the "Zone of Proximal Development" (ZPD) (зона ближайшего развития). Vygotsky has been most closely tied to constructivism and constructivist learning theories, but this is actually the result of a number of significant misunderstandings of his work. Given how ubiquitous Vygotsky and his work is in contemporary educational discourse, it is probably worth briefly exploring both his work and how it has been misunderstood.

Vygotsky was born in 1896 in what was then the Russian Empire, and was a university student at the time of the Russian Revolution; the corpus of his work thus developed in the early years of the Soviet Union (see Vygotsky, 2005a, 2005b, 2008). An important objective of the new Soviet state was the creation of the "Socialist Man," and Vygotsky was most interested in the genesis of developmental psychology as a means of understanding how such a person might be created (see Yasnitsky, 2019). Focusing, then, on the study of infant and child behavior, as well as on language acquisition (including what is called "inner speech"),[4] Vygotsky's psychological studies underwent a number of shifts and changes before his premature death from tuberculosis in 1934, at the age of only 37. His earliest work, which took place in the 1920s, was characterized by what has been "instrumentalism," a doctrine that he later strongly rejected. Between 1929 and 1932, Vygotsky underwent a period of significant self-criticism during which he radically revised his earlier thinking, which led to what is called the "holistic period" of his work, between 1932 and his death in 1934 – a period of incredible creativity but also one that resulted in far fewer publications than his earlier work (Frawley, 1997; Moll, 1990). Although Vygotsky was known in the West from his work in the 1920s, it was not really until the 1980s when constructivist psychology began gaining traction that his work gained significant attention. Unfortunately, due to an overreliance on a very small number of translations of his work (see Vygotsky, 2012), distortions in other published works from the Soviet era, and often a lack of understanding of Vygotsky's own social, political, and cultural context, his contributions have on all too many occasions been misunderstood and oversimplified (see Van der Veer & Valsiner, 1991).

Focusing on the relationship between the child's learning and their cognitive development, Vygotsky recognized that there were three major theoretical approaches to understanding this relationship. Basically, these approaches consisted of fundamentally different views of the relationship between learning and cognitive development:

---

[4] To some extent, it could be argued that some of Vygotsky's greatest contributions were not so much concerned with learning theory as with language, inner speech, and the relationship between language and speech (see Alderson-Day & Fernyhough, 2015).

Behaviorism, which essentially assumes that learning *is* development.

Constructivism, which is based on the broad idea that the child has to *first* reach a certain developmental level *before* learning can occur.

Gestaltism, which suggests that learning and development are separate and distinct, but also *overlapping* and *interactive* processes.

Vygotsky rejected all three of these positions, and instead proposed the idea of the ZPD as a better and more appropriate way of viewing the relationship between learning and cognitive development. Specifically, Vygotsky believed that learning needed to *precede* development, but that it needed to do so *within* the ZPD. For Vygotsky, the ZPD explained the relationship between the child's learning and their cognitive development, specifically by distinguishing between the child's current knowledge and the unmatured abilities of the child that can be developed with the guidance of the teacher.

Bloom's Taxonomy

In 1956, Benjamin Bloom and his colleagues published the first volume of *The Taxonomy of Educational Objectives* (Bloom, Engelhard, Furst, & Hill, 1956), which provided a rubric for the classification of learning objectives that has continued to play an important role in educational practice to the present day. As G. M. Seddon noted in 1978, "There is no doubt that Bloom's *Taxonomy of Educational Objectives* … has had a considerable impact on educational thought and practice all over the world" (p. 303), and if anything this is even more true today than it was then. "Bloom's Taxonomy," as this system is commonly known, consists of three hierarchical models that allow us to classify learning objectives into levels of complexity and specificity. In essence, what Bloom's Taxonomy does is to give us a multi-layered model that demonstrates how different kinds of learning take place through a number of distinct stages of increasing complexity, moving from lower order thinking skills to higher level thinking skills. The domains addressed by Bloom's Taxonomy include the cognitive (knowledge-based) domain, the affective (emotion-based) domain, and the psychomotor (action-based) domain. The 1956 volume addressed objectives in the cognitive domain, and it has been primarily with cognitive objectives that Bloom's Taxonomy has continued in large part to be identified. The original cognitive domain taxonomy consisted of six levels, ranging from the lowest level, which is concerned with knowledge, to the highest level, concerned with evaluation. The six levels were:

Evaluating
Synthesizing
Analyzing
Applying
Comprehending
Knowing (Bloom et al., 1956)

The taxonomy was updated and revised by Lorin Anderson and David Krathwohl in 2001, and several of the levels were renamed and some changes in the hierarchy were also made. The revised cognitive domain is now as follows:

Creating
Evaluating
Analyzing
Applying
Understanding
Remembering (Anderson & Krathwohl, 2001)

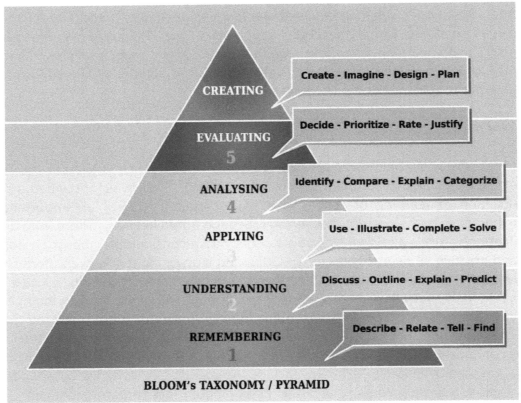

Bloom's Taxonomy Pyramid
©Artelloa/Shutterstock.com

Table 3.1 offers a summary of some of the key elements of the cognitive domain in the revised version of Bloom's Taxonomy, including a brief explanation of each of the six levels in the hierarchy, the core or fundamental classroom-based question that each level seeks to answer, and finally, a sample of some of the verbs that can be used in the writing of instructional objectives for learning at each of the levels.[5]

---

[5] One of the most common uses of Bloom's Taxonomy, and especially the cognitive domain component of Bloom's Taxonomy, is its use in constructing learning objectives. As a general rule, it is preferable to utilize learning objectives that are written with measurable verbs (e.g., list, compare, contrast) than with vague or non-measurable verbs (e.g., discuss, explain, talk about). This is true especially in terms of relating the learning objectives in a class to the process of evaluation and assessment.

Cognitive Level	Explanation	Core Question	Verbs for Learning Objectives
Creating	Elements can be put together to form a new, coherent whole.	Can the student create a new product or point of view?	*assemble, construct, create, design, develop, devise, formulate, generate, imagine, organize, plan*
Evaluating	Judgments based on criteria and standards can be made by checking and critiquing.	Can the student justify a position or decision?	*appraise, argue, decide, defend, judge, justify, prioritize, rate, select, verify*
Analyzing	Information can be broken into parts, and the relationship among the parts can be shown.	Can the student distinguish and differentiate among different parts of the content being learned?	*categorize, classify, compare, contrast, criticize, differentiate, discriminate, distinguish, experiment, explain, identify, question*
Applying	What was learned in Remembering and Understanding can be implemented in practice.	Can the student use information in new ways?	*complete, convert, demonstrate, discover, discuss, dramatize, illustrate, interpret, prepare, solve, use*
Understanding	Meaning is constructed by interpreting and summarizing information.	Can the student explain new ideas and concepts?	*classify, discuss, exemplify, explain, infer, interpret, outline, explain, paraphrase, predict, summarize*
Remembering	Information from long-term memory can be recalled.	Can the student remember or recall information?	*define, describe, duplicate, find, list, memorize, relate, repeat, reproduce, tell*

Table 3.1 Bloom's Taxonomy: The Cognitive Domain (2001 Revision)

The hierarchy for the affective domain in Bloom's Taxonomy, which focuses on human emotions, is summarized in Table 3.2. In essence, the affective domain seeks to address the ways that we deal with different kinds of issues emotionally, including such topics as feelings, values, motivations, and attitudes (see Krathwohl, 2002; Krathwohl, Bloom, & Masia, 1973).

Cognitive Level	Explanation	Core Question	Verbs for Learning Objectives
Characterizing	Internalizes and believes in the new value; works cooperatively and collaboratively with group members.	Does the student act consistently with the new value?	*avoid, manage, rate, resist, require, resolve, revise*
Organizing	Accepts different viewpoints and builds on them to construct new perspectives and understandings.	Has the student combined and conceptualized a new value, giving it priority?	*balance, discuss, examine, formulate, prioritize, theorize*

Valuing	Attaches importance and worth to the information gained; shares one's own perspectives while remaining open to those of others in the group.	Does the student show involvement and commitment?	*debate, measure proficiency, subsidize, support*
Responding	Inquires and asks questions; makes unique comments that lead to the development of conversations.	Can the student demonstrate a new behavior due to an experience?	*acclaim, commend, comply, engage in, follow, volunteer*
Receiving	Listens to comments of peers and other group members, reads, seeks other information.	Is the student aware of the new environment?	*accept, differentiate, listen, respond*

Table 3.2 Bloom's Taxonomy: The Affective Domain

Finally, the hierarchy for the psychomotor domain in Bloom's Taxonomy, which focuses on physical activities, is summarized in Table 3.3.[6] The psychomotor domain basically includes physical movement, coordination, and the development of motor skills, all of which require practice and which are measured in terms of factors such as speed, precision, accuracy, distance, procedures, and techniques with respect to execution (Simpson, 1971).

Cognitive Level	Explanation	Core Question	Verbs for Learning Objectives
Naturalization	High level of performance is achieved with actions becoming second nature.	Is the student able to demonstrate a high level of competence performing selected physical activities?	*arrange, build, construct, initiate*
Articulation	Several skills can be performed together in a harmonious manner.	Does the student have advanced and complex physical skills and abilities? Can the student perform multiple physical activities simultaneously?	*alter, rearrange, vary, revise*
Precision	Performance becomes more exact, and actions are more precise.	Does the student have the stamina, strength, and ability needed for particular actions?	*assemble, calibrate, fasten, measure, mend*

---

[6] The psychomotor domain is sometimes presented with different categories. The most common alternative to those we have provided here, from the lowest level to the highest level, is one that includes perception, set, guided response, mechanism, complex overt response, adaptation, and origination. When structured in this manner, the psychomotor domain has six rather than five levels.

Manipulation	Actions are performed through memorization or following directions.	Can the student demonstrate basic physical abilities independently or with limited guidance?	*copy, react, reproduce, trace*
Imitation	Learning by watching and imitating actions.	Does the student demonstrate reflex and born reactions and abilities?	*begin, move, show, state*

Table 3.3 Bloom's Taxonomy: The Psychomotor Domain

Learning Styles

Classroom teachers have long been aware of the fact that students seem to learn in different ways. Most often, in education we talk about three different orientations in learners -- visual learners, auditory learners, and kinesthetic learners.[7] The basic idea is that some students learn best by *seeing* content, others by *hearing* content, and still others as a result of more *tactile* or *"hands on"* kinds of learning experiences. The assumption that there are these three major learning styles has also led to the common belief that there should be different teaching styles, oriented to each of the learning styles, and that we should attempt to tie or to match our teaching approaches to the specific needs of different learners. Thus, the most appropriate way to meet the educational needs of visual learners is by making maximal use of visual teaching materials, while the needs of auditory learners can be best addressed using more auditory teaching methods, and the needs of kinesthetic learners requires more experiential kinds of teaching. So, for visual learners, who typically benefit most from actually seeing what they need to learn, the use of techniques such as readings, graphics, and videos are especially useful. For auditory learners, hearing information and receiving instruction orally, as well as being able to repeat such information and instruction themselves, is generally believed to work best. Finally, kinesthetic learners are usually very tactile, and often learn best when they can get a physical "sense" of what they are learning. At the same time, it is extremely important to understand that every person actually uses all three learning styles – the issue is not simply one of identifying which learning style works best for an individual student; rather, it entails understanding which style is dominant, as well as the relative importance of each learning style for the individual.

The idea that there are different learning styles is popular not only with classroom teachers, but also with students themselves – most of whom can fairly easily identify and discuss what they believe to be the style that best describes their own learning. As a result of the "common sense" element of these ideas, discussions and activities concerned with identifying and addressing different learning styles has become ubiquitous in the educational literature. However, in spite of this, the empirical evidence of the significance of different learning styles, as well as for the effectiveness of matching learning styles with teaching styles,

---

[7] Somewhat distinct from the common idea of differing learning styles is the theory proposed by the Harvard psychologist Howard Gardner about "multiple intelligences" (see Gardner, 1983, 1991, 1993).

is far from overwhelming. As Harold Pashler, Mark McDaniel, Doug Rohrer, and Robert Bjork (2009) have argued,

> Although the literature on learning styles is enormous, very few studies have even used an experimental methodology capable of testing the validity of learning styles applied to education. Moreover, of those that did use an appropriate method, several found results that flatly contradict the popular meshing hypothesis …. We conclude, therefore, that at present, there is no adequate evidence base to justify incorporating learning-styles assessments into general educational practice. Thus, limited educational resources would better be devoted to adopting other educational practices that have a strong evidence base, of which there are an increasing number. However, given the lack of methodologically sound studies of learning styles, it would be an error to conclude that all possible versions of learning styles have been tested and found wanting; many have simply not been tested at all. (p. 105)

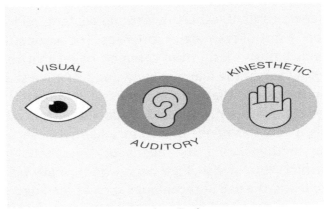

Learning Styles
© Jeremyah/Shutterstock.com

It is important to understand both what Pashler et al. are arguing here and what they are *not* arguing. Claims about different learning styles clearly make a great deal of intuitive sense to both learners and teachers, and Pashler et al. are by no means suggesting that they do not exist or that they are not important. What they *are* arguing, and which is important in its own right for educators to understand, is that the empirical evidence for such learning styles is not clear, and that it is a mistake to assume that simply by matching a student's preferred learning style with an appropriate teaching style we can be assured of meeting the student's needs, let alone of ensuring effective and adequate learning.

Questions for Reflection and Discussion

1. In our daily lives, we actually do recognize that there are different "ways of knowing." Can you identify some of the contexts, settings and ways in which we do so? What are the advantages and disadvantages of utilizing multiple "ways of knowing" in making sense of the world around us?

2. What would behaviorists, cognitivists, and constructivists say about the role of social relationships in learning and the learning process? What are the implications of this answer for teaching in the classroom? Of these three perspectives, which most closely reflects your own views?

3. According to feminist scholarship, what are some of the features of epistemology? What are the implications of this for the classroom, and for teaching and learning?

4. Describe how we use metaphors in discussing teaching. What metaphors best describe your own view or ideas about teaching and learning? What metaphors are commonly used to describe students and student learning?

5. How can Bloom's Taxonomy be used to create learning objectives for a lesson? In what ways might learning objectives created using Bloom's Taxonomy be useful for the classroom teacher? What limitations do you think that the use of Bloom's taxonomy might create?

References

Abu-Saad, I., & Champagne, D. (Eds.). (2006). *Indigenous education and empowerment: International perspectives.* Lanham, MD: Rowman & Littlefield.

Alcoff, L., & Potter, E. (Eds.). (1993). *Feminist epistemologies.* New York, NY: Routledge.

Aldersoon-Day, B., & Fernyhough, C. (2015). Inner speech: Development, cognitive functions, phenomenology, and neurobiology. *Psychological Bulletin, 141*(5), 931-965.

Anderson, E. (1995). Feminist epistemology: An interpretation and a defense. *Hypatia: A Journal of Feminist Philosophy, 10*(3), 50-84.

Anderson, L., & Krathwohl, D. (Eds.). (2001). *A taxonomy for learning, teaching, and assessing: A revision of Bloom's taxonomy of educational objectives.* New York, NY: Wesley Longman.

Baum, W. (2017). *Understanding behaviorism: Behavior, culture, and evolution* (3rd ed.). Oxford, UK: Wiley Blackwell.

Beatty, B. (1998). From laws of learning to a science of values: Efficiency and morality in Thorndike's educational psychology. *American Psychologist, 53*(10), 1145-1152.

Belenky, M., Clinchy, B., Goldberger, N., & Tarule, J. (1997). *Women's ways of knowing: The development of self, voice, and mind.* New York, NY: Basic Books. (Original work published 1986)

Bernal, D. (1998). Using a chicana feminist epistemology in educational research. *Harvard Educational Review, 68*(4), 555-582.

Bird, A. (2000). *Thomas Kuhn*. New York, NY: Routledge.

Bloom, B., Englehard, M., Furst, E., Hill, W., & Krathwohl, D. (1956). *Taxonomy of educational objectives: Handbook I: Cognitive domain*. New York, NY: David McKay.

Boudourides, M. (2003). Constructivism, education, science, and technology. *Canadian Journal of Learning and Technology/La Revue Canadienne de l'Apprentissage et de la Technologie, 29*(3). Retrieved from https://www.learntechlib.org/p/43187/.

Brush, S. (2000). Thomas Kuhn as a historian of science. *Science and Education, 9*, 39-58.

Chiesa, M. (1992). Radical behaviorism and scientific frameworks: From mechanistic to relational accounts. *American Psychologist, 47*(11), 1287-1299.

Chiesa, M. (1994). *Radical behaviorism: The philosophy and the science*. Boston, MA: Authors Cooperative.

Christie, M. (2006). Transdisciplinary research and Aboriginal knowledge. *The Australian Journal of Indigenous Education, 35*, 78-89.

Condon, M., Clyde, J., Kyle, D., & Hovda, R. (1993). A constructivist basis for teaching and teacher education: A framework for program development and research on graduates. *Journal of Teacher Education, 44*(4), 273-278.

Duncan, G. (2005). Critical race ethnography in education: Narrative, inequality and the problem of epistemology. *Race, Ethnicity and Education, 8*(1), 93-114.

Ertmer, P., & Newby, T. (2013). Behaviorism, cognitivism, constructivism: Comparing critical features from an instructional design perspective. *Performance Improvement Quarterly, 26*(2), 43-71.

Feyerabend, P. (1970). Consolations for the specialist. In I. Lakatos & A. Musgrave (Eds.), *Criticism and the growth of knowledge* (pp. 197-230). Cambridge, UK: University of Cambridge Press.

Feyerabend, P. (1981a). *Probleme des Empirismus: Schriften zur Theorie der Efklärung, der Quantentheorie und der Wissenschaftsgeschichte, Ausgewählte Schriften, Band 2*. Braunschweig, Germany: Vieweg & Sohn.

Feyerabend, P. (1981b). *Realism, rationalism and scientific method: Philosophical papers Volume 1*. Cambridge, UK: Cambridge University Press.

Feyerabend, P. (1983). *Science in a free society*. London, UK: Verso. (Original work published 1978)

Feyerabend, P. (1991). *Three dialogues on knowledge.* Oxford, UK: Basil Blackwell.

Feyerabend, P. (1995). *Killing time: The autobiography of Paul Feyerabend.* Chicago, IL: University of Chicago Press.

Feyerabend, P. (2002a). *Against method: Outline of an anarchistic theory of knowledge* (3rd ed.). London, UK: Verso. (Original work published 1975)

Feyerabend, P. (2002b). *Farewell to reason* (2nd ed.). London, UK: Verso. (Original work published 1987)

Feyerabend, P. (2006). *Paul K. Feyerabend: Knowledge, science and relativism* (3 volumes). Cambridge, UK: Cambridge University Press. (Original work published 1999)

Feyerabend, P. (2010). *Against method* (4th ed.). London, UK: Verso. (Original work published 1975)

Fosnot, C. (1993). Preface. In J. Grennon Brooks & M. Brooks (Eds.), *The case for constructivist classrooms* (pp. vii-viii). Alexandria, VA: Association for Supervision and Curriculum Development.

Fosnot, C. (Ed.). (1996a). *Constructivism: Theory, perspectives, and practice.* New York, NY: Teachers College Press.

Fosnot, C. (1996b). Constructivism: A psychological theory of learning. In C. Fosnot (Ed.), *Constructivism* (pp. 8-33). New York, NY: Teachers College Press.

Foucault, M. (1975). *Surveiller et punir: Naissance de la prison.* Paris, France: Éditions Gallimard.

Foucault, M. (1976). *Histoire de la folie à l'âge classique.* Paris, France: Éditions Gallimard.

Foucault, M. (2000). *Naissance de la clinique.* Paris, France: Presses Universitaires de France. (Original work published 1963)

Foucault, M. (2001). *Dits et écrits, Volume 2.* Paris, France: Éditions Gallimard.

Foucault, M. (2008). *L'archéologie du savoir.* Paris, France: Éditions Gallimard. (Original work published 1969)

Frawley, W. (1997). *Vygotsky and cognitive science: Language and the unification of the social and computational mind.* Cambridge, MA: Harvard University Press.

García, R. (2013). De los sistemas orgánicos a los sistemas simbólicos. La cultura y la articulación de lo real apuntes para una etnoepistemología desde Wittgenstein. *Revista de Filosofía, 74*(2), 43-70.

Gardner, H. (1983). *Frames of mind: The theory of multiple intelligences.* New York, NY: Basic Books.

Gardner, H. (1991). *The unschooled mind: How children think and how schools should teach.* New York, NY: Basic Books.

Gardner, H. (1993). *Multiple intelligences: The theory in practice.* New York, NY: Basic Books.

Gélinas, C., & Bouchard, Y. (2014). An epistemological framework for indigenous knowledge. *Revista de Humanidades de Valparaíso, 4,* 47-62.

Gergen, K. (1982). *Towards transformation in social knowledge.* New York, NY: Springer.

Gergen, K. (1995). Social construction and the educational process. In L. Steffe & J. Gale (Eds.), *Constructivism in education* (pp. 17-39). Hillsdale, NJ: Lawrence Erlbaum.

Goldberger, N., Tarule, J., & Clinchy, B. (1996). *Knowledge, difference, and power: Essays inspired by women's ways of knowing.* New York, NY: Basic Books.

Green, T. (1971). *The activities of teaching.* New York, NY: McGraw-Hill.

Grennon Brooks, J., & Brooks, M. (1993). *The case for constructivist classrooms.* Alexandria, VA: Association for Supervision and Curriculum Development.

Habermas, J. (1972). *Knowledge and human interests* (2nd ed.). London, UK: Heinemann.

Henning, E. (1995). Problematising the discourse of classroom management from the view of social constructivism. *South African Journal of Education, 15*(3), 124-129.

Holub, R. (1991). *Jurgen Habermas: Critic in the public sphere.* New York, NY: Routledge.

Jha, A., & Devi, R. (2014). Social epistemology and social constructivist pedagogy for school reforms. *Pedagogy of Learning, 2*(1), 12-18.

Johnson, J. (2014). *Radical behaviorism for ABA practitioners.* Cornwall-on-Hudson, NY: Sloan Educational Publishing.

Jones, M., & Brader-Araje, L. (2002). The impact of constructivism on education: Language, discourse, and meaning. *American Communication Journal, 5*(3). Retrieved from https://pdfs.semanticscholar.org/11e2/5b4e83ec8d804d125a4eddf02ceaca39d6fd.pdf?_ga=2.261817163.772962529.1574727270-522058878.1574727270.

Kafai, Y., & Resnick, M. (Eds.). (1996). *Constructivism in practice: Designing, thinking, and learning in a digital world.* Mahwah, NJ: Lawrence Erlbaum.

Kaufman, D., & Grennon Brooks, J. (1996). Interdisciplinary collaboration in teacher education: A constructivist approach. *TESOL Quarterly, 30*(2), 231-251.

Krathwohl, D. (2002). A revision of Bloom's Taxonomy: An overview. *Theory into Practice, 41*(4), 212-218.

Krathwohl, D., Bloom, B., & Masia, B. (1973). *Taxonomy of educational objectives: Handbook II: Affective domain*. New York, NY: David McKay.

Kuhn, T. (1970). *The structure of scientific revolutions* (2nd enlarged ed.). Chicago, IL: University of Chicago Press. (Original work published 1962)

Kuhn, T. (1977). *The essential tension*. Chicago, IL: University of Chicago Press.

Lakoff, G., & Johnson, M. (1980). *Metaphors we live by*. Chicago, IL: University of Chicago Press.

Laughlin, C. (2013). The ethno-epistemology of transpersonal experience: The view from transpersonal anthropology. *International Journal of Transpersonal Studies, 32*(1), 43-50.

Lennon, K., & Whitford, M. (Eds.). (1994). *Knowing the difference: Feminist perspectives in epistemology*. New York, NY: Routledge.

Lilienfeld, S., Lynn, S., Namy, L., Woolf, N., Jamieson, G., Marks, A., & Slaughter, V. (2015). *Psychology: From inquiry to understanding* (2nd ed.). Melbourne, Australia: Pearson Australia.

Maffie, J. (2013). Ethno-epistemology. In B. Kaldis (Ed.), *Encyclopedia of philosophy and the social sciences* (pp. 277-279). Los Angeles, CA: Sage.

Mandler, G. (2002). Origins of the cognitive (r)evolution. *Journal of the History of the Behavioral Sciences, 38*(4), 339-353.

Matthews, M. (2002). Constructivism and science education: A further appraisal. *Journal of Science Education and Technology, 11*(2), 121-134.

Mazzocchi, F. (2018). Why 'integrating' Western science and indigenous knowledge is not an easy task: What lessons could be learned for the future of knowledge? *Journal of Futures Studies, 22*(3), 19-34.

McLaren, P. (2003). *Life in schools: An introduction to critical pedagogy in the foundations of education* (4th ed.). Boston, MA: Allyn & Bacon.

Merrill, M. (1992). Constructivism and instructional design. In T. Duffy & D. Jonassen (Eds.), *Constructivism and the technology of instruction* (pp. 99-114). Hillsdale, NJ: Lawrence Erlbaum.

Miller, S., & Fredericks, M. (1988). Uses of metaphor: A qualitative case study. *International Journal of Qualitative Studies in Education, 1*(3), 263-272.

Mintzes, J., Wandersee, J., & Novak, J. (Eds.). (1997). *Teaching science for understanding: A human constructivist view.* San Diego, CA: Academic Press.

Moll, L. (Ed.). (1990). *Vygotsky and education: Instructional implications and applications of sociocultural psychology.* Cambridge, UK: Cambridge University Press.

National Research Council. (2000). *How people learn: Brain, mind, experience, and school.* Washington, DC: National Academy Press.

Nattinger, J. (1993). Communicative language teaching: A new metaphor. In L. Cleary & M. Linn (Eds.), *Linguistics for teachers* (pp. 599-612). New York, NY: McGraw-Hill.

Nicaise, M., & Barnes, D. (1996). The union of technology, constructivism, and teacher education. *Journal of Teacher Education, 47*(3), 205-212.

Nickles, T. (Ed.). (2003). *Thomas Kuhn.* Cambridge, UK: Cambridge University Press.

Noddings, N. (1990). Constructivism in mathematics education. In R. Davis, C. Maher, & N. Noddings (Eds.), *Constructivist views on the teaching and learning of mathematics* (pp. 7-18). Reston, VA: National Council of Teachers of Mathematics.

Nola, R. (1997). Constructivism in science and science education: A philosophical critique. *Science and Education, 6*(1-2), 55-83.

Nuessel, F. (2000). The use of metaphor to comprehend and explicate scientific theory. In P. Perron, L. Sbrochhi, P. Colilli, & M. Danesi (Eds.), *Semiotics as a bridge between the humanities and the sciences* (pp. 479-500). New York, NY: Legas.

O'Neil, W. (1995). American behaviorism: A historical and critical analysis. *Theory and Psychology, 5*(2), 285-305.

Ortony, A. (Ed.). (1980). *Metaphor and thought.* Cambridge, UK: Cambridge University Press.

Outhwaite, W. (2009). *Habermas: A critical introduction* (2nd ed.). Cambridge: Polity Press.

Oxford, R. (1997). Constructivism: Shape-shifting, substance, and teacher education applications. *Peabody Journal of Education, 72*(1), 35-66.

Parker, S. (1997). *Reflective teaching in the postmodern world: A manifesto for education in postmodernity.* Buckingham, UK: Open University Press.

Pashler, H., McDaniel, M., Rohrer, D., & Bjork, R. (2009). Learning styles: Concepts and evidence. *Psychological Science in the Public Interest, 9*(3), 105-119.

Paul, P., & Moores, D. F. (2012). Toward an understanding of epistemology and deafness. In P. Paul & D. Moores (Eds.), *Deaf epistemologies: Multiple perspectives on the acquisition of knowledge* (pp. 3-15). Washington, DC: Gallaudet University Press.

Piaget, J. (1928). Logique génétique et sociologie. *Revue Philosophique de la France et de l'Étranger, 105,* 167-205.

Piaget, J. (1932). *The moral judgment of the child.* London, UK: Routledge & Kegan Paul.

Piaget, J. (1948a). *Le langage et la pensée chez l'enfant* (new ed.). Paris, France: Delachaux et Niestlé. (Original work published 1923)

Piaget, J. (1948b). *La naissance de l'intelligence chez l'enfant* (new ed.). Paris, France: Delachaux et Niestlé. (Original work published 1923)

Piaget, J. (1976). *Psychologie et epistémologie.* Paris, France: Éditions Gonthier. (Original work published 1970)

Piaget, J. (1979). *L'epistémologie génétique* (3e ed.). Paris, France: Presses Universitaires de France. (Original work published 1950)

Piaget, J. (1993). *Le jugement et le raisonnement chez l'enfant* (8ᵉ ed.). Paris, France: Delachaux & Niestlé.

Piaget, J. (1996). *La construction du réel chez l'enfant* (6ᵉ ed.). Neuchatel, Switzerland: Delachaux & Niestlé. (Original work published 1950)

Piaget, J. (2012). *La psychologie de l'intelligence* (3ᵉ ed.). Paris, France: Armand Collin. (Original work published 1947)

Polyani, M. (1958). *Personal knowledge: Towards a post-critical philosophy.* Chicago, IL: University of Chicago Press.

Polyani, M. (1966). *The tacit dimension.* Chicago, IL: University of Chicago Press.

Rainer, J., & Guyton, E. (1994). Developing a constructivist teacher education program: The policy-making stage. *Journal of Teacher Education, 45*(2), 140-146.

Reagan, T., Case, C., & Brubacher, J. (2000). *Becoming a reflective educator: How to build a culture of inquiry in the schools* (2nd ed.). Thousand Oaks, CA: Corwin.

Richards, J., & Lockhart, C. (1994). *Reflective teaching in second language classrooms.* Cambridge, UK: Cambridge University Press.

Richardson, V. (Ed.). (1997a). *Constructivist teacher education: Building a world of new understandings.* London, UK: Falmer Press.

Richardson, V. (1997b). Constructivist teaching and teacher education: Theory and practice. In V. Richardson (Ed.), *Constructivist teacher education* (pp. 3-14). London, UK: Falmer Press.

Salazar Pérez, M. S., & Saavedra, C. (2017). A call for onto-epistemological diversity in early childhood education and care: Centering global south conceptualizations of childhood/s. *Review of Research in Education, 41*(1), 1-29.

Simpson, E. (1971). Educational objectives in the psychomotor domain. In M. Kapfer (Ed.), Behavioral objectives in curriculum development: Selected readings and bibliography (pp. 60-67). Englewood Cliffs, NJ: Educational Technology Publications.

Scheffler, I. (1960). *The language of education.* Springfield, IL: Charles C. Thomas.

Scheffler, I. (1979). *Beyond the letter: A philosophical inquiry into ambiguity, vagueness and metaphor in language.* London, UK: Routledge & Kegan Paul.

Schwandt, T. (1994). Constructivist, interpretivist approaches to human inquiry. In N. Denzin & Y. Lincoln (Eds.), *Handbook of qualitative research* (pp. 118-137). Thousand Oaks, CA: Sage.

Scott, D. (2010). *Education, epistemology and critical realism.* New York, NY: Routledge.

Seddon, G. (1978). The properties of Bloom's *Taxonomy of Educational Objectives* for the cognitive domain. *Review of Educational Research, 48*(2), 303-323.

Siegel, H. (2010). Knowledge and truth. In R. Bailey, R. Barrow, D. Carr, & C. McCarthy (Eds.), *The Sage handbook of philosophy of education* (pp. 283-295). London, UK: Sage.

Siegelman, E. (1990). *Metaphor and reasoning in psychotherapy.* New York, NY: Guilford.

Sinclair, H., Berthoud, I., Gerard, J., & Venesiano, E. (1985). Constructivisme et psycholinguistique génétique. *Archives de Psychologie, 53*(204), 37-60.

Skinner, B. F. (1971). *Beyond freedom and dignity.* Indianapolis, IN: Hackett.

Skinner, B. F. (1974). *About behaviorism.* New York, NY: Random House.

Slavin, R. (2018). *Educational psychology: Theory and practice* (12ᵗʰ ed.). New York, NY: Pearson.

Slezak, P. (2010). Radical constructivism: Epistemology, education and dynamite. *Constructivist Foundations, 6*(1), 102-111.

Smith, N. (Ed.). (1981). *Metatphors for evaluation: Sources of new methods.* Beverly Hills, CA: Sage.

Spivey, N. (1997). *The constructivist metaphor: Reading, writing and the making of meaning.* San Diego, CA: Academic Press.

Steffe, L., & Gale, J. (Eds.). (1995). *Constructivism in education.* Hillsdale, NJ: Lawrence Erlbaum.

Steffe, L., & Kieren, T. (1994). Radical constructivism and mathematics education. *Research in Mathematics Education, 25*, 711-733.

Stokoes, P. (2004). *Philosophy: 100 essential thinkers.* New York, NY: Enchanted Lion Books.

Tarsitani, C. (1996). Metaphors in knowledge and metaphors of knowledge: Notes on the constructivist view of learning. *Interchange, 27*(1), 23-40.

Taylor, W. (Ed.). (1984). *Metaphors of education.* London, UK: Heinemann.

Thorndike, E. (2000). *Animal intelligence: Experimental studies.* New York, NY: Routledge. (Original work published 1911)

Tobin, K. (Ed.). (1993). *The practice of constructivism in science education.* Hillsdale, NJ: Lawrence Erlbaum.

Van der Veer, R., & Valsiner, J. (1991). *Understanding Vygotsky: A quest for synthesis.* Oxford, UK: Basil Blackwell.

Vanier, F. (2011). *Une conception naturaliste et normative de l'axiologie scientifique contemporaine: Analyse et dépassement de la théorie de Laudan.* Unpublished M.A. thesis, Université de Montréal, Montréal, Canada.

Von Glasersfeld, E. (1993). Questions and answers about radical constructivism. In K. Tobin (Ed.), *The practice of constructivism in science education* (pp. 23-38). Hillsdale, NJ: Lawrence Erlbaum.

Von Glasersfeld, E. (1995). A constructivist approach to teaching. In L. Steffe & J. Gale (Eds.), *Constructivism in education* (pp. 3-15). Hillsdale, NJ: Lawrence Erlbaum.

Von Glasersfeld, E. (Ed.). (2002). *Radical constructivism in mathematics education.* New York, NY: Kluwer.

Vygotsky, L. S. (2005a). *Мышление и речь* [Thinking and speech]. Moscow, Russia: Labirint.

Vygotsky, L. S. (2005b). *Психология развития ребенка* [Psychology of the child's development]. Moscow, Russia: Eksmo.

Vygotsky, L. S. (2008). *Психология искусства* [Psychology of art]. Moscow, Russia: Labirint.

Vygotsky, L. (2012). Thought and language (rev. and exp. ed.). Cambridge, MA: Massachusetts Institute of Technology.

Watson, J. B. (1970). *Behaviorism.* New York, NY: W. W. Norton. (Originally published 1924)

Williams, M., & Burden, R. (1999). *Psicología para profesores de idiomas: Enfoque del constructivismo social.* Cambridge, UK: Cambridge University Press.

Winitzky, N., & Kauchak, D. (1997). Constructivism in teacher education: Applying cognitive theory to teacher learning. In V. Richardson (Ed.), *Constructivist teacher education* (pp. 59-83). London, UK: Falmer Press.

Wolfmeyer, M. (2017). Anarchist epistemologies and the separation of science and state: The critique and relevance of Paul Feyerabend to educational foundations. *Educational Studies, 53*(4), 327-341.

Wood, T., Cobb, P., & Yackel, E. (1995). Reflections of learning and teaching mathematics in elementary school. In L. Steffe & J. Gale (Eds.), *Constructivism in education* (pp. 401-422). Hillsdale, NJ: Lawrence Erlbaum.

Yasnitsky, A. (Ed.). (2019). *Questioning Vygotsky's legacy: Scientific psychology or heroic cult.* New York: Routledge.

Zambrano, I., & Greenfield, P. (2004). Ethnoepistemologies at home and school. In R. Sternberg & E. Grigorenko (Eds.), *Culture and competence: Contexts of life success* (pp. 251-272). Washington, DC: American Psychological Association.

Zeichner, K., & Liston, D. (1987). Teaching student teachers to reflect. *Harvard Educational Review, 57*(1), 23-48.

Zeichner, K., & Liston, D. (1996). *Reflective teaching: An introduction.* Mahwah, NJ: Lawrence Erlbaum.

Zietsman, A. (1996). Constructivism: Super theory for all educational ills? *South African Journal of Higher Education, 10*(1), 70-75.

Chapter 4

Schooling, Education, and the "Educated Person"

I have never let my schooling interfere with my education. (Mark Twain)

Education is what survives when what has been learned has been forgotten. (B. F. Skinner)

In this chapter, we will examine several important concepts for educators to understand, and we will do so utilizing what are essentially philosophical methods – methods that we will discuss in greater detail in Chapter 6. We will consider the concepts of "schooling," "education," and "training," and discuss how each of these is unique – and why the differences among them matter. We will then study the ways in which the ideal of the "educated person" has evolved and developed and what it represents in our own society.

There is a tension between the concepts of "schooling" and "education." These two things are related, sometimes very closely, but they are not actually quite the same thing. Most of our discussion thus far in this book has really been focused on and concerned with schooling. We have looked at the politics and ideology, the purposes, the legal influences, and at the legal and the organizational structures of public schooling in the United States. These are all important things, and they are matters of considerable importance not only for anyone considering a career as a teacher but also for anyone who wishes to be a well-informed citizen. The concept of education is different from that of schooling, however. Schooling, in essence, is an institutional process – the word refers to whatever happens in the context of, and under the auspices of, the school as an institution. Education – which has to do with very particular kinds of mental and cognitive development – can and does take place in schools, but it also takes place in many other settings. Furthermore, much (perhaps even most) of what occurs in the school is *not* educational.

Schooling

Schooling, in essence, is whatever takes place in schools. This may sound like a circular definition, but it is actually far more than that. As we saw in Chapter 1, there are many things that take place in schools and classrooms every day, some of them educational (such as learning to read), some of them institutional (such as taking attendance), some of them vocational (preparing future workers for the labor market), some of them social and cultural (socialization and acculturation), and so on. Also learned in schools, however, are many less desirable things: whether deliberately or not, children are exposed to sexism, racism, linguicism, and so on, in powerful and lasting ways. These, too, are part of schooling, just as are efforts to counter such things. We will discuss aspects of bias (and counter-bias) in schooling later in this book; for now, we want to focus our attention on what might be considered to be for formal and institutional aspects of schooling.

Children Leaving School
© Rido/Shutterstock.com

One useful way to think about schooling institutionally is to try to devise a "formula" or set of necessary conditions that would describe what we can consider to be schooling, and which will also help us determine what is not schooling, even if it is very much educational. So, what do we have to have for something to count as "schooling"? A good place to begin is that schooling must involve both a student (let's call this student *S*) and a teacher (*T*). A teacher in this philosophical sense is not necessarily limited to a licensed professional. Any number of adults in a school setting function as teachers, including administrators, coaches, librarians, school resource officers, cafeteria workers, bus drivers, and so on. Of course, an individual may well be studying or learning on their own – say, by reading books on a topic, or conducting experiments to better understand something – and this can certainly be both valuable and educational. It is not, though, what we generally have in mind when we think about schooling.[1]

The presence of a teacher and a student is necessary for schooling to be taking place, but it is not sufficient – there must be a specific kind of interaction between the two. Specifically, the teacher must engage in the process of actually *teaching* the student, and further, there must be some sort of identifiable content that is being taught (let's call the content *x*). This leaves us with a good starting point for a formula that will help us lay out the conditions for schooling: *T teaches x to S*.

Although a good starting point, *T teaches x to S* is not yet sufficient for our needs. For the formula to have meaningful and logical force, there must be a reason – a goal, objective, or

---

[1] Self-paced home schooling might initially appear to be an exception to this, and to a certain extent it is. At the same time, it could certainly be argued that in such a situation the learner actually functions as *both* the student *and* as the teacher.

purpose – for the teacher to teach *x* to the student. This is a bit more complicated than it might at first appear because we can imagine two different kinds of goals here: long-term goals and short-term goals. Long-term goals are those that we most often talk about when we are providing a justification or rationalization for the curriculum: Why should students learn to do specific things, or to know particular kinds of information? In the age of the Internet, when one can access pretty much any factual knowledge on one's cellphone, why should we care if a student knows particular content? If you can use the calculator on your cellphone far more quickly, and sometimes get far more accurate results, than you can by solving a problem yourself, what is the point, say, of learning the multiplication tables? We believe that there are very compelling reasons for knowing certain kinds of information, and for possessing certain sorts of skills, but we also believe that it is important for educators to be able to offer students good answers to the question, "Why do I need to learn this?" Indeed, if we do not have a satisfactory answer to this question, then perhaps we should reconsider whatever it is that we are teaching our students. In addition to long-term goals, there are also short-term goals: What do we need to accomplish to help students pass a mandated and standardized assessment? Of course, one hopes that long-term and short-term goals are at least not contradictory, but sometimes that is not always the case. Taking the need for long-term and short-term goals (which we can label *Y* and *y*) into account, our formula for conceptualizing schooling is now: *T teaches x to S, so that Y/y.*

Finally, imagine that the teacher and the student happen to meet one day at a grocery store. They greet each other, and make small talk for a few moments. The student then glances over toward the fruits and vegetable section of the store and sees pomegranates on sale. With a puzzled expression, the student says, "By the way, see those things over there? I've seen them before, but I don't really know what they are, or what you'd use them for." Seizing the "teachable moment," the teacher explains what pomegranates are (a fruit), where they come from (originally from Iran and northern India, and now also grown in the Mediterranean region as well as in Latin America and California), and some of the ways in which they can be used (as a source of juice, in baking and cooking, in smoothies, and in different alcoholic beverages). Here we have a teacher engaged in teaching a student particular content with a long-term goal in mind: *T teaches x to S, so that Y*. And yet, if you think about it for a moment, you will realize that while this may very well have been excellent teaching, and was certainly educational, it wasn't actually *schooling*.

School Bus
© MaxyM/Shutterstock.com

95

What is missing is an explicit tie to the institutional nature and structure of public schooling. Many things entail teaching and learning, and there are a host of activities that are educational, but they are not schooling because they do not take place *under the auspices of the school*. Notice the way that we worded that sentence, though: In order to be schooling, an activity must take place *under the auspices of the school* – but that does not mean that it must take place *in* the school. Field trips, for instance, are still examples of schooling even though they may involve considerable planning and travel away from the school. A trip to see Washington, DC, as part of a high school social studies unit is, despite the fact that the teacher and students are far from the actual school building, very much an example of schooling. Thus, the formula that we end up with that provides us with all of the necessary conditions for schooling (and, which taken together, are sufficient for us to describe something as schooling), is *T teaches x to S, under the auspices of the school, so that Y/y.*

Education

If schooling is an institutional concept, "education" is at least potentially and in some contexts something quite different. It takes place in virtually every domain and part of human life, it can be personal and individual in nature or can involve a group, it can take place formally or informally, and it can be organized or unorganized. Indeed, one of the challenges that we face in discussing education is that the word itself is ambiguous – in everyday conversation and discourse, we actually use the word "education" in a number of quite different ways, and with very different meanings. One of these meanings, called the "institutional sense" of the term, is in fact often used synonymously with "schooling." When we ask how many years of education a person has, for instance, what we are actually asking is how many years of formal schooling they have completed. There is a second sense in which we use the word "education," which is basically as a synonym for "childrearing" – that is, it refers to the social and cultural processes by which children in a society are prepared for their lives as adults. In this sense, every human culture engages in informal educational processes – although the same is not true (or at least has not been true traditionally) with respect to formal schooling, without which some societies have historically done quite well (see Reagan, 2018). Thus, the term "education" is commonly employed in two senses – the institutional sense and the sociological sense – in which there are other words that perhaps better describe what is taking place. The third way in which "education" is used, though, is unique, and is the sense in which it is generally used in philosophy of education. We call this sense of the term the "General Enlightenment" conceptualization of "education," and it is similar to the ancient Greek notion of *paideia* (παιδεία; see Jaeger, 1967, 1971a, 1971b; see also Park, 1984). It is this third sense of the term "education" that we will be focusing on here.

The Attributes of Education

For an activity to constitute an educational activity, there are two conditions, or attributes, that it must meet. The first of these attributes is that it must involve the student being introduced to a body of *knowledge*. Indeed, the acquisition of knowledge (including certain skills) is a necessary part of education. As Cornel Hamm (1989) noted, "The fact that educated people are knowledgeable is not merely an interesting observation about some people; it is a definitional truth" (p. 36). Education is thus a special sort of initiation, and this is precisely the term that Peters employs in describing the process of education (see Peters, 1963). Although the acquisition of knowledge is indeed a necessary aspect of education, there are two further conditions with respect to knowledge that must be met – not all knowledge is of equal weight or value, and furthermore, while some things might well be worth knowing, they are probably not required for us to consider an individual to be "educated," just as there are, in any society, certain things that we would expect any "educated" person to know or to be able to do. Therefore, the knowledge of the educated person needs to be both broad and deep. In other words, it must cover a number of different disciplinary areas and in at least some of these areas, it must entail more than simply being vaguely familiar with the topics in a field. An excellent way to think about this relationship is with respect to the "general education" requirements at most colleges and universities. For their first two years, students typically complete a variety of courses representing a number of different disciplinary areas. This coursework usually involves classes in composition and writing, mathematics, literature, social sciences, natural and biological sciences, foreign languages, physical education, and so on. It is the "general education" curriculum that is intended to provide college and university students with educational breadth.[2] In the third and fourth years, college and university students most often concentrate on courses in their major and minor(s); it is here that they are supposed to acquire some degree of depth in particular subject areas.[3]

The second attribute of any educational activity is that it must be of *value*. Education requires, then, more than simply that knowledge is acquired. Think about the difference between these two claims:

> *John has been schooled.*

> *John has been educated.*

---

[2] Actually, although this is a good example of the point that we are trying to make here, we should note that while this is related to the concept of education, it is actually definitionally an example of schooling.

[3] This is of course an incredible overgeneralization. General education requirements differ significantly from one college or university to another, and there are any number of general education models that have been developed. The description provided here is intended to be illustrative only, although the fundamental concept of how and why general education works the way that it does is basically correct.

Father and Daughter Working
© goodluz/Shutterstock.com

The claim that "John has been schooled" clearly indicates that John attended a school. It does not actually say anything about what he may (or may not) have learned or accomplished. To be sure, we would hope that one of the outcomes of schooling had to do with learning things of value, but we also know that that is not always true. There are, after all, high school graduates in our society who remain illiterate. This is not something to be proud of, of course, but it is true nevertheless. On the other hand, when we say that "John has been educated," we are indicating that John has accomplished something cognitively and intellectually of value. As the British philosopher of education R. S. Peters (1966) noted,

> "Education" … does have normative implications … It implies that something worthwhile is being or has been intentionally transmitted in a morally acceptable manner. It would be a logical contradiction to say that a man had been educated but that he had in no way changed for the better, or that in educating his son a man was attempting nothing that was worthwhile. (p. 25)

The value attribution of education is extremely important, since there are many examples in which both teaching and learning are taking place, but where we would still not call an activity "educational." Consider the example presented in the 19th century novel *Oliver Twist*, written by Charles Dickens (and later turned into the musical and later the movie *Oliver!*). In that novel, the character Fagin teaches a group of children to engage in pickpocketing and other sorts of criminal activities in exchange for food and shelter.[4] Fagin thus teaches the children something (i.e., how to pick pockets), which the children in turn use (and which they have therefore presumably learned). We thus have both teaching and learning taking place, but for most of us we would be extremely reluctant to describe this as an example of "education" – and the reason for our reluctance is that we sense that it violates the value attribute.

---

[4] It is worth noting here that the character of Fagin has been the focus of considerable debate when *Oliver Twist* was written and today. The ongoing concern has been the question of whether the portrayal of Fagin is blatantly and offensively anti-Semitic. In the original publication, Fagin is described as "the Jew" more than 250 times. In later additions, Dickens eliminated about 180 of these references, and he himself always denied any anti-Semitism in his description of Fagin.

In addition to the knowledge and value attributes, in order to count as "education," an activity must also be in compliance with what is called the "procedural criterion." Basically, the procedural criterion is a way of addressing what has also been referred to as the difference between product goals and process goals. Product goals are the outcomes that we wish to achieve, while process goals are essentially the limitations on how we go about achieving the product goals. For instance, in a third-grade classroom, if we wish the students to learn the multiplication table by heart, one potentially effective, but highly unethical, way to accomplish this might be to arrange for each child to be given a small electrical shock any time they make a mistake and give a wrong answer. Even if it turned out that this was an incredibly effective and efficient manner of teaching the multiplication table, it is hard to imagine any educator advocating such a practice – in short, it clearly violates a process goal. One way to think about this distinction was provided by Cornell Hamm (1989), who suggested that virtually any activity might count as an educational one so long as (i) the procedure or activity results in an educationally valuable or worthwhile achievement, and (ii) the manner of proceeding to reach the outcome does not impinge on the willingness and voluntariness of the learner (p. 38).[5]

The Nature of Training

There is a word that often comes up in discussions about teaching, learning, schooling, and education that requires our consideration at this point, and that word is "training." Training is a somewhat slippery word, as Thomas Green (1971) observed in his book *The Activities of Teaching*:

> The concepts "teaching" and "training" are closely related. How do we know? Simply because there are many contexts within which either of these terms may be substituted for the other without changing the meaning of our statement … There are many contexts …within which it is a matter of indifference whether the term "training" is used or the term "teaching," and this is a good reason for concluding that the meanings of the two terms overlap. They are closely related. (p. 23)

The two words are indeed closely related, as Green says, but they are not synonymous. There are many situations in which one rather than the other is used, and where the alternative term is either inappropriate or misleading.

Let us start by considering some cases that we would all accept as examples of training. We can begin with a non-human example: We routinely talk about training a dog. Such training refers to teaching the dog to obey certain commands (sit, stay, heel, play dead, fetch, etc.). When we train a dog, the entire point of the exercise is to change and control the dog's behavior. This is the heart of behaviorism as a learning theory: There is a stimulus, followed by

---

[5] Interestingly, for Peters while this does rule out the use of indoctrination, it does not rule out compulsion, which can still be justified so long as the learner still has a choice and can resist it.

a response. With human beings, the connection between training and stimulus-response bonds is often a characteristic feature of the activity. For instance, we talk about potty-training a young child. This involves largely the same sort of stimulus-response bonding as does that used with dogs. We are not discussing an intellectual activity, nor are we asking the child to engage in any sort of logical or reflective practice. Indeed, such things are precisely what we are trying to eliminate. We also talk about basic training in the military. Although some of basic training may have greater cognitive elements than other parts, such training is again primarily concerned with the soldier learning and being able to perform specific tasks in specific ways at specific times. The U.S. Army is not interested in hearing from a recruit that they have a better idea about how a squad should march, or about how a weapon should be taken apart and put back together. Finally, when we talk about physical training, to a considerable degree we are concerned with the development of particular motor skills and related skills intended to develop and maintain physical fitness. Many of the activities that are part of physical training have single, specific ways in which they should take place – there is a correct way to lift weights, and many incorrect ways. Training is focused on learning and engaging in the correct ways,

Dog Training
© SpeedKingz/Shutterstock.com

These cases – dog training, potty-training, basic training in the military, and physical training – are all relative clear-cut examples of training. There are also examples of training that are more complex than these cases might suggest. We routinely talk about medical training, legal training, pilot training – but we also talk about medical education, legal education, and so on. To be sure, in each of these cases there are certain kinds of activities in which the kind of trained response that we have been discussing thus far makes a great deal of sense. Consider the case of the physician. In an emergency room setting, there are some things that we would hope that a physician would not need to think about or reflect upon – things of such urgency that saving a life may require an instantaneous decision and action. Detailed study and reflection, research and experimental trials, and so on, may well underlie what takes place when a patient is having a heart attack,[6] but in the context of an emergency room, there is no time to consider these things. Rather, the physician needs to determine whether the patient is actually having a heart attack and, if so, must respond in fairly predictable ways. There is some degree of reflection in making the determination about whether the patient is indeed having a heart attack, since not everyone has the same symptoms or severity of symptoms, but basically the physician is looking for such things as:

- Chest pain.
- Shortness of breath.
- Coughing.
- Nausea.
- Vomiting.
- Dizziness.
- Face appearing grey in color.
- Patient feeling clammy and sweaty.
- Patient reporting their arms feel heavy.

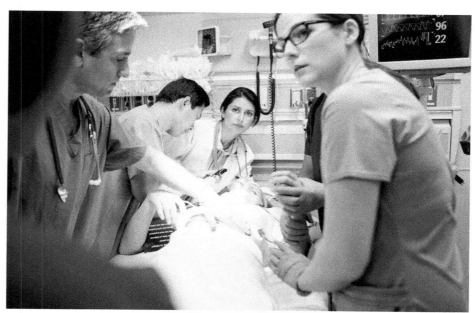

Emergency Room
© Monkey Business Images/Shutterstock.com

If a patient exhibits some or all of these conditions, then there are a number of likely things that will take place. In addition to taking a medical history and doing a physical examination, and putting the patient on intravenous (IV) fluids, an electrocardiogram (EKG) may be given to diagnose a heart attack and electrocardiographic monitoring to screen for arrhythmias may be used, blood tests may be used to confirm a heart attack, certain medications may be given to the

---

[6] This is an overgeneralization. Although we often use the term "heart attack," the term conflates five different kinds of heart attacks: stable angina, unstable angina, STEMI (ST-segment elevation myocardial infarction), and coronary artery spasm.

patient (nitroglycerin, aspirin, clot-busting drugs), oxygen may be given to the patient, and cardiac catheterization may take place. It is in the decision-making about which of these things will take place that the physician's medical *education* will come into play. However, if the electrocardiographic monitor indicates that the heart has stopped, the time for reflection has stopped, and instant responses are called for – again, moving into the medical *training* that the physician has received.

Pilots are another example of a group whose preparation involves both activities that are clearly training and activities that are educational in nature. As Green (1971) explained,

> Not all teaching is a kind of training. For example, it is possible for a pilot to be trained to fly a certain airplane, and a part of [their] training may involve learning the stall properties of the airplane. But although we may speak of training [them] to fly the plane, we do not speak of training [them] that the stall properties are such and such. We may teach [them] or tell [them] that the plane will stall at 100 knots, but we do not speak of training [them] that it will stall at 100 knots. (p. 24)

On the other hand, there are clearly many things that a pilot must know and be able to do almost instantaneously. We can see this in cases in which there are airline disasters and near-disasters, when pilots have had only seconds to make incredibly complex decisions. A powerful example of such a situation was provided on January 15, 2009, when US Airways flight 1549 took off from New York's LaGuardia Airport on its way to Charlotte Douglas International Airport. The plane, an Airbus A320 with 150 passengers and 3 flight attendants, as well as the pilot and co-pilot, on board, was cleared for takeoff at 3:24:56 p.m., and reported being airborne at 3:25:51, when it had reached an altitude of 700 feet. At 3:27:11, at an altitude of 2,818 feet, the plane hit a flock of Canada geese about 4.5 miles from LaGuardia, and both of the plane's engines shut down. Unable to restart the engines, at 3:27:33 the plane radioed a mayday call, and indicated that it was turning back to LaGuardia. Moments later, after Air Traffic Control directed it to land on Runway 13, the pilot, Captain Chesley Sullenberger answered simply, "Unable." At 3:31 p.m., the plane made an unpowered ditching in the Hudson River. Fortunately, no one died in the incident, which came to be called "the Miracle on the Hudson." The point here is the timing of what took place with US Airways flight 1549. Consider the timeline:

3:24:56	Cleared for Takeoff
3:25:51	Reported Being Airborne
3:27:11	Hit Flock of Canada Geese
3:27:33	Mayday Call
3:31	Ditches in Hudson River

US Air Flight 1549
© Sonder Quest/Shutterstock.com

The time between hitting the Canada geese and ditching in the Hudson River was *at most* slightly under 3 minutes. During that 3 minutes, the pilots tried to restart the plane's engines, radioed a mayday call, made several judgments about possible emergency landings, engaged in ongoing efforts to control both the altitude and location of the plane, had several brief radio interactions with New York Terminal Radar Approach Control (TRACON), warned the passengers and crew to brace for impact, and performed a successful unpowered ditching of the aircraft in the Hudson River. The incident ended as well as it did because of the training that the pilots had had and the checklists they were trained to use (as well as the extensive experience of Captain Sullenberger). That training was grounded in a great deal of education, of course, but there was simply no time available for reflective consideration of the situation.

This brings us to a somewhat problematic case, and that is how one becomes a teacher. In our society, in order to teach in a public school, with some notable exceptions, one must hold a teaching certificate or license issued by a state Department of Education. In order to gain such certification or licensure, **a person usually has to complete a university-based program that includes courses and field experiences designed and intended to prepare them for a career in the classroom.**[7] **Interestingly, what takes place in such university-based programs is often called one of three things: teacher** *education,* **teacher** *training,* **and teacher** *preparation.* Although it is certainly true that the label used to describe how individuals are prepared to become teachers does not necessarily indicate any particular view of teaching or teachers, we would suggest that in at least some cases the terminology actually does make a difference. Insofar as we hold the view that teachers are indeed professionals comparable to other professionals – a view that we both hold (see Reagan, 2009) – **then** it makes a great deal of sense to recognize that there are elements of both education and training involved in the preparation of teachers. At the same time, though, it should be kept in mind that the balance between the educative and training

---

[7] In some states, there are a growing number of exceptions to the prerequisite of university-based programs, but some form of teacher education as well as standardized testing is required in all cases.

components of teacher preparation is important and significant, since it has various implications, including teacher input to curricular, assessment, and organizational policies in the schools, teacher evaluation, teacher licensure, and last but not least, how teachers are compensated for their work.

The Ideal of the "Educated Person"

Philosophers have long been concerned with the concept of education, but even more, with the concept of the "educated person," and there is a vast literature in the philosophy of education on this precise topic (see, for example, Barrow & Woods, 1988; Hamm, 1989; Hirst, 1974; Peters, 1966, 1973a, 1973b). Indeed, the concept of the "educated person," and its relationship to liberal education, has been a matter of considerable interest to philosophers throughout Western history. In the decades since the 1960s, several different approaches have been taken to understanding what the educated person should know and be able to do.

At the outset of our discussion here, it is important to note that the ideals of both the educated person and of liberal education more broadly are neither static nor immutable; indeed, both are clearly socially constructed, and both have changed (and will continue to change) over time, from place to place, and community to community. We would argue that not only what constitutes an educated person is necessarily tied to time and place, but further, that there cannot be any neutral conception of either education or the educated person (see Levinson, Foley, & Holland, 1996; Reagan, 2018). What constituted an educated person in Athens during the time of Plato was radically different than what constituted an educated person during the time of St. Thomas Aquinas, as it would have been from that of 17th century colonial America, or indeed from our own 21st century Anglophone North American perspective. It is important to note that we are concerned here solely with the contemporary Western educational tradition and that our argument is focused on that tradition, especially (although not exclusively) as it is manifested in the U.S. context. While we do believe that some elements of a liberal education are likely to be of more universal value for virtually any society, the discussion presented here is very much culturally and temporally grounded and specific.

In the 1960s, 1970s, and 1980s, the work of R. S. Peters, Paul Hirst, and others (see Barrow, 1976, 1981; Barrow & Woods, 1988; Brent, 1978; Chambers, 1983; Dearden, Hirst, & Peters, 1972a, 1972b, 1972c; Doyle, 1973; Elvin, 1977; Hamlyn, 1978; Hirst, 1974, 1993; Hirst & Peters, 1970; Lloyd, 1976; Peters, 1973a, 1973b; Schofield, 1972; Straughan & Wilson, 1983) focused on articulating the nature and characteristics of the "educated man." The Peters-Hirst ideal of the "educated man," as it was called, was based on the idea that the student should be exposed to the various forms of knowledge, which included pure mathematics and logic, physical (empirical) sciences, history and human sciences, aesthetics, morals, philosophy, and religion (see Hamm, 1989, pp. 67-71). This approach emphasized theoretical rather than practical knowledge, as a number of critics noted (see Pring, 1976), and ultimately led Hirst himself to re-evaluate the forms of knowledge (see Hirst, 1993).

A form of knowledge, on Hirst's account, is far more than merely knowledge or skill *per se*; it is a very particular *type* of knowledge and skill and one that meets certain clear criteria. Specifically, Hirst (1973) argued that:

By a form of knowledge is meant a distinct way in which our experience becomes structured round the use of accepted public symbols. The symbols thus having public meaning, their use is in some way testable against experience and there is the progressive development of series of tested symbolic expressions. In this way experience has been probed further and further by extending and elaborating the use of the symbols, and by means of these it has become possible for the personal experience of individuals to become more fully structured, more fully understood. The various forms of knowledge can be seen in low-level developments within the common area of our knowledge of the everyday world. From this there branch out the developed forms which, taking certain elements in our common knowledge as a basis, have grown in distinctive ways. (p. 102)

This means, as Robin Barrow (1981) has explained, that the forms of knowledge are characterized by three criteria:

- They have their own distinctive concepts, as, for example, gravity, acceleration and hydrogen are characteristic of the sciences.
- They have their own logical structure. That is to say, largely because of the meanings of the distinctive concepts, there is a limit to what may meaningfully be said employing such concepts. (Ways of talking that may make sense in one form [of knowledge] do not necessarily make sense in another.)
- They have their own distinctive manner of testing the truth of their claims. (p. 40)

One of the reasons for studying a variety of disciplines in the tradition of liberal education is that each discipline approaches problems in its own unique manner. Thus, by studying history students learn something about the way in which historians think, just as by studying biology they learn how biologists think. To be sure, initial study in a discipline does not mean that students master the epistemological approaches used in the discipline – that comes only with in-depth, long-term study – but the basic idea in liberal education is that the student should gain a clearer understanding of how each discipline organizes the world.

The Peters-Hirst ideal has been critiqued on a number of grounds: Marxists and neo-Marxists quite correctly argued that it was based in and derived from a class-based set of principles and an educational tradition that was grounded firmly in a particular social class system (see Matthews, 1980). Even more powerful has been the feminist critique, offered cogently by Jane Roland Martin and others (Martin, 1984, 1985, 1986, 1994, 2000; Mulcahy, 2002, 2008). Martin argued that the "educated man" represented by the Peters-Hirst ideal was just that: an ideal that presupposed certain gender-specific assumptions. More recent efforts to address the complexities of identifying a justifiable conceptualization of the educated person and of liberal education more broadly still remain incomplete. For example, some have argued for thinking about liberal education as preparation for life (Mulcahy, 2008; see also Campbell, 2009) which constitutes significant improvements on earlier discussions. Although we are sympathetic to Richard Pring's (1976) observation that "I cannot lay down what precisely should be the content of the curriculum" (p. 115) because of the varying needs of distinct individuals, we nevertheless do believe that there are core areas of knowledge – along the lines of the forms of knowledge – that can, and indeed must, be identified.

Alternative Conceptions of the "Educated Person"

While the Peters-Hirst model of the "educated person" is a powerful one that has received a great deal of attention, it is by no means the only such model. Although it does not make a great deal of sense to explore alternative conceptions of the "educated person" fully at this point, there are three 20th century models that have had disproportionate impacts on educational thought and practice and which we believe are worth briefly discussing and commenting upon: those offered by Robert Maynard Hutchins, John Dewey, and Mortimer Adler.

Robert Maynard Hutchins

Robert Maynard Hutchins (January 17, 1899 -- May 14, 1977) was the Dean of the Yale Law School from 1927 to 1929, and the President (1929 to 1945) and Chancellor (1945 to 1951) of the University of Chicago, where he made significant contributions to debates about the undergraduate curriculum and, ultimately, offered a very powerful view of what an educated person should know and be able to do – a view that still has many advocates. While at the University of Chicago, Hutchins made a number of controversial decisions that reflected deeply held views about what a university should be. For example, he eliminated the varsity football program and argued for the disbanding of fraternities and religious organizations on campus. Hutchins was a major defender of academic freedom, and in both 1935 and 1949 he fought claims that the University of Chicago was supporting communism, arguing that professors should be allowed to teach without interference and, further, that the best way to defeat communism was through public exposure and debate. He is best known for what was called the "Hutchins Plan," which was based on Socratic dialogue and exposure to the "Great Books," and was also an early advocate for interdisciplinary studies (his role in promoting the Great Books will be discussed below, in the section dealing with Mortimer Adler). It is worth noting that Hutchins' curricular proposals were actually rejected on three separate occasions by the faculty at the University of Chicago in the late 1930s before he was able to implement many of them. Hutchins left the University of Chicago to lead the Ford Foundation, and in 1959 he founded the Center for the Study of Democratic Institutions in Santa Barbara, California.

John Dewey

John Dewey (October 20, 1859 -- June 1, 1952) was among the most significant American philosophers and public intellectuals of the first half of the 20th century. Dewey received his PhD from Johns Hopkins University in 1884, after which he taught at the University of Michigan and the University of Minnesota before moving to the University of Chicago in 1894. In 1904, Dewey moved once again to the faculty at Teachers College at Columbia University in New York, where he completed many of his major works. Often considered to be the "Father of Progressive Education," Dewey wrote extensively about education, teaching and learning, and tested many of his educational theories in practice at the University of Chicago Laboratory Schools, which he founded in 1896 in Hyde Park in Chicago. The central focus of Dewey's work was democracy, not only in education but also as a political, social, and economic system to promote civil society. Although best known as an educator and educational philosopher, Dewey also wrote extensively about social theory, ethics, epistemology, logic, psychology, metaphysics, aesthetics, and art. In essence, Dewey argued that schools are profoundly social institutions and that education is an interactive, social process. One quote of Dewey's that is frequently cited, and which reflects these ideas, is that "Education is, not a preparation for life; education is life itself." He believed that students should play a role in their own learning rather than being seen simply as vessels into which knowledge should be poured. He also believed that it was pedagogically important for the curriculum to reflect student interests and concerns. This did not mean, for Dewey, that the curriculum should simply be handed over to students – the teacher plays a central role in guiding students, but must do so in a way that nevertheless honors and respects their individual interests. Throughout his work on education, his commitment to both democracy and social reform is clear. Among his better-known educational writings are *My Pedagogic Creed* (1897), *The School and Society* (1899), *The Child and the Curriculum* (1902), *Democracy and Education* (1916), *Schools of Tomorrow* (1915) (which he co-authored with his daughter Evelyn Dewey), and *Experience and Education* (1938).

John Dewey Stamp
©Lefteris Papaulakis/Shutterstock.com

Mortimer Adler

Mortimer Adler (December 28, 1902 -- June 28, 2001) was an important 20th century American philosopher and educator who worked in the Aristotelian and Thomistic traditions. At various points, he worked at Columbia University, the University of Chicago, *Encyclopaedia Britannica*, and his own Institute for Philosophical Research. Adler was born and raised in New York City; he dropped out of school at the age of 14 and became a copy boy for the *New York Sun* newspaper. Seeking to become a journalist, he began taking night courses, and ultimately matriculated at Columbia University, receiving a doctoral degree in psychology.[8] As a student, he read and was deeply impressed by Plato, Aristotle, St. Thomas Aquinas, John Locke, among others. He became a good friend of Robert Maynard Hutchins, who brought him to the University of Chicago as a professor of the philosophy of law in the university's law school (he was rejected as a potential faculty member by the Department of Philosophy). Working collaboratively, Hutchins and Adler created the "Great Books of the Western World" program and the Great Books Foundation. He also served on the Board of Editors of the *Encyclopaedia Britannica* and followed Hutchins as its Chair in 1974. In 1982, Adler published *The Paideia Proposal: An Educational Manifesto*, which was a reform plan for K-12 schooling in the United States. In essence, *The Paideia Proposal* proposed that all students should be given an education grounded in the liberal arts tradition, regardless of their age, background, whether they are likely to go to a college or university, and so on. In Adler's view, the contemporary system of public education in the United States is anti-democratic since it denies the "best" education to many, while reserving such learning for a small élite in society. Although presupposing some degree of flexibility at both the state and local levels, Adler argued that the core curriculum to which all students should be exposed ought to include:

- Language, literature and fine arts.
- Mathematics and natural science.
- History, geography and social studies.
- Physical education and manual training.[9]
- A general introduction to the world of work.[10] (Adler, 1982, 1983)

Adler's Paideia Proposal gained a great deal of popularity in the 1980s, especially as concerns about the need for curriculum reform and accountability in the public schools increased. It is probably worth noting, incidentally, that the very sorts of accountability that emerged in the *No Child Left Behind* era make the implementation of the type proposed by Adler almost impossible to imagine in the context of a public school.

Questions for Reflection and Discussion

1. In your own words, explain the distinction between *schooling* and *education*. What are three examples of each that have taken place in your own life?

---

[8] Adler actually did not graduate and receive a bachelor's degree from Columbia University because he refused to take the required swimming test. In 1983, Columbia University rectified this situation when it awarded him an honorary degree.

[9] Adler argues that physical education should entail 12 years in the curriculum, while manual training (including things such as cooking, sewing, typing, and machine repair) should take 6 years.

[10] This should, on Adler's account, last 2 years.

2. The authors provide several examples of *training* and argue that training is appropriate and legitimate for many different kinds of learning. This suggests, though, that there are also kinds of learning for which training is *not* appropriate or legitimate. Can you identify some examples of learning where this would be the case? Why would training not be appropriate in these cases?

3. The authors point out that there are different ways that the preparation of teachers is described: teacher preparation, teacher education, and teacher training. They appear to believe that the terminology that we chose to use to describe this process reflects differences in how we conceptualize the role and job of classroom teachers. Do you agree? If so, how would you suggest that each of these phrases is used in practice? What are the implications of this?

4. In this chapter, the Peters-Hirst ideal of the "educated person" is discussed. An important aspect of this ideal is the assumption that the individual must have mastered a number of different "forms of knowledge." How would you explain a "form of knowledge"? Do you agree with the "forms of knowledge" that Peters and Hirst identify as necessary requirements for the "educated person"?

5. The outcome of education should be the production of an "educated person," but the way that we identify and discuss what this actually means is very controversial. In your view, what are the requirements for a person to be an "educated person" in 21st century American society? How would you defend each of the requirements that you identify?

References

Adler, M. (1982). *The Paideia proposal: An educational manifesto*. New York, NY: Simon & Shuster.

Adler, M. (1983). *Paideia problems and possibilities: A consideration of questions raised by the Paideia proposal*. New York, NY: Macmillan.

Barrow, R. (1976). *Common sense and the curriculum*. London, UK: George Allen & Unwin.

Barrow, R. (1981). *The philosophy of schooling*. Brighton, UK: Harvester.

Barrow, R., & Woods, R. (1988). *An introduction to philosophy of education* (3rd ed.). New York, NY: Routledge.

Brent, A. (1978). *Philosophical foundations for the curriculum*. London, UK: George Allen & Unwin.

Campbell, E. (2009). The educated person. *Curriculum Inquiry, 39*(3), 371-379.

Chambers, J. (1983). *The achievement of education*. New York, NY: Harper & Row.

Dearden, R., Hirst, P., & Peters, R. S. (Eds.). (1972a). *Education and the development of reason, Part 1: A critique of current educational aims.* London, UK: Routledge & Kegan Paul.

Dearden, R., Hirst, P., & Peters, R. S. (Eds.). (1972b). *Education and the development of reason, Part 2: Reason.* London, UK: Routledge & Kegan Paul.

Dearden, R., Hirst, P., & Peters, R. S. (Eds.). (1972c). *Education and the development of reason, Part 3: Education and reason.* London, UK: Routledge & Kegan Paul.

Dewey, J. (1897). *My pedagogic creed.* New York, NY: E. L. Kellogg.

Dewey, J. (1899). *The school and society.* Chicago, IL: University of Chicago Press.

Dewey, J. (1902). *The child and the curriculum.* Chicago, IL: University of Chicago Press.

Dewey, J. (1916). *Democracy and education: An introduction to the philosophy of education.* New York, NY: Macmillan.

Dewey, J. (1938). *Experience and education.* New York, NY: Collier.

Dewey, J., & Dewey, E. (1915). *Schools of tomorrow.* New York, NY: E. P. Dutton.

Doyle, J. (Ed.). (1973). *Educational judgments.* London, UK: Routledge & Kegan Paul.

Elvin, L. (1977). *The place of commonsense in educational thought.* London, UK: George Allen & Unwin.

Green, T. (1971). *The activities of teaching.* New York, NY: McGraw-Hill.

Hamlyn, D. (1978). *Experience and the growth of understanding.* London, UK: Routledge & Kegan Paul.

Hamm, C. (1989). *Philosophical issues in education: An introduction.* New York, NY: Falmer Press.

Hirst, P. (1973). Liberal education and the nature of knowledge. In R. S. Peters (Ed.), *The philosophy of education* (pp. 87-111). Oxford, UK: Oxford University Press.

Hirst, P. (1974). *Knowledge and the curriculum.* London, UK: Routledge & Kegan Paul.

Hirst, P. (1993). Education, knowledge and practices. In R. Barrow & P. White (Eds.), *Beyond liberal education* (pp. 184-199). New York, NY: Routledge.

Hirst, P., & Peters, R. S. (1970). *The logic of education.* London, UK: Routledge & Kegan Paul.

Jaeger, W. (1967). *Paideia: The ideals of Greek culture, Volume I: Archaic Greece: The mind of Athens* (2nd ed.). Oxford, UK: Oxford University Press. (Original work published 1933)

Jaeger, W. (1971a). *Paideia: The ideals of Greek culture, Volume II: In search of the divine center.* Oxford, UK: Oxford University Press. (Original work published 1944)

Jaeger, W. (1971b). *Paideia: The ideals of Greek culture, Volume III: The conflict of cultural ideals in the age of Plato.* Oxford, UK: Oxford University Press. (Original work published 1947)

Levinson, B., Foley, D., & Holland, D. (Eds.). (1996). *The cultural production of the educated person.* Albany: State University of New York Press.

Lloyd, D. (Ed.) (1976). *Philosophy and the teacher.* London, UK: Routledge & Kegan Paul.

Martin, J. R. (1984). Bringing women into educational thought. *Educational Theory, 34*(4), 341-353.

Martin, J. R. (1985). *Reclaiming a conversation: The ideal of the educated woman.* New Haven, CT: Yale University Press.

Martin, J. R. (1986). Redefining the educated person: Rethinking the significance of gender. *Educational Researcher, 15*(6), 6-10.

Martin, J. R. (1994). *Changing the educational landscape: Philosophy, women, and curriculum.* New York, NY: Routledge.

Martin, J. R. (2000). *Coming of age in academe: Rekindling women's hopes and reforming the academy.* New York, NY: Routledge.

Matthews, M. (1980). *The Marxist theory of schooling: A study of epistemology and education.* Brighton, UK: Harvester.

Mulcahy, D. (2002). *Knowledge, gender, and schooling.* Westport, CT: Bergin & Garvey.

Mulcahy, D. (2008). *The educated person: Toward a new paradigm for liberal education.* Lanham, MD: Rowman & Littlefield.

Park, C. (1984). A reconsideration: Werner Jaeger's *Paideia. Modern Age, 28*(2), 152-155.

Peters, R. (1963, December 9). *Education as initiation.* Inaugural lecture delivered at the University of London, Institute of Education.

Peters, R. (1966). *Ethics and education.* London, UK: George Allen & Unwin.

Peters, R. S. (Ed.). (1973a). *The concept of education.* London, UK: Routledge & Kegan Paul.

Peters, R. S. (Ed.). (1973b). *The philosophy of education.* Oxford, UK: Oxford University Press.

Pring, R. (1976). *Knowledge and schooling.* London, UK: Open Books.

Reagan, T. (2009). The professional status of teachers. In R. Bailey, D. Carr, R. Barrow, & C. McCarthy (Eds.), *The Sage handbook of philosophy of education* (pp. 209-221). London, UK: Sage.

Reagan, T. (2018). *Non-Western educational traditions: Alternative approaches to educational thought and practice* (4th ed.). New York, NY: Routledge.

Schofield, H. (1972). *The philosophy of education.* London, UK: George Allen & Unwin.

Straughan, R., & Wilson, J. (1983). *Philosophizing about education.* London, UK: Cassell.

Chapter 5

Curriculum and Instruction

*If we have learned anything from the intense and
continuing conflicts over what and whose knowledge
should be declared "official" that have raged
throughout the history of the curriculum
in so many nations, it should have been one lesson.
There is an intricate set of connections between
knowledge and power.* (Michael Apple)

*Learning and teaching is messy stuff. It
doesn't fit into bubbles.* (Michele Forman)

In this chapter, we will be examining two of what most educators would consider to be the "core" elements of teaching: curriculum and instruction. In the preceding chapter, we defined "schooling" using the formula *T teaches x* to *S, under the auspices of the school, so that Y/y*. Two of the key components of this formula – *teaches* and *x* – are essentially the focus of this chapter. Both of these topics can be understood and conceptualized in what are basically technical terms: We can define "instruction" as nothing more than the collection of the techniques and methods used by the classroom teacher in attempting to accomplish their identified learning objectives, and "curriculum" as the content that is manifested in those learning objectives. Although such definitions are not intrinsically wrong, as Michael Apple (2006, p. 25) argues in the above quote, there are also alternative ways of thinking about both curriculum and instruction that emphasize their political and ideological nature, and which can provide us with what are sometimes far more powerful and useful understandings of what actually goes on in public schools.

The Curriculum

Discussions about the curriculum often begin with references to the etymology of the term "curriculum." The word "curriculum" can be traced back to the Latin verb *currere*, which means "to run (in a race)," and so the curriculum is the course that the student "runs" in going through the educational process. Although this explanation is true to a certain extent, it does not really adequately explain the contemporary use of the term "curriculum." In fact, we would suggest that it is not particularly helpful to rely on etymology here – rather, what seems to us to make the most sense is simply to provide a clear definition of the term, and then to outline the details embedded in this definition. Essentially, the curriculum is the sum total of all aspects of the student's experiences as they go through the learning process. Grant Wiggins and Jay McTighe (2005), in their popular work on "learning by design," suggest that:

curriculum refers to the specific blueprint for learning that is derived from *desired results* — that is, content and performance standards (be they state-determined or locally developed). Curriculum takes content (from external standards and local goals) and shapes it into a plan for how to conduct effective and engaging teaching and learning. It is thus more than a list of topics and lists of key facts and skills (the "inputs"). It is a *map* for how to achieve the "outputs" of desired student performance, in which appropriate learning activities and assessments are suggested to make it more likely that students achieve the desired results. (pp. 5-6, emphasis added)

Although this definition has a number of advantages when conceptualizing the curriculum within the formal and institutional context of the school, it is far too narrow to encompass all of the significant aspects of what students experience. Critiquing the fundamental assumptions of such a definition of curriculum, Peter McLaren (1989) has pointed out that critical pedagogues challenge the notion that schools are places where knowledge alone is passed on. This includes consideration how schools act as sites for sorting and empowering students based on some set or combination of sets of criteria, identifying elements of these criteria within planned curriculum and standards, and even challenging these criteria (see Arnowitz & Giroux, 1985, 1991). Furthermore, as Joel Spring (2011) has noted,

Educational goals are a product of what people think schooling should do for the good of society. Consequently, they often reflect opinions and beliefs about how people should act and how society should be organized. Since there is wide variation in what people believe, educational goals often generate a great deal of debate. (p. 4)

In fact, the curriculum is an immensely complex and diverse matter, as well as sometimes a divisive one, and can be understood in a number of quite different ways. Some of these ways of conceptualizing the curriculum (which can and do overlap) are discussed below.

The Planned and Unplanned Curricula

The most obvious and commonly used way in which the term curriculum is used is to refer to what can be thought of as the "planned" or "formal" curriculum. The planned curriculum is the "official" curriculum, in the sense that it is what the teacher and the school would claim to be a description of what is and should be occurring in the classroom. The planned curriculum will normally reflect the mission and vision of the school, as well as the goals and objectives of the particular subject area being taught. The planned curriculum is the explicit articulation of the content to be covered, as well as how that content is to be taught, and the ways in which the learning of the content will be assessed, both formatively and summatively. In the context of the typical classroom, the planned curriculum is often closely tied to the textbook used in the class. This is a very important point, since, as Allan Ornstein (1982) has observed, the most fundamental concern of schooling is curriculum. Students tend to view schooling largely as subjects or courses to be taken. Teachers and professors give much attention to adoption and revision of subject matter. Parents and community members frequently express concern about what schools are for and what they should teach. In short, all of these groups are attending to one thing: curriculum. (p. 404)

The "unplanned curriculum," in contrast to the planned curriculum, is basically everything else that takes place in the classroom: unintended and unplanned events, content, learning, and so on. The unplanned curriculum may be either positive or negative in nature. It is possible that students in a class might learn something very valuable about respecting other people, or about how to interact with others appropriately or about how to politely and civilly disagree with others – all of which would be positive outcomes of the classroom experience but none of which are likely to have been included in the formal, planned curriculum. At the same time, there is considerable evidence about the teaching and learning of racism, sexism, ableism, and other kinds of bias in the classroom, none of which, one might wish to assume, is deliberate – but which is nevertheless an outcome of many educational experiences (see Jay, 2003; Ladson-Billings, 2003; Peters, 2015; Shaffer & Shevitz, 2001; Singer, 1995). To be sure, while we believe that a great deal of explicit bias in textbook and instructional materials may have been eliminated in recent years, many ideological and cultural biases *do* remain largely unexamined and unaddressed. As Susan Shaffer and Linda Shevitz (2001) have noted, "all aspects of the curriculum, including the 'evaded' curriculum, that which is not [explicitly] taught, can contain … forms of bias that impede the learning and educational opportunities of all students" (p. 115).

The Excluded Curriculum

In every society, there are many topics, perspectives, issues, ideas, and so on that are deliberately excluded from the curriculum. This is not, of course, an intrinsically bad thing – no curriculum in any discipline or field of study could possibly include *all* of the knowledge that exists in that discipline. *All* curricula involve making choices about what should and should not be included, and this is a perfectly legitimate aspect of the design and development of any curriculum. What is left out of the curriculum is called the "excluded curriculum" (also sometimes the "null curriculum"), and almost by definition it is far larger than the planned, formal, overt curriculum. While many of the things that are excluded from the formal curriculum are excluded for sound reasons, other things that are excluded from the curriculum are left out for less defensible reasons. The curriculum can be a source of considerable controversy, and it is not uncommon for topics and issues that might offend parents, politicians, religious figures, and so on, to be excluded from the curriculum. In some cases, such exclusion might not be particularly problematic, but in other cases, this can lead to what is essentially censorship in the curriculum. Such censorship is most common in subject areas such as social studies, literature, and sometimes in the sciences, but it can and does occur in all disciplines. The areas in which such censorship is most likely to occur are politics and ideological topics, sexual and lifestyle issues, religious matters, and similar areas in which there are significant and ongoing debates in U.S. society.

One valuable way to think about issues of the excluded curriculum and censorship is to distinguish between censorship and indoctrination. The key difference here is that while censorship involves decisions about the inclusion or exclusion of content, indoctrination is a far deeper, and arguably far more serious, matter. In his landmark study of indoctrination, I. A. Snook (1972) argued that "indoctrination is the teaching of any subject matter with the intention that it be believed regardless of the evidence," and further, that "indoctrination, so defined, is morally reprehensible" (p. 75). Although Snook's fundamental concern is actually with the teaching of religion, his definition applies equally to other subjects. There is an important difference, in short, between teaching about a topic, and teaching about a topic in order that a particular belief is accepted by the student regardless of the evidence supporting or not supporting that belief. In the U.S. context, we often utilize this distinction in discussing "teaching religion" and "teaching about religion" – the former being unacceptable in a public school setting, while the latter is not only acceptable, but arguably necessary and even essential.[1]

The Hidden Curriculum

The phrase "the hidden curriculum" was first used by Philip Jackson in his 1968 book *Life in Classrooms*. Jackson (1990) described the hidden curriculum as follows:

> The crowds, the praise, and the power that combine to give a distinctive flavor to classroom life collectively form a hidden curriculum which each student (and teacher) must master if [they are] to make [their] way satisfactorily through the school. The demands created by these features of classroom life may be contrasted with the academic demands – the "official" curriculum, so to speak – to which educators traditionally have paid the most attention. As might be expected, the two curriculums are related to each other in several important ways. (pp. 33-34)

Although a powerful insight, Jackson's conceptualization of the hidden curriculum was not tied to the political socialization and ideological aspects of public schooling, but rather simply to the non-academic aspects of schooling. Later scholars, however, extended the notion of the hidden curriculum in ways that emphasized such issues. Samuel Bowles and Herbert Gintis provided a critique of common views of the role of public schooling in the United States as agencies of social mobility, arguing that rather than encouraging upward mobility the schools reproduce existing social class structures for the vast majority of students, in part by sending messages to students about their intellectual abilities, personal traits, and appropriate educational and occupational choices (see Bowles & Gintis, 1976, 2002; Kentli, 2009). Jane Roland Martin suggested that the hidden curriculum can be seen in the social structure of the classroom, in

---

[1] Our focus here is on what takes place in the context of the public schools. Although there is a very broad, general consensus that it is inappropriate to teach religion in *public* schools, there are a number of other settings in which such instruction is perfectly appropriate. Private and parochial schools, Sunday school classes, and so on, are often concerned in large part (if not entirely) in teaching religion – that is, in inducting children into a specific religious tradition.

116

the teacher's exercise of classroom authority, and in the rules that govern the relationship between the teacher and their students (Kentli, 2009; Martin, 1976). Writing in the context of the United Kingdom, Paul Willis suggested that there are actually two hidden curricula – one that of the formal structures of the school, which determine in large part the reproduction of social class relations in society, and the other being constituted by the resistance of pupils to this process. Thus, on Willis' account, there is a far more complex dynamic with respect to social class reproduction and the role of the school in such reproduction (see Kentli, 2009; Willis, 1997).[2] Finally, Henry Giroux has defined the hidden curriculum as the unstated norms, values and beliefs that area embedded in and transmitted to students through the underlying (and often unstated) rules that structure the routines and social relationships in the school and classroom (see Giroux, 1983, 1988, 1997; Kentli, 2009).

The Historical Evolution of the Curriculum in the United States

During the colonial era, schooling was for the most part restricted to a relatively small part of the population, and was far more common in New England than in the other colonies. Even in New England, many children were actually educated at home, by their parents, rather than in any sort of formal institution of schooling. For most children, schooling consisted of the development of the basic skills of literacy, numeracy and the acquisition of religious knowledge – typically, the Protestant denominational version of Christianity that was dominant in each town or community. As early as the mid-17th century, schooling was mandated in parts of New England for all children (the *Old Deluder Satan Act* of 1647 in Massachusetts is often cited as the first legislation dealing with public schooling in America). In the remainder of colonial America, schooling was less common and formal, and institutional schooling tended to develop later. In the South, the Planter élite provided tutors to educate their own children, while the enslaved people upon whom the economy relied received no education. For the male colonial élite, there was higher education either in a North American or British university, grounded in the classical liberal arts curriculum. The rise of the Common Schools in the mid-19th century led to an institutionalization of schooling in most parts of the United States (excluding the South), and an expansion of the curriculum (Katz, 1968). To a significant extent, the Common School curriculum consisted of what some historians have called the "four R's": reading, writing, arithmetic, and "rules of conduct." The "rules of conduct" were essentially the common, shared elements that were believed to be necessary for the maintenance of a social order grounded in republican democratic institutions, the emerging industrial capitalism that was increasingly the foundation of the American economy, the assimilation and acculturation of immigrants and the concomitant creation of a shared national identity, and, not least, what Horace Mann called "those great Christian truths" that were shared by "all rational men" – essentially, a sort of pan-Protestantism (see Tozer, Violas & Senese, 1993, pp. 58-59).

Secondary schools serving most students developed long after the Common Schools. Indeed, the emergence of secondary schools in the United States was largely a phenomenon of the late 19th and early 20th centuries. In 1892, the National Education Association (NEA) established a group of educators called the "Committee of Ten" to examine contemporary

---

[2] Although Willis was indeed writing in the context of the United Kingdom, his observations are every bit as valid in the American context as in the British context.

secondary school practice and to make recommendations for how secondary education might be improved. Among the recommendations offered by the Committee of Ten were that public schooling be expanded to 12 years (8 years of elementary schooling followed by 4 years of secondary schooling), that the quality of instruction should be improved, and that the curriculum should be simplified and unified. In terms of subject matter, the Committee of Ten's recommendations resulted in a fairly standardized national curriculum that included English, mathematics, history and/or civics, chemistry, and physics. Perhaps one of the most important outcomes of the work of the Committee of Ten was its strong commitment to equity and unity in the curriculum. Unlike common practice in many other societies, the Committee of Ten unanimously recommended that "every subject which is taught at all in a secondary school should be taught *in the same way* and *to the same extent* to every pupil so long as he pursues it, no matter what the probable destination of the pupil may be, or at what point his education is to cease" (National Education Association, 1894, p. 17, emphasis added).

As public secondary education expanded and spread, additional pressures came to bear on the schools, and the NEA once again created a commission, this time the "Commission on the Reorganization of Secondary Education," to establish clear objectives for American secondary schools. The Commission of the Reorganization of Secondary Education began its work in 1915, and released its final report, the *Cardinal Principles of Secondary Education*, in 1918. The *Cardinal Principles of Secondary Education* was, in effect, the last of a whole series of reports concerned with the standardization of American public schooling (see Kliebard, 2002, p. 39). Written at the height of the progressive education movement, the *Cardinal Principles of Secondary Education* had as its organizing theme the ideal of democracy as the guiding principle for all students. Focusing not on subject matter or disciplinary knowledge, the seven objectives identified in the *Cardinal Principles of Secondary Education* included:

(1) Health.
(2) Command of Fundamental Processes.
(3) Worthy Home Membership.
(4) Vocation.
(5) Civic Education.
(6) Worthy Use of Leisure.
(7) Ethical Character.

The development of and increasing access to higher education may well be considered to have provided the origin of much of the standard or prescribed curriculum at the secondary school level. The university, with its expectation of a curriculum that prepared students for college admission, was originally intended to have a fairly classical focus (see Ornstein & Hunkins, 1993). However, as more and more students began attending universities, secondary schools increasingly sought to include curricula and curricular options that would best prepare students for higher education. What is most interesting about the *Cardinal Principles of Secondary Education* for us today, slightly more than a century later, is not how different they are from the objectives of contemporary schooling, but rather, how profoundly similar they are.

More recently, the most significant curricular development in public schooling in the United States has been the widespread adoption of the "Common Core State Standards Initiative," or, as it is more commonly known, simply the "Common Core." Introduced in 2010, and initially adopted by more than 40 states, the Common Core was an effort to dramatically improve the academic achievement of American students in two areas: literacy and mathematics. In part a response to the poor results of American students on the OECD's "Programme for International Student Assessment" (PISA),[3] which is given every 3 years (see Tables 5.1 and 5.2), the Common Core standards were created to "provide clear and consistent learning goals to help prepare students for college, career, and life" (Common Core State Standards Initiative, 2020). Advocates for the Core Curriculum maintain that the standards are:

- Research and evidence based.
- Clear, understandable, and consistent.
- Aligned with college and career expectations.
- Based on rigorous content and the application of knowledge through higher-order thinking skills.
- Building upon the strengths and lessons of current state standards.
- Informed by other top-performing countries to prepare all students for success in our global economy and society. (Common Core State Standards Initiative, 2020)

Country	2012	2015	2018
Argentina	396	425	402
Australia	512	503	503
Austria	490	485	484
Belgium	509	499	493
Brazil	410	407	413
Bulgaria	436	432	420
Canada	523	527	520
Chile	441	459	452
China (PRC)	494	494	555
China (Taiwan)	523	497	502
Czech Republic	493	487	490
Denmark	496	500	501
Estonia	516	519	523
Finland	524	526	520
France	505	499	493
Germany	508	509	498
Greece	477	467	457
Hong Kong	545	527	524
Hungary	488	470	476
Iceland	483	482	474
Ireland	523	521	518

[3] The focus in the United States, and especially as a consequence of the rise of the Common Core, has been on literacy and mathematics. The PISA actually provides comparative data in three areas: reading, mathematics, and science.

Israel	486	479	470
Italy	490	485	476
Japan	538	516	504
Korea (South)	536	517	514
Latvia	489	488	479
Lithuania	477	472	476
Mexico	424	423	420
Netherlands	511	503	485
New Zealand	512	509	506
Norway	504	513	499
Peru	384	398	401
Poland	518	506	512
Portugal	488	498	492
Russian Federation	475	495	479
Singapore	542	535	549
Slovenia	481	N/A	495
Sweden	483	500	506
Switzerland	509	492	484
Turkey	475	428	466
United Arab Emirates	442	434	434
United States	498	497	505
United Kingdom	499	498	504

Table 5.1 Comparative 2012-2018 PISA Results: Reading (Mean Scores)

Country	2012	2015	2018
Argentina	388	409	379
Australia	504	494	491
Austria	506	497	499
Belgium	515	507	508
Brazil	391	377	384
Bulgaria	439	441	436
Canada	518	516	512
Chile	423	423	417
China (PRC)	531	531	591
China (Taiwan)	560	542	531
Czech Republic	499	492	499
Denmark	500	511	509
Estonia	521	529	523
Finland	519	511	507
France	495	493	495
Germany	514	506	500
Greece	453	454	451
Hong Kong	561	548	551
Hungary	477	477	481

Iceland	493	488	495
Ireland	501	504	500
Israel	466	470	463
Italy	485	490	487
Japan	536	532	527
Korea (South)	554	524	526
Latvia	491	482	496
Lithuania	479	478	481
Mexico	413	408	409
Netherlands	523	512	519
New Zealand	500	495	494
Norway	489	502	501
Peru	368	387	400
Poland	518	504	516
Portugal	487	492	492
Russian Federation	482	494	488
Singapore	573	564	569
Slovenia	501	510	509
Sweden	478	494	502
Switzerland	531	521	515
Turkey	448	420	454
United Arab Emirates	434	427	427
United States	481	470	478
United Kingdom	494	492	502

Table 5.2 Comparative 2012-2018 PISA Results: Mathematics (Mean Scores)

In spite of its initial popularity and bipartisan support, the Common Core has become increasingly controversial among both conservative critics and progressive educators. Conservatives have been largely concerned with what they see as an attempt to impose a national curriculum on the states and local school districts. Progressive educators are concerned that the Common Core takes decision-making away from teachers and imposes a one-size-fits all approach to schooling that ignores the cultural and linguistic diversity of our society. Indeed, the educational writer Jonathan Kozol (2005) has described the effect of the Common Core as "cognitive decapitation" (p. 119). Diane Ravitch, formerly U.S. Assistant Secretary of Education and a well-known educational historian, as well as a specialist in educational policy issues, has noted an additional problem with the Common Core:

The financial cost of implementing Common Core has barely been mentioned in the national debates. All Common Core testing will be done online. This is a bonanza for the tech industry and other vendors. Every school district must buy new computers, new teaching materials, and new bandwidth for the testing. At a time when school budgets have been cut in most states and many thousands of teachers have been laid off, school districts across the nation will spend billions to pay for Common Core testing. Los Angeles alone committed to spend $1 billion on iPads for the tests; the money is being taken from a bond issue approved by voters for construction and repair of school facilities. Meanwhile, the district has cut teachers of the arts, class size has increased, and necessary repairs are deferred because the money will be spent on iPads. The iPads will be obsolete in a year or two, and the Pearson content loaded onto the iPads has only a three-year license. The cost of implementing the Common Core and the new tests is likely to run into the billions at a time of deep budget cuts. (Quoted in Strauss, 2014)

The results of the implementation of the Common Core have, at best, been mixed. Certainly with respect to the PISA results, as Tables 5.1 and 5.2. make clear, there have been slight increases in the performance of U.S. students (especially in reading and science), and our overall ranking has improved in comparison to many other countries – but this is due almost as much to declines elsewhere as to increases in the United States in many cases.

The Curriculum and the Textbook

There is sometimes an unfortunate tendency to confuse and conflate the *curriculum* in a particular course or subject area with the *textbook* that is being used This problem is not unique to any particular subject, but it does seem to be more common in certain content areas (such as mathematics and world languages) than in others. There are a number of possible explanations for this tendency: institutional requirements that the teacher follow the textbook, the ease of simply following the pre-determined course structure provided by a textbook, teacher insecurity about their own competence in the subject matter being taught, and understandable (though perhaps somewhat inappropriate) assumptions about the knowledge, skills, and competence of the creators and authors of textbooks. Taken together, all of these factors lead to what can be termed the "hegemony of the textbook," which refers to an unwillingness to question or challenge the textbook (see Ornstein, 1992, 1994). This is not meant to be an attack on textbooks *per se*; indeed, as Allan Ornstein (1994) has noted, there is much that is positive in the use of textbooks:

> Good textbooks have many desirable characteristics. They are usually well-organized, coherent, unified, relatively up-to-date, accurate, and relatively unbiased. They have been scrutinized by scholars, educators, and minority groups. Their reading level and knowledge base match the developmental level of their intended audience. They are accompanied by teacher's manuals, test items, study guides, and activity guides. The textbook is an acceptable tool for instruction *as long as it is selected with care and is kept in proper perspective so that it is not viewed as the only source of knowledge, and it does not turn into the curriculum*. (p. 70, emphasis added)

The caveat added by Ornstein, though, is an extremely important one. Despite their utility, it is a serious error to conflate the textbook with the curriculum – a mistake that is all too often made. Properly utilized, the textbook can serve as a very valuable tool in the classroom, but the teacher should always be willing to modify it, to challenge it, and to go beyond it with their students.

Curricular Nullification

Although it is clearly desirable for teachers to go beyond the textbook with respect to the curriculum, there is a process by which the critical pedagogue can challenge the hegemony of the textbook in a far more profound way than simply providing students with various kinds of supplementary materials and exploring additional topics. This process is called "curricular nullification," and it is analogous to the phenomenon of "jury nullification" in the United States, in which the members of a jury choose to ignore legal mandates in coming to a finding that they believe to be more just and appropriate (see Osborn, 2000, pp. 98-103). Curricular nullification refers to the teacher's ability to reject the set curriculum (whether this means the textbook or more formal and established institutional curricula), either to exclude certain features or units or to include features or units that were absent in the original textbook or curriculum (i.e., both additive and subtractive curricular nullification; see Osborn, 2000, 2006; Reagan, 2016).

The Role of Interdisciplinary Units in the Critical Curriculum

During the past several decades, a growing number of educators working within and among the core content areas have advocated the development and implementation of interdisciplinary curricula[4] as an important aspect of educational reform and renewal (see Lonning & DeFranco, 1997; Lonning, DeFranco & Weinland, 1998; National Council of Teachers of Mathematics, 1991). An important aspect of the literature concerned with the interdisciplinary curriculum has been its emphasis on the hurdles faced by educators in integrating course content across disciplinary lines, which constitute a challenge of considerable scope and difficulty (Davison, Miller & Methany, 1995). The education literature in general tends to be strongly supportive of interdisciplinary approaches to teaching and learning, and we would certainly agree that the linking of content across parts of the curriculum (or ideally, across the whole curriculum) is certainly a worthwhile goal. However, desire alone is insufficient to direct and guide efforts of this type to successful fruition. A model for the initial planning stages of interdisciplinary curriculum development in and for content area courses is crucial. This is especially true because of the general difficulty involved in developing and implementing interdisciplinary curricula, as David Ackerman (1989) has stressed:

> While it unquestionably has high rhetorical appeal, curriculum integration presents daunting challenges to those who would like to see it more widely embraced as an alternative or counterpart to subject-based curriculum … With its promise of unifying knowledge and modes of understanding, interdisciplinary education represents the pinnacle of curriculum development. (p. 37)

Heidi Jacobs (1989) has noted that, "in contrast to a discipline-field based view of knowledge, interdisciplinarity does not stress delineations but linkages" (p. 8). Ackerman has moved the interdisciplinary agenda forward by proffering intellectual and practical criteria to be considered as a "framework for teachers and curriculum developers deliberating over whether

---

[4] What we are calling "interdisciplinary" here actually refers to several related but distinct approaches to the curriculum, including not only interdisciplinary approaches but also multidisciplinary and transdisciplinary approaches.

to adopt a curriculum integration approach for some portion of their instructional program" (Ackerman, 1989, p. 25). Perhaps the most significant elements of Ackerman's framework are the concepts of *validity for, validity within,* and *validity beyond* the discipline (see Lonning et al., 1998, p. 315). Briefly summarized, these criteria require that an interdisciplinary theme or organizing center be important to relevant fields of study – that is, that they not be just a contrived connection. Furthermore, the criteria must facilitate the learning of other concepts within the individual disciplines, and must give the student a "metaconceptual bonus" (Ackerman, 1989, pp. 27-30). Within these parameters, however, one finds the genesis of new ways of thinking about such units and about the limitations of current models for the classroom.

As Rob Lonning, Thomas DeFranco, and Tim Weinland (1998) have pointed out, the "selection of appropriate themes seems to be the key to providing instruction that is potentially more meaningful when taught in an interdisciplinary fashion than when the concepts are taught separately" (p. 312). The model they propose for the integration of mathematics and science includes moving from standards and state frameworks, through a revision and evaluation process in selecting an applicable theme, to a refinement of activities that balance mathematics and science content. In an analogous fashion, units in other content areas can become interdisciplinary as they move from the usual textbook chapter topics to overarching and extendable curricular themes, especially insofar as such themes overlap and are tied to curricular content in other subject areas.

Instruction

One of the core activities in which teachers engage – if not *the* core activity -- is teaching. Teaching, or instruction,[5] is at the heart not only of what teachers do, but also is central to the very reason that we have schools. Although we might, therefore, expect that it would be fairly easy and straight-forward to define what constitutes teaching, this is not actually the case. The problem is that teachers do *many* different things during the course of the day, some of which are certainly are teaching, but others that – while perhaps necessary for the operation of the school – are not so much *teaching* as some other sort of activity. In order to allow us to conceptualize what is and what is not teaching, a good place to begin is to examine what takes place in the classroom. Let's imagine that we are observing a third-grade teacher in a fairly typical elementary school in the United States. What kinds of things would we expect that teacher to engage in over the course of the day? A list of their activities might include all of the following:

---

[5] Although we are utilizing the terms "teaching" and "instructing" here synonymously, there is actually sometimes a distinction with respect to how the two words are used, with "teaching" (to some extent) referring more to the acquisition of knowledge and beliefs, and "instructing" (to some extent) referring more to the acquisition of habits (see Green, 1971, p. 28; Hirst & Peters, 1970, p. 84).

talks
disciplines
demonstrates
collects money
provides guidance
(Green, 1971, p. 2)

takes attendance
drinks coffee
evaluates
explains
completes reports

defines
motivates
plans
asks questions
concludes

Teacher in Classroom
© Monkey Business Images/Shutterstock.com

All of these activities are perfectly reasonable, and it is easy to imagine a classroom teacher doing each of them. Some are clearly teaching, but many – in fact, of those listed above, most – may be important, valuable, and even essential but may not really count as "teaching." Only a few of these activities would be likely to be included in any way in the formal curriculum, and many would not be subject to some sort of assessment. The teacher would not have a lesson plan for most of these. Finally, while some of these are definitely examples of teaching, and while others are almost certainly not examples of teaching, still others might be considered to be "border-line" depending on how they actually take place in the classroom. What this tells us is useful, not the least of which is that although observing what takes place in the classroom can be a valuable starting point for understanding teaching – indeed, even an essential part of this process – it will not be sufficient for us to fully describe teaching. As Thomas Green (1971) has commented,

One way to find out how to engage in an activity is to watch somebody else engaged in it. To find out how to bake bread, for example, or how to lay a wall, or how to do something very complex like building a house, we might begin by watching someone who excels at that activity and observe carefully what [they do] and how [they do] it. Such observation, of course, would not, by itself, carry us very far toward either understanding or emulation. It would be a beginning, but little more, for engaging in a practical activity like baking or building involves not only doing certain things, but doing them for certain reasons. Therefore, we need to do more than merely observe what is done. We need also to ask many questions about why it is being done, and why it is being done in a particular way. (p. 1)

The Acts of Teaching

One of the fairly obvious issues that arises from the above list is that there is a fundamental distinction between what might be called the "institutional acts of teaching" and what can be labeled the "logical and strategic acts of teaching" (Green, 1971, pp. 5-7). The former – the institutional acts of teaching – are exactly what they sound like. They include all of the many different things in which classroom teachers engage as members (and, indeed, as employees) of complex institutional organizations. For instance, teachers take attendance, complete forms, sit in meetings, monitor hallways and playgrounds, and do a host of other things. These "institutional acts of teaching" also play a key role in the distinction that we drew between the concepts of schooling and education in the previous chapter.

The institutional acts of teaching play essential, and necessary, roles in public schools. For the most part, though, we do not expect students to learn a great deal as a consequence of the institutional acts of teaching. They may, of course, learn elements of the hidden curriculum, but the institutional acts of teaching are not really concerned with teaching the formal curriculum. Consider, though, visiting a class for one period in a secondary school. During the class, a number of things take place: The teacher takes attendance, walks around the room, talks informally, with students, looks out the window, sits at their desk, and so on. However, at no point does the teacher give reasons for something, ask or answer questions, offer evidence for a claim, explain something, draw or suggest a conclusion, offer a definition, or demonstrate something. By taking attendance, they have performed an institutional act of teaching, but what have they actually taught – or even tried to teach? There is clearly something that is missing here; most of us would be puzzled by the idea that this teacher was actually engaged in teaching, at least in a strong sense (see Green, 1971, p. 6). What is missing in this scenario is what are called the logical and strategic acts of teaching.

Girls Throwing Ball
© 2xSamara.com/Shutterstock.com

The logical and strategic acts of teaching are at the heart of what teaching is really all about. The best way to think about these two kinds of acts of teaching is with respect to how each can be evaluated (Green, 1971, pp. 7-9). Logical acts can be evaluated on the basis of the quality of the material taught – are the reasons, evidence, explanations, and conclusions presented true? Strategic acts are evaluated by asking a very different question -- what are their consequences, that is, have students learned what was taught? This points to a paradox in the teaching process, which has to do with the relationship between teaching and learning (see Hirst & Peters, 1970, pp. 76-79). This paradox can be understood using two metaphors. The first metaphor is that of two children playing catch. If the first child throws the ball, and the second child catches it, then we would all agree that both throwing and catching took place. However, if the first child throws the ball, but the second child falls to catch it, we would still agree that the first child had thrown the ball. Throwing the ball is unrelated to whether or not the ball is caught. In the context of teaching and learning, it is thus possible for a logical act of teaching to successfully take place even if no learning occurs. The second metaphor for teaching and learning, though, offers an explanation for strategic acts of teaching. Instead of picturing two children throwing a ball, think about a Farmer's Market. At this Farmer's Market, there is a stand where a person is selling jars of honey. If a customer comes to their stand and buys a jar of honey, then we would all agree that they have sold the jar of honey. If a customer decides not to buy the honey, though, they have clearly not sold a jar of honey. In this second metaphor, selling can take place *only* if buying also takes place. In the same way, a strategic act of teaching can only be seen as successful if learning actually does take place. Of course, what these two different examples also demonstrate is that a necessary condition for teaching is the intentionality of the teacher (see Hirst & Peters, 1970, pp. 78-79; Wringe, 1976, pp. 8-10).

Farmer's Market
© Ness Pris/Shutterstock.com

Questions for Reflection and Discussion

1. In this chapter, the authors distinguish among the formal curriculum, the excluded curriculum, and the hidden curriculum. In your own words, describe each of these, and provide an example from your own teaching or observations in classrooms.

2. What are additive and subtractive curricular nullification? Can you provide examples of each from a classroom experience that you have had?

3. In the section on "Instruction," the authors list a number of verbs that they assert might be common activities in which teachers engage. Are there any that you disagree with? What are some other things that you believe that classroom teachers do?

4. Can you explain the difference between institutional acts of teaching and logical and strategic acts of teaching as these might apply in your own classroom? Why do you believe that this distinction is an important one?

5. Consider the two metaphors offered in this chapter for the relationship between teaching and learning. Is one of these metaphors more appropriate or more accurate than the other? Why?

References

Ackerman, D. (1989). Intellectual and practical criteria for successful curriculum integration. In H. Jacobs (Ed.), *Interdisciplinary curricula: Design and implementation* (pp. 25-38). Alexandria, VA: Association for Supervision and Curriculum Development.

Apple, M. (2006). Understanding and interrupting neoliberalism and neoconservatism in education. *Pedagogies: An International Journal, 1*(1), 21-26.

Arnowitz, S., & Giroux, H. (1985). *Education under siege: The conservative, liberal, and radical debate over schooling.* South Hadley, MA: Bergin and Garvey.

Arnowitz, S., & Giroux, H. (1991). *Postmodern education: Politics, culture, and social criticism.* Minneapolis: University of Minnesota Press.

Bowles, S., & Gintis, H. (1976) *Schooling in capitalist America.* New York, NY: Basic Books.

Bowles, S., & Gintis, H. (2002). *Schooling in capitalist America* revisited. *Sociology of Education, 75*(1), 1-18.

Common Core State Standards Initiative (2020). Read the standards. Retrieved from http://www.corestandards.org/read-the-standards/.

Davison, D., Miller, K., & Methany, D. (1995). What does integration of science and mathematics really mean? *School Science and Mathematics, 95*(5), 226-230.

Giroux, H. (1983). *Theory and resistance in education.* London, UK: Heineman.

Giroux, H. (1988). *Escola crítica e política cultural* (2nd ed.). São Paulo, Brazil: Cortez Editora.

Giroux, H. (1997). *Pedagogy and the politics of hope: Theory, culture and schooling.* Boulder, CO: Westview Press.

Green, T. (1971). *The activities of teaching.* New York, NY: McGraw.

Hirst, P., & Peters, R. S. (1970). *The logic of education.* London, UK: Routledge & Kegan Paul.

Jackson, P. (1990). *Life in classrooms.* New York, NY: Teachers College Press. (Original work published 1968)

Jacobs, H. (Ed.). (1989). *Interdisciplinary curricula: Design and implementation.* Alexandria, VA: Association for Supervision and Curriculum Development.

Jay, M. (2003). Critical race theory, multicultural education, and the hidden curriculum of hegemony. *Multicultural Perspectives, 5*(4), 3-9.

Katz, M. (1968). *The irony of early school reform: Educational innovation in mid-19th century Massachusetts.* New York, NY: Teachers College Press.

Kentli, F. (2009). Comparison of hidden curriculum theories. *European Journal of Education, 1*(2), 83-88.

Kliebard, H. (2002). *Changing course: American curriculum reform in the 20th century*. New York, NY: Teachers College Press.

Kozol, J. (2005). *The shame of the nation: The restoration of apartheid schooling in America*. New York, NY: Three Rivers Press.

Ladson-Billings, G. (Ed.). (2003). *Critical race theory perspectives on the social studies: The profession, policies, and curriculum*. Greenwich, CT: Information Age.

Lonning, R., & DeFranco, T. (1997). Integration of science and mathematics: A theoretical model. *School Science and Mathematics, 97*(4), 18-25.

Lonning, R., DeFranco, T., & Weinland, T. (1998). Development of theme-based, interdisciplinary, integrated curriculum: A theoretical model. *School Science and Mathematics, 98*(6), 312-318.

Martin, J. R. (1976). What should we do with a hidden curriculum when we find one? *Curriculum Inquiry, 6*(2), 135-151.

McLaren, P. (1989). *Life in schools: An introduction to critical pedagogy in the foundations of education*. New York, NY: Longman.

National Council of Teachers of Mathematics. (1991). *Professional standards for teaching mathematics*. Reston, VA: Author.

National Education Association of the United States. (1894). *Report of the Committee of Ten on Secondary School Studies*. New York, NY: American Book Co.

Ornstein, A. (1982). Curriculum contrasts: A historical overview. *Phi Delta Kappan, 63*(6), 404-408.

Ornstein, A. (1992). The textbook curriculum. *Educational Horizons, 70*(4), 167-169.

Ornstein, A. (1994). The textbook-driven curriculum. *Peabody Journal of Education, 69*(3), 70-85.

Ornstein, A., & Hunkins, F. (1993). *Curriculum: Foundations, principles and issues* (2nd ed.). Boston, MA: Allyn & Bacon.

Osborn, T. A. (2000). *Critical reflection and the foreign language classroom*. Westport, CT: Bergin & Garvey.

Osborn, T. A. (2006). *Teaching world languages for social justice: A sourcebook of principles and practices*. Mahwah, NJ: Lawrence Erlbaum.

Peters, M. (2015). Why is my curriculum white? *Educational Philosophy and Theory, 47*(7), 641-646.

Reagan, T. (2016). Language teachers in foreign territory: A call for a critical pedagogy-infused curriculum. In L. Cammarata, T. Osborn, & D. Tedick (Eds.), *Content-based foreign language teaching: Curriculum and pedagogy for developing advanced thinking and literacy skills* (pp.173–191). New York, NY: Routledge.

Shaffer, S., & Shevitz, L. (2001). She bakes and he builds: Gender bias in the curriculum. In H. Rousso & M. Wehmeyer (Eds.), *Double jeopardy: Addressing gender equity in special education* (pp. 115-131). Albany: State University of New York Press.

Singer, A. (1995). Challenging gender bias through a transformative high school social studies curriculum. *Theory and Research in Social Education, 23*(3), 234-259.

Snook, I. A. (1972). *Indoctrination and education.* London, UK: Routledge & Kegan Paul.

Spring, J. (2011). *American education* (15th ed.). New York, NY: Routledge.

Strauss, V. (2014, January 18). Everything you need to know about Common Core – Ravitch. *The Washington Post*. Retrieved from https://www.washingtonpost.com/news/answer-sheet/wp/2014/01/18/everything-you-need-to-know-about-common-core-ravitch/.

Tozer, S., Violas, P., & Senese, G. (1993). *School and society: Educational practice as social expression.* New York, NY: McGraw-Hill.

Wiggins, G., & McTighe, J. (2005). *Backward design* (exp. 2nd ed.). Alexandria, VA: Association for Supervision and Curriculum Development.

Willis, P. (1997). *Learning to labour.* New York, NY: Columbia University Press.

Wringe, D. (1976). The teacher's task. In D. Lloyd (Ed.), *Philosophy and the teacher* (pp. 6-18). London, UK: Routledge & Kegan Paul.

Chapter 6

Philosophy of Education and Reflective Practice

Long before there were professional philosophers of education, philosophers and educators debated questions familiar to contemporary philosophers of education: What should be the aims or purposes of education? Who should be educated? Should education differ according to natural interests and abilities? What role should the state play in education? (Nel Noddings)

Reflective teaching means looking at what you do in the classroom, thinking about why you do it, and thinking about if it works – a process of self-observation and self-evaluation. (Julie Tice)

When one hears the phrase "philosophy of education," it can mean a number of quite different things, as the contemporary philosopher of education Nel Noddings (1995) suggests here (p. 4). First, and very commonly, it is used to refer to an individual educator's ideas, beliefs, and values with respect to teaching and learning. It is not at all unusual in the context of an interview for a teaching position to be asked about one's philosophy of education. When used in this way, all the phrase means really is what one believes based on personal experience, reading, and consideration of educational matters. A statement of personal philosophy of education is often included in job applications, teaching portfolios, and the like. A second way in which the phrase "philosophy of education" is used is in reference to a number of historical perspectives on education – perspectives, or philosophies, such as Idealism, Realism, Pragmatism, Existentialism, Perennialism, Essentialism, Progressivism, Reconstructionism, and so on. These are also sometimes called "schools of thought," or somewhat disparagingly, the "isms" approach to philosophy of education. Each of these philosophies of education is typically associated with one or more famous philosophers – Idealism is associated with Plato, Realism with Aristotle, Perennialism with Robert M. Hutchins, Progressivism with John Dewey, and so on (see Table 6.1). Another way that the phrase philosophy of education has been used is with respect to the kinds of activities in which professional philosophers, and especially those working in the analytic tradition, engage in trying to better understand concepts and ideas that are of importance in education. All of these ways of conceptualizing "philosophy of education" have value, and in this chapter we will explore all of them. We will also discuss the concept of reflective practice as an outcome of philosophical considerations in education.

Developing a Personal Philosophy of Education

A good place to begin a discussion about how one should go about writing a personal philosophy of education statement is by noting that there is no single model or format that is necessary to accomplish this, nor is there a "right" or "wrong" way to do this. Writing your personal philosophy of education statement is very much an individual activity that is intended to express *your* views about teaching and learning. If there is no single "correct" way of composing your personal philosophy of education statement, though, there are some general guidelines that will be of help to you. One way to help to conceptualize your personal philosophy of education is to try to provide answers to the following six questions:

- Why do I want to be a teacher? How do I see my role as a teacher?
- How do I view my students? What is my students' role in the learning process?
- How do I believe that people learn? What does it mean to learn?
- What do I want to teach, and why is it important for students?
- How do I want to teach? What constitutes "good teaching"?
- How do I believe that students should be assessed and evaluated? How should learning be assessed?

A well-thought-out personal philosophy of education statement will provide answers to these questions. The answers need not be long and involved – in fact, they should be clear, short, and to the point. They should also provide the reader with a good sense of the kind of teacher that you wish to be. In writing your personal philosophy of education statement, as a general rule it is a good thing to think about the different historical philosophies of education (Idealism, Realism, Perennialism, Progressivism, Reconstructionism, etc.) and consider the advantages and disadvantages of each. It is generally *not* a good idea to simply say, for instance, "My teaching philosophy is that I am a Progressive Educator." Remember that the primary purpose for writing a personal philosophy of education statement is to present *your* views.

Philosophical Schools of Thought

The different historical philosophies of education, or "schools of thought," are often taught in basic courses in philosophy of education and social foundations of education. There is nothing at all wrong with this, as long as you understand that it is only one of the approaches to philosophy of education as an academic discipline and, further, that the study of these "schools of thought" is really more a part of intellectual history or the history of ideas than it is of philosophy of education. In order to understand the foundations of the "schools of thought" approach to philosophy of education, it is important to understand the way in which philosophy as a discipline is organized. For our purposes, there are three branches to philosophical inquiry: metaphysics, epistemology, and axiology.[1]

---

[1] Alternative ways of organizing philosophy as an academic discipline are sometimes suggested. For example, some philosophers argue that there are four "branches" -- metaphysics, epistemology, ethics,

134

Metaphysics is concerned, in a nutshell, with the study of existence. It is the most theoretical of the different domains of philosophy, and is concerned with understanding the principles of reality and the fundamental nature of the universe. Epistemology is the branch of philosophy that is most relevant for educators; it is concerned with theories about the nature of knowledge.[2] The kinds of specific questions that are asked in epistemology are:

- What is knowledge, and what does it mean "to know"?
- How do we acquire knowledge?
- What can we know?
- How do we know what we know?
- Is human knowledge trustworthy?
- Can we trust our senses?
- What is the difference between knowledge and opinion?

One of the key concepts in epistemology is that knowledge is "justified true belief." In other words, for us to say that something constitutes knowledge, we must believe it to be true, there must be compelling reasons for us to believe that it is true, and it must actually be true.[3] Finally, axiology is concerned with theories of value, and is relevant in such areas as ethics and aesthetics.

There are a large number of different philosophical "schools of thought" that we could identify here, but there are five that are the most common in contemporary educational settings. These five are Perennialism, Essentialism, Progressivism, Humanism/Existentialism, and Social Reconstructionism. In Table 6.1, a summary is presented offering an overview of each of these "schools of thought," indicating its view of the goal of education, the nature and content of the curriculum, the role of the student, the role of the teacher, and the preferred teaching methods associated with the "school of thought."

School of Thought	Perennialism	Essentialism	Progressivism	Humanism/ Existentialism	Social Reconstructionism
Goal of Education	To encourage learning for the sake of	To ensure that all students are culturally	Makes use of student interests as a basis for	Assist students to blend cognitive and	Make use of education to help solve important social problems

---

and logic; others divide axiology into ethics, aesthetics, and political theory. Interestingly, metaphysics and epistemology are always considered to be distinct branches of philosophy.

[2] Epistemology was dealt with extensively in Chapter 3.

[3] There is actually a problem with this notion of justified true belief that has been raised. In a 1963 paper, the philosopher Edmund Gettier offered two counterexamples to the fundamental claims of the theory of justified true belief – two cases in which a person might have a justified, true belief regarding a claim but still fail to know it because the reasons for the belief, while justified, turn out to be false. Thus, on Gettier's account, the justified true belief theory is inadequate. This critique, called the Gettier Problem, has proven to be extremely controversial among philosophers (see Floridi, 2004; Lycan, 2006; Sturgeon, 1993; Turri, 2011).

	learning, and to instill timeless virtues.	literate, and that they have mastered a common core of knowledge.	understanding and organizing students' experiences.	academic learning in their daily lives, and to create a climate of freedom in which students can learn to be responsible for their own decisions.	and make democracy more effective.
Curriculum	Subject matter and common core curriculum, with an emphasis on the arts and sciences.	A common, uniform curriculum that emphasizes subject matter and cultural knowledge.	Emphasis on student interests and needs; concern with democracy, morality, and social development.	Social studies and humanities are stressed; helping students to develop physically and emotionally.	Integration of knowledge about and solutions to social problems into the curriculum.
Role of Student	Acquire knowledge; demonstrate the use of virtues in making daily decisions.	Acquire and use cultural knowledge; employ critical thinking skills.	Participate in formulating a student-centered curriculum.	Develop healthy attitudes; accept responsibility for choices, engage in making decisions and problem-solving.	Identify social problems and use critical thinking skills and knowledge to engage in problem solving.
Role of Teacher	Know subject matter, instill virtues.	Provide a common core of cultural literacy.	Act as a facilitator for student learning.	Create environment for independent action; enable students to make decisions and choices and learn to be responsible for their behavior.	Facilitate the process of students identifying and solving community-based problems.

Preferred Teaching Methods	Teacher centered; lectures.	Primarily teacher and subject-centered.	Cooperative learning; student led and initiated discussions.	Group processes; analysis and discussion of student decisions and choices.	Facilitation of cooperative learning and group problem-solving; encourage students to use problem-solving skills.

Table 6.1 Philosophical "Schools of Thought" (adapted from Gutek, 1997; Ornstein, Levine, Gutek, & Vocke, 2017)

Analytic Philosophy of Education

The "schools of thought" approach to philosophy of education seeks to provide teachers and others interested in education and educational topics with broad, systematic frameworks for guiding and justifying educational practice. In doing so, these "philosophies of education" attempt to offer educational theories based on the metaphysical, epistemological, and axiological assumptions of particular individual philosophers or groups of philosophers. Such an approach to philosophy of education is essentially content-oriented, asking the teacher to study what the "great thinkers" have had to say about different educational issues, such as the nature of knowledge, the learning process, the goals of education, and so on, and to then apply the insights gained from such study to the classroom.

In the 1960s, 1970s, and into the 1980s, a very different approach to philosophy of education developed in the anglophone world. Grounded in the more general analytic philosophical movement in philosophy, what is called "analytic philosophy of education" was concerned not with articulating any particular set of claims about what schools should seek to accomplish but rather sought to clarify and explicate important educational concepts. In describing the goals of analytic philosophy of education, the British philosopher of education John Wilson (1983) suggested, "the philosopher, after all, merely asks people to consider whether they are doing, or meaning, A or B; whether their aims are clear, admirable, disastrous, wicked, muddled, or whatever. [They] simply interrogate. But, as we know from Socrates, for most people, that is more than enough" (p. 191). Furthermore, as Cornel Hamm (1989) noted,

> Philosophy of education … is not a matter of drawing conclusions, making extrapolations, and eliciting implications from bodies of systematic and doctrinaire thought of a metaphysical, socio-political, or religious nature. Such an activity can be thought of as the "isms" approach to philosophy of education … These various "isms" take a particular position on a variety of highly speculative issues and attempt to build some sort of practical educational system around the core ideas … Many of the core ideas are highly questionable and the implications drawn from them extremely weak and tenuous. Modern philosophy of education fortunately has turned away from this type of enterprise. (p. 3)

As Hamm suggests, modern philosophers of education are for the most part in agreement in their rejection of the "isms" approach as demonstrative of contemporary philosophy of education, but this does not mean that they are in agreement of what philosophy of education *is* or *should be* all about. Indeed, as an academic discipline philosophy of education is broadly eclectic in nature, ranging from historical approaches to the study of educational thought to critical theory and critical pedagogy (see, for instance, Giroux, 1988, 1991; Giroux & McClaren, 1986). It is not our purpose here to provide a complete introduction to the incredible richness and diversity that has characterized work in analytic philosophy of education. Rather, our purpose here is to provide you with a general overview of the analytic approach to philosophy of education.

Analytic philosophy of education does not seek to provide teachers, or anyone else for that matter, with prepackaged guidelines for educational practice, nor does it try to provide set answers to the difficult normative questions that arise in discussions of educational issues. Rather, analytic philosophy of education seeks to utilize the tools of logical and conceptual analysis in helping us to understand educational doctrines, dilemmas, and debates more clearly. The value of such work for classroom teachers was explained by Richard Peters (1967) when he argued that:

> There was a time, I suppose, when the view was defensible that teachers could pick up their art entirely on an apprenticeship system from experienced practitioners on the job. Education had relatively few agreed upon aims; procedures were more or less standardized; few fundamental questions were raised about principles underlying school organization, class management and the curriculum; the general standards of the community, which they were meant to pass on in training the character of children, were relatively stable; and little was known about the psychology of children and the social conditions under which they lived which transcended common-sense …. I do not want to minimize the importance of this learning on the job under skilled direction. Indeed I think we would all agree that it must be the lynchpin of any system of training. I need hardly comment much either on its limitations as a sufficient type of training under modern conditions. The point is that nowadays just about none of the conditions obtain which provided the milieu in which the old apprenticeship system was viable. Education no longer has agreed aims; procedures are constantly under discussion and vary according to what different people conceive themselves as doing in teaching the various subjects; fundamental questions concerned with principles underlying school organization, class management and the curriculum are constantly being raised; and in the area of moral education the task is made more perplexing by the variations of standards which characterize a differentiated society. The question therefore is not *whether* a modern teacher indulges in philosophical reflection about what [they are] doing; it is rather *whether [they do] it in a sloppy or a rigorous manner* … (pp. 152-153, emphasis added)

In short, analytic philosophy of education is simply a methodology that we can use to help us to clarify our meanings, strengthen our arguments, and in general think more clearly and cogently. It provides a basis for us to become critical thinkers. Analytic philosophers of education do not claim to have what John Wilson (1983) calls "grand thoughts about Life or Reality," nor do they have any particular "ism" to give to others to resolve educational questions (p. 191). Instead, they work in the Socratic tradition to help us think analytically and reflectively about what we do and believe in the classroom and in terms of educational policies and practices more generally. Teachers today are increasingly asked not merely to be competent technicians; rather, as we shall see, they are expected to be "reflective practitioners" as well as thoroughly professional educators (see Reagan, Case, & Brubacher, 2000; Schön, 1983, 1987; Sparks-Langer & Colton, 1991). To function in such a role, critical and analytic thinking skills of the sort employed in analytic philosophy of education are essential. As Roger Straughan and John Wilson (1983) explain,

> Philosophy requires that you temporarily shelve or abandon partisan commitment to political or religious views; the object of the exercise is to inspect the concepts inherent in the views, not to advocate or spurn the views themselves … The point is that merely feeling strongly about something is no substitute for a clear-headed analysis and at times can be an obstacle to it. (p. 4)

In fact, you have already read a great deal of analytic philosophy of education – in Chapter 4, the analysis of the concept of the "educated person" was drawn largely from the analytic philosophy of education tradition.

Reflective Practice and the Classroom Teacher

One of the more recent developments in philosophy of education has been concerned with the idea of the classroom teacher as a "reflective practitioner." The concept of the teacher as reflective practitioner is not a new one. John Dewey wrote about the need for reflective thinking as early as 1903 and dealt with the role of reflection extensively in both *How We Think* (1910, 1933) and *Logic: The Theory of Inquiry* (1938). For Dewey, logical theory and analysis was a generalization of the reflective process in which we all engage from time to time. Dewey recognized that we can "reflect" on a whole host of things in the sense of merely "thinking about" them; however, logical, or *analytic*, reflection can take place only when there is a real problem to be solved. As Dewey (1976) explained,

> The general theory of reflection, as over against its concrete exercise, appears when occasions for reflection are so overwhelming and so mutually conflicting that specific adequate response in thought is blocked. Again, it shows itself when practical affairs are so multifarious, complicated, and remote from control that thinking is held off from successful passage into them. (p. 300)

In other words, *true* reflective practice can be said to take place only when the individual is faced with a *real* problem or situation that they need to resolve, and seeks to resolve that problem in a rational manner.

In 1983, Donald Schön published the first edition of his *The Reflective Practitioner: How Professionals Think in Action.* Schön's focus in that work was not exclusively on teachers, but rather on professionals in a host of fields including architecture, social services, and various health service professions (social work, architecture, and nursing). In all of these areas, it had a huge impact, but arguably nowhere was its impact greater than in teacher education. Indeed, nearly 40 years after the initial publication of *The Reflective Practitioner,* most teacher preparation programs include among their explicit and articulated goals the development of "reflective practitioners" – although precisely what that phrase means is often less than crystal clear. Most recently, the idea that our goal should be not simply preparing teachers to be reflective practitioners, but rather *critical* reflective practitioners, has gained support, especially among those committed to critical pedagogy more generally (see Brookfield, 2005; Fook, 2006). In this section of the chapter, we will begin with an examination of the knowledge basis that is necessary for an individual to become an effective teacher, and then turn to an analysis of the real-world tasks of the teacher. Next, we will focus on the meaning and implications of reflective practice in general, and then of *critical* reflective practice in particular, as these are manifested in the classroom.

The Knowledge Base of the Classroom Teacher

What does a person need to know in order to be an effective teacher? Although it is often suggested that a knowledge of the subject matter to be taught is sufficient to teach a subject, this is clearly not really the case. We have all had teachers who are, without a doubt, very knowledgeable in their subject areas but who, for whatever reason, are not particularly good or effective teachers. There is in fact an entire constellation of knowledge, skills, and dispositions that are required to be effective in the classroom (see Ghaye, 2010; Jay & Johnson, 2002; Loughran, 1996, 2002; van Manen, 1995). Some years ago, the educational psychologist Lee Shulman identified seven broad categories of knowledge that would, taken together, constitute the major components of the knowledge base for the classroom teacher, and Shulman's categories have remained largely unchallenged since he proposed them. Shulman (1987) argued that any teacher should have mastered:

- The appropriate content knowledge.
- General pedagogical knowledge, with special reference to those broad principles and strategies of classroom management and organization that appear to transcend subject matter.
- Curriculum knowledge, with particular grasp of the materials and programs that serve as "tools of the trade" for teachers.
- Pedagogical content knowledge, that special amalgam of content and pedagogy that is uniquely the province of teachers, their own special form of professional understanding.
- Knowledge of learners and their characteristics.
- Knowledge of educational contexts, ranging from the workings of the group or classroom, the governance and financing of school districts, to the character of communities and cultures.
- Knowledge of educational ends, purposes, and values, and their philosophical and historical grounds. (p. 54)

It is important to note that Shulman's conceptualization of the teacher education knowledge base is, by its nature, very general, and not tied to any particular subject matter.

Content knowledge is at the top of Shulman's conceptualization of the teacher education knowledge base, and this is obviously as it should be. Clearly, we would argue, one must know a subject in order to teach it effectively. In the context of a teacher of mathematics, for instance, we would assume that the teacher would have achieved a fairly high degree of competence in mathematics. The same would be true of the teacher of history, or of biology, or of French. This would seem to be axiomatic; it is somewhat puzzling to imagine any subject matter being taught by someone who has not actually mastered it themselves – and yet, it is not uncommon to find a teacher assigned to teach a subject in which they are simply not adequately prepared (in some places, it is in fact common practice for a teacher to "teach out of certification area" – and as the teacher shortage grows, this is likely to become more rather than less common). This concern with subject area competence applies in all subjects and at all grade levels, incidentally – it is just as important for an elementary teacher to have a solid grasp of mathematics, science, history, and so on, to teach at the elementary school level as it is for teachers at higher grade levels to know their content. The difference is one of the necessary breadth and depth of knowledge, but not of the necessity of content knowledge *per se*.

Beyond content knowledge, there is general pedagogical knowledge that is necessary for effective teaching practice regardless of one's area of specialization. Included here, on Shulman's account, "are those broad principles and strategies of classroom management and organization that appear to transcend subject matter" (Shulman, 1987, p. 54). Such principles and strategies are not particularly difficult to identify; they include the knowledge and skills that often allow us to differentiate between successful and unsuccessful classroom teachers. Among the principles and strategies that are core pedagogical knowledge and skills are instructional planning, lesson presentation skills, questioning skills, interpersonal communication skills, classroom management skills, and knowledge of evaluation approaches and strategies.

This brings us to what Shulman called pedagogical content knowledge, which is a powerful combination of content, pedagogical and curricular knowledge. This combination, though, is an instance in which the whole is greater than the sum of its parts, since it refers to the specialized articulated and unarticulated knowledge that world language educators are able to manifest in classroom practice. This knowledge goes far beyond merely content or pedagogical knowledge; it is, at its base, the understanding not only of the subject area content, but also of how particular features of the subject area content are most likely to be acquired by learners. In addition, pedagogical content knowledge includes an awareness of how learners make sense (or do not make sense) of elements of the subject matter, and of ways of assisting them master that content. As an example of pedagogical content knowledge, consider a Spanish teacher faced with teaching their students the difference between *ser* and *estar*, the two verbs "to be" in Spanish. Since English has only one verb "to be," this is often a challenge for students in a beginning Spanish class. In order to teach this concept and usage effectively, the teacher must know and understand the difference themself. The teacher must also know at what point in the curriculum the distinction is most likely to be taught, ways that it can be taught effectively, and how the difference is covered in the textbook and other instructional materials. Finally, the teacher needs to be aware of the kinds of difficulties and misunderstandings that English-speaking students are most likely to have in learning how to use the two verbs correctly. All of this taken together would constitute the pedagogical content knowledge for teaching *ser* and *estar*.

The effective educator must also have a detailed and in-depth knowledge of learners, learning and teaching styles, and possible barriers to learning. This includes such knowledge as that typically included in courses in areas like educational psychology, learning theories, child and adolescent development, and so on. Finally, the educator must also be familiar with the broader social and cultural context in which they are to teach. This includes not only an understanding of the interpersonal interactions among students but also the power relations in the classroom, the school, and society in general.

All of this taken together constitutes the knowledge base for the teacher. It is important to understand that this compilation is in fact merely a heuristic device, since each individual world language educator will inevitably construct their own knowledge base. Thus, although an impressive (and even, perhaps, intimidating) summary, this conceptualization of the knowledge base is still inadequate, because it relies on an idealized, and simplistic, conception of what the educator actually does, and indeed only hints at what the real tasks of the teacher in the classroom actually are.

The Real World of the Classroom Teacher

We have already suggested that much of what the classroom teacher does during the school day is to act as a decision-maker. In fact, Richard Shavelson (1973) has gone so far as to suggest that, "any teaching act is the result of a decision, either conscious or unconscious .... What distinguishes the exceptional teacher is not the ability to ask, say, a higher-order question, but the ability to decide when to ask such a question" (pp. 143-145). Consider the many different kinds of judgments and decisions that the typical teacher makes during their normal, daily routine. Every teacher makes curricular decisions, methodological decisions, decisions about individual children and their needs and problems, decisions about classroom management and organization, decisions about both personal and professional ethics, all areas that are reflected in, and reflective of, the knowledge base for teaching as a profession. The educational philosopher Robert Fitzgibbons has suggested that teachers make three types of decisions: those concerned with *educational outcomes* (i.e., with what the goals or results of the educational experience should be), those concerned with the *matter of education* (i.e., with *what* is, could be, or should be taught), and those concerned with the *manner of education* (that is, with *how* teaching should take place; Fitzgibbons, 1981, pp. 13-14).

When a teacher makes decisions, they are doing more than merely taking a course of action or acting in a certain way. The process of decision-making should be a rational one, which means that the teacher (whether consciously or unconsciously) considers and weighs alternatives, and employs criteria to select a given option or course of action. Unfortunately, as Jere Brophy, a well-known educational researcher, once reported, "most studies of teachers' interactive decision-making portray it as more reactive than reflective, more intuitive than rational, and more routinized than conscious" (quoted in Irwin, 1987, p. 1).[4] *Good* teaching, however, inevitably requires reflective, rational, and conscious decision-making. As Charles Silberman argued almost 50 years ago in his book *Crisis in the Classroom*, "We must find ways of stimulating public school teachers ... to think about what they are doing and why they are doing it" (Silberman, 1971, p. 380). An important element in this process of reflective, rational and conscious decision-making is that we should be able to expect a teacher to be able to justify their decisions and actions in the classroom. Justification of decisions and actions, as Cornel Hamm (1989) explains, is actually a fairly simple and straightforward matter: "To provide a justification for a course of action is to provide good reasons or grounds for that course of action" (p. 163). To be able to provide such justification, the teacher cannot rely either on instinct alone or on prepackaged sets of techniques. Instead, they must think about what is taking place and what options are available in a critical, analytic way. In other words, the teacher must engage in *reflection* about their practice.

Reflective Practice in the Classroom

Reflective practice can be understood as a cyclical process, moving from *reflection-for-practice* through *reflection-in-practice* and to *reflection-on- practice,* which then leads on to new *reflection-for-practice* (see Killion & Todnem, 1991; Norlander-Case, Reagan, & Case, 1999; Reagan et al., 2000; Schön, 1983, 1987).[5] Reflection-for-practice refers to the reflective planning and preparation that precedes the classroom teaching event. Included here are not only the formal lesson and unit planning engaged in by the teacher, but also, and arguably more important, the teacher's analysis of likely pedagogical, learning and management problems and challenges that might emerge in a particular class when dealing with a specific topic. All teachers, to some extent, engage in reflection-for-practice, though they do so with varying degrees of thoroughness and effectiveness. Reflection-on-practice takes place at the other end of the classroom teaching event; it refers to retrospective reflection on what took place, both positive and negative, during the classroom teaching event. All teachers engage in reflection-on-practice, though again, they do so in very different ways, some of which are far more

---

[4] It is important to note here that this criticism is not so much directed toward teachers as it is of the environment in which teachers work. For the quality of teacher decision-making to improve, more is required than simply changing teacher preparation. In addition, the many structural and organizational barriers to reflective practice must also be addressed – hence, calls for reflective practice properly understood inevitably involve concomitant changes in school organization and culture.

[5] "Reflective practice" in educational contexts is, then, far more than simply "thinking about" teaching. It involves a deliberate, critical, and on-going kind of self-evaluation, and is oriented not just to the understanding of classroom practice but also toward its improvement through rational thought.

productive and useful than others. Good reflection-on-practice leads, of course, to new reflection-for-practice, thus completing the cycle of reflective practice.

Cat and Lion
© canbedone/Shutterstock.com

Distinct in kind from reflection-for-practice and reflection-on-practice is *reflection-in-practice*, which is concerned with the application of what Michael Polyani (1958, 1966) has called "tacit knowledge" in the classroom setting. Reflection-in-practice involves the teacher's ability to utilize their unarticulated (and often unconscious) knowledge about content, pedagogy, and learners in the classroom context. It is this ability to engage in reflection-in-practice that, to a very significant extent, distinguishes the experienced master teacher from the novice.   Both may well engage in effective, even exemplary, reflection-for-practice and reflection-on-practice, but only the experiential base of the master teacher allows for consistently effective reflection-in-practice. This experiential base develops only as a result of practice; it helps to explain why no new teacher is likely to be as effective as many more experienced classroom teachers. Table 6.2 provides some key questions related to reflection-for-practice, reflection-on-practice, and reflection-in practice that may be useful to you as you try to conceptualize the broad idea of reflective practice.

	Reflection-for-Practice	Reflection-on-Practice	Reflection-in-Practice
Effective Application of Skills and Knowledge	What am I going to teach? What activities and procedures will I use to teach it? What will I include in my lesson plan?	Did I achieve my objectives for the lesson? Was each individual procedure or activity optimal? How could this lesson be improved next time?	Is this activity working to achieve my objective? Do I need to conduct more review or move more slowly? Is there another way that I should teach this to improve student understanding?

Assumptions Underlying Specific Class Practices	What are likely pedagogical, learning, and management problems that I might face in this lesson?	How did my assumptions line up with what I actually experienced? What assumptions, strategies, curricular, or assessment approaches should I change?	Would it be better if I employed group work now to help students understand better? Are they prepared for the test that I created, or should I delay – or create a different kind of assessment?
Questions About Moral, Ethical and Other Normative Issues (Critical Reflection)	Are my methods, activities, and examples ethical and professional? Could there be implications along those lines of my decisions?	Are there moments that impact the ethical, moral, or other criteria that I value in my practice as a teacher? How? Am I satisfied with the outcome?	What moral and ethical messages am I sending right now with my choices, examples, and behavior?

Table 6.2 Types of Reflective Practice

Another way of thinking about the relationships among the different kinds of reflective practice is to note that both reflection-in-practice and reflection-on-practice are essentially *reactive* in nature, being distinguished primarily by *when* reflection takes place -- with reflection-in-action referring to reflection in the midst of practice, and reflection-on-practice referring to reflection that takes place after an event. Reflection-for-action, on the other hand, is: "the desired outcome of both previous types of reflection. We undertake reflection, not so much to revisit the past or to become aware of the metacognitive process one is experiencing (both noble reasons in themselves), but to guide future action (the more practical purpose)" (Killion & Todnem, 1991, p. 15). In other words, reflection-for-practice is *proactive* in nature.

All three of these types of reflection – reflection-for-practice, reflection-on-practice, and reflection-in-practice -- will be necessary components of reflective practice on the part of the teacher. It is important to note that the relative significance of each of these three components of reflective practice may change over the course of a teacher's career; thus, as was noted earlier, for the novice teacher, reflection-for-practice and reflection-on-practice may be the most obvious ways in which their practice is distinguished, while for the more experienced teacher, reflection may be most clearly manifested in their reflection-in-practice. Furthermore, the process of engaging in reflection-for-practice should be seen not as a linear one, but as an on-going spiral, in which each of the elements of reflective practice are constantly involved in an interactive process of change and development. As we have seen, reflective practice involves what the teacher does *before* entering the classroom (in terms of their planning and preparation, for instance), *while* in the classroom (both while functioning as an educator and in all of the other roles expected of the classroom teacher), and retrospectively, *after* they have left the classroom.

A useful way of thinking about both the reflective teacher and the nature of the reflective practice in which they will engage has been provided by Judee Irwin (1987), who has suggested that:

A reflective/analytic teacher is one who makes teaching decisions on the basis of a conscious awareness and careful consideration of (1) the assumptions on which the decisions are based and (2) the technical, educational, and ethical consequences of those decisions. These decisions are made before, during and after teaching actions. In order to make these decisions, the reflective/analytic teacher must have an extensive knowledge of the content to be taught, pedagogical and theoretical options, characteristics of individual students, and the situational constraints in the classroom, school and society in which they work. (p. 6)

Notice that this description includes virtually all of the issues that have been discussed thus far. We see that the reflective teacher is first and foremost a decision-maker, who must make their decisions consciously and rationally. Furthermore, the reflective teacher must base their decisions and judgments on a solid body of content, including both technical and content knowledge, which are organized and reinterpreted according to their unique experiences.

From Reflective Practice to Critical *Reflective Practice*

What we have been discussing thus far is reflective practice and its implications for the classroom teacher. However, reflective practice on its own – whatever its many benefits may be – is not our ultimate objective. Rather, we are concerned with practice that is not merely reflective, but which is *both* reflective *and* critical (see Reagan & Osborn, 2021) – practice that combines theory and practice in a way that is often called *praxis*. One way of thinking about this important distinction was provided in the 1970s by Max van Manen (1977), who suggested a hierarchical model of *levels of reflectivity* (pp. 205-208). He argued that there are three distinct levels of reflective practice, which can be seen, at least ideally, as paralleling the growth of the individual teacher from novice to expert or master teacher. The first level is concerned with the effective application of skills and technical knowledge in the classroom setting. At this first level, reflection entails the appropriate selection and use of instructional strategies and the like in the classroom. The second level involves reflection about the assumptions underlying specific classroom practices, as well as about the consequences of particular methodological strategies, curricula, and assessment approaches. In other words, at this second level of reflectivity teachers begin to apply educational criteria to teaching practice in order to make individual and independent decisions about pedagogical matters. Finally, the third level of reflectivity (the level at which the reflection becomes *critical reflection*) entails the questioning of moral, ethical and other types of normative criteria related directly and indirectly to the classroom (see Irwin, 1996). At this level, we are concerned not only with pedagogical matters but also with issues of equity, social justice, ethics, and so on. It is also at this level of reflectivity that we would expect the classroom teacher to become an active advocate for the role and place of world language study both in the curriculum and in our society more generally.

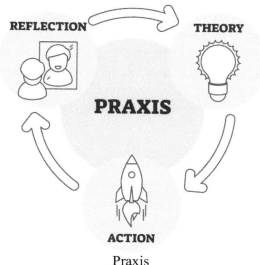

Praxis
© VectorMine/Shutterstock.com

Another way of conceptualizing the distinction between reflective practice and critical reflective practice is to view reflective practice not in a hierarchical manner but instead focus on elements that appear to play significant roles in fostering reflection and reflective practice on the part of the classroom teacher. Georgea Sparks-Langer and Amy Colton (1991), in a synthesis of the research on teachers' reflective thinking, have argued that there are three such elements: the *cognitive element*, the *narrative element,* and the *critical element*. The cognitive element of reflective thinking is concerned with the knowledge that teachers need to master in order to make good decisions in and about the classroom situation. It is important to recognize that while all teachers, whether novice or expert, will for the most part have similar bodies of knowledge at their disposal, the *organization* and *structuring* of this knowledge may differ radically. Research conducted by cognitive psychologists has suggested that the *schemata*, or organized networks of facts, concepts, generalizations and experiences, of beginning and experienced teachers are very different in significant ways (see Sparks-Langer & Colton, 1991, pp. 37-38). Since such *schemata* are constructed by teachers over time as a result of their experiences, it is not surprising that those who have been teaching for longer periods of time will often be able to make sense of and respond to a problematic or challenging situations in the classroom more quickly and effectively than are novices.[6] Studies that suggest that expert teachers are able to deal with changes in lesson plans and classroom situations far more successfully than are new teachers can be explained, according to Sparks-Langer and Colton (1991), "because (1) many of the routines and the content were available [to the expert teachers] in memory as automatic scripts and (2) their rich schemata allowed the experts to quickly consider cues in the environment and access appropriate strategies" (p. 38). *Schemata* of the sort discussed here are constructed naturally over time, but their development can be encouraged and supported by reflective practice. In other words, while good teaching practice

---

[6] It is important to note that we tend to assume that more experience in the classroom automatically translates into greater pedagogical skill – an assumption that is demonstrably false in many cases. There is an old saying in educational circles that there is an important difference between having 30 years of teaching experience and one year of teaching experience repeated 30 times.

does indeed depend on a strong experiential base, reflective practice can help us to speed up the development of such an experiential base in new teachers. At the same time that experience can, and frequently does, help the expert teacher to respond to changes and challenges in the classroom, it is important to note that there is also a risk of "negative socialization" – the process by which new teachers are assimilated into existing, traditional models and approaches in the school context, in spite of whatever they might have learned in their teacher preparation programs.

The second element of reflective thinking, the *narrative element*, has to do with teachers' narratives – that is, with their ability to describe and analyze what has taken place in their classroom, why it has taken place, what might have been done to change what took place, and what should be done following particular classroom events (see Connelly & Clandinin, 1990; Goswami & Stillman, 1987; Zeichner & Liston, 1987, 1996). Teacher accounts of their own experiences in the classroom take many forms, and serve a variety of different functions. A pre-service student's journal is an example of one fairly common type of narrative (see, for example, Vélez-Rendón, 2008a, 2008b). Other kinds of narrative discourse on the part of teachers include descriptions of critical events in the classroom, various types of logs and journals, conference reports completed jointly by teachers and supervisors or mentors, self-interviewing, peer observations followed by collaborative and cooperative discussions, and so on. The key aspect of the narrative element of reflective thinking is that such narratives, whatever their form, serve to contextualize the classroom experience both for the teacher themself and for others, and by so doing, provide us with a much richer understanding of what takes place in the classroom and of the teacher's construction of reality than would otherwise be possible. Narrative accounts are extremely common, especially in the preparation of teachers as well as in qualitative research on classroom practices (see Antonek, McCormick, & Donato, 2011; Bolton, 2010; Orland-Barak & Yinon, 2007), and there can be little doubt that they provide one of the most effective ways in which reflective practice can be encouraged and promoted.

The third element of reflective thinking is the *critical element*, which is concerned with "the moral and ethical aspects of social compassion and justice" (Sparks-Langer & Colton, 1991, p. 39). Concerns with issues of social justice and ethics in education have been common to educators and educational theorists throughout the history of education, and are clearly manifested in such common and important distinctions made by educators as that between educational *product goals* (i.e., what we want to achieve in the classroom or the school) and *process goals* (i.e., the restrictions that exist on how our product goals can be achieved; see Teal & Reagan, 1973). Furthermore, as part of their concern with critical reflective practice, the teacher must also demonstrate both ethical behavior and sensitivity as well as sociocultural awareness.[7] As Charles Case, Judith Lanier, and Cecil Miskel (1986) have noted, "The attendant

---

[7] The ethical dimensions of teaching are an incredibly important aspect of teaching as a profession. John Goodlad's discussions of the "moral dimensions of schooling" are central to this point, as are the more focused explorations of "teacher ethics" and professional codes of ethics in the teacher education literature (see Goodlad, 1994, 1997; Strike, Haller, & Soltis, 1988; Strike & Soltis, 1992).

characteristics of professions include conditions of practice that allow professionals to apply this knowledge freely to the practical affairs of their occupation and to use their knowledge, judgment, and skill within the structures of the ethical code of the profession" (p. 36). The critical element of reflective practice is a necessary part of all reflective practice, but as we shall see, *critical* reflective practice takes this element to a new and more powerful level – one more in keeping with our earlier discussion of critical pedagogy and education.

Such a conceptualization of the reflective practitioner makes clear how much is being expected of the classroom teacher by advocates of reflective practice. Why, one might ask, should a teacher devote so much time and energy to becoming a reflective practitioner? What are the benefits of reflective practice? There are in fact a number of benefits to be gained from reflective practice, but perhaps among the more compelling is that reflective practice is useful in helping to *empower* classroom teachers. As Catherine Fosnot (1989) has noted, "An empowered teacher is a reflective decision maker who finds joy in learning and in investigating the teaching/learning process -- one who views learning as construction and teaching as a facilitating process to enhance and enrich development" (p. xi). Most important, though, reflective practice is a tool for individual teachers to improve their own teaching practice, and to become better, more proficient, and more thoughtful professionals in their own right (see Zeichner & Liston, 1987, 1996), and, hence, to improve student learning (Osterman & Kottkamp, 2004; Zubizarreta, 2009). *Critical* reflective practice, in short, entails all of the elements of reflective practice more generally but also emphasizes the need to place educational practice in its social, historical and ideological context, and to deeply explore the underlying assumptions that govern both educational theory and pedagogical practice in a genuinely deep manner (see Brookfield, 2000; Howard, 2010).

Critical Literacy and Education

An important part of critical reflective practice is the development of critical literacy. There is a substantial body of literature devoted to critical literacy, much of it outstanding, but it tends to focus on the nurturing and development of critical literacy for students rather than for teachers (see Cadiero-Kaplan 2002; McDaniel, 2004; Mulcahy, 2010). Although we share the concern with and commitment to promoting critical literacy in students, our concern here is more on the development of critical literacy in pre- and in-service teachers. The key facet of critical literacy is learning to read in a far different way than most of us are used to. Critical literacy is not synonymous with simply reading – it refers to a very special type of reading. Reading can be (and typically is) understood to refer to the process of decoding a text and comprehending that text. It also includes placing the text in a broader context, to ensure a clear, cogent, and accurate understanding of the author's intention in producing the text. Critical literacy, however, goes far beyond this, asking us to join in what is better thought of as an on-going intellectual discussion and debate. This on-going discussion has been called the "human conversation" by some scholars, and basically means that we are placing the text not only in a particularistic context, but in a much broader one that takes into account the setting in which it was produced, the setting in which we are reading it, and the socio-historical, political, and ideological frameworks in which it was developed and in which it is being read and (perhaps) applied. This means that reading a text critically is a much more in-depth process than simply reading a text.

A valuable way of conceptualizing critical literacy, at least metaphorically, is provided by the Jewish *Talmud*. Traditional study of the *Talmud* is a lifelong undertaking that involves intense study, discussion, comparison, debate, and argument (see Freedman, 2014; Küng, 1991, pp. 169-222; Steinsaltz, 1989). The *Talmud*,[8] which is the core text of Rabbinic Judaism, was produced between the third and sixth centuries CE. It constitutes the source of both *halakha* (religious law) and Jewish theology. It is not, however, a collection of straightforward, logical arguments of the sort that most of us are familiar with. Rather, it employs its own unique logic and forms of reasoning.

The way that a page of *Talmud* is laid out provides us with an excellent way of thinking about what critical literacy might look like in practice. At the top of the page, all the way on the left, is the page number, while centered on the page is the page heading. In the center of the page is the Talmudic text itself. One the right-hand side of the page, next to the Talmudic text, is Rashi's commentary[9] on the text (written in a special script, called "Rashi Script"[10]). On the left-hand side of the page are commentaries by other Talmudic scholars and other references. So, on a single page one finds the basic text, the Rashi commentary on the text, several other (often disagreeing) commentaries, and additional reference materials. It is thus, as suggested earlier, an entire conversation that is taking place – but a conversation among different Rabbinic scholars that actually took place over centuries, in many different locales and among people who never actually meet one another. Although the case of the *Talmud* is an unusual one taken from a very particular religious context, the basic idea of approaching a text as part of an on-going conversation across time and place, and involving many readers, is an extremely valuable one in attempting to develop critical literacy.

---

[8] Although we are discussing "the" *Talmud* here, there are actually two different *Talmuds*: the *Babylonian Talmud* (*Talmud Bavli*) and the *Jerusalem Talmud* (*Talmud Yerushalmi*). The former was first produced in Babylon around the year 500 CE, although its final form was only determined later. The *Talmud Yerushalmi* was produced somewhat earlier (around the 4th century CE) in Galilee. In general, when the term *Talmud* is used, it is the *Babylonian Talmud* that is being discussed.

[9] Rashi was Rabbi Shlomo Yitzchaki, a medieval French rabbi and scholar, who is generally referred to by the acronym "Rashi"; Rashi wrote a comprehensive commentary of the *Talmud*, as well as one on the *Tanakh*. His work is recognized for its clear, concise and accurate approach to the fundamental meaning of texts.

[10] "Rashi script" is a special typeface in which Rashi's commentaries are traditionally printed. It is, basically, a semi-cursive typeface. There is no connection between Rashi script and Rashi himself; the script was introduced by printers at some point in the 15th century CE.

Rashi
© Rook76/Shutterstock.com

A Caveat

At the outset of this chapter, we argued that there is no "right" or "wrong" way to create your own personal philosophy of education, and we want to reiterate that point here. At the same time, however, it is imperative to understand that there are ethical guidelines to guide the content of that philosophy. The Council for the Accreditation of Educator Preparation (CAEP) requires that educator preparation programs produce candidates for the classroom who are competent and caring. It defines these criteria even further, including understanding professional expectations, standards of practice, codes of ethics, and appropriate laws and policies. As a result, there are examples of content in a philosophy of education statement that could be problematic, if not disqualifying, for a teacher candidate.

Returning to our list of possible questions for you to consider responding to in your personal philosophy of education statement, the answers below, although hypothetical, come remarkably close to answers that we have actually seen over the course of our careers.

Why do I want to be a teacher? How do I see my role as a teacher?

I want to be a teacher because I enjoy having power and control over other people. The teacher should be the ultimate authority over everything that happens in the classroom. Any student who challenges that authority should be called out and embarrassed in front of peers. That will make them behave in the future.

How do I view my students? What is my students' role in the learning process?

I want my students to be my friends, and to think of me first and foremost as a friend. I believe that if we hang out together socially, they will be more likely to respect me and learn in the classroom. I would feel very comfortable giving them my phone number so that if they ever need to talk, or need a ride, they would feel comfortable calling me.

How do I believe that people learn? What does it mean to learn?

I really don't think that education is for everyone. Some kids just can't learn, and it's not fair to expect them to do so. They really shouldn't be in the classroom at all. Most of the students in my school have parents who don't care about their children anyway.

Although one might consider these absurd examples, unfortunately they are, on occasion, actually voiced. Such attitudes and beliefs, we would emphasize, are inconsistent and incompatible with any sort of career in a teaching profession.

Questions for Reflection and Discussion

1. In this chapter, the authors consider the concept of the knowledge base for a classroom teacher. Can you add specificity to the different elements that they identify as necessary for effective teaching practice? What content have you learned in your (a) subject matter classes, (b) education classes, (c) general education classes, and (d) other classes, that you believe will prove to be essential in functioning as a classroom teacher?

2. What are the implications of the idea that reflective practice can occur "only when the individual [student] is faced with a *real* problem that they need to resolve" for the classroom?

3. Describe an instance in which you changed your teaching *during a lesson*. Explain your rationale for the change, and discuss the consequences.

4. In their discussion of analytic philosophy of education, the authors quote R. S. Peters, who writes that, "The question therefore is not *whether* a modern teacher indulges in philosophical reflection about what [they are] doing; it is rather *whether [they do] it in a sloppy or a rigorous manner.*" Can you offer some examples that support Peters' claim? Are there examples that might serve to challenge his claim?

5. In the last section of this chapter, the authors provide three sets of answers for why individuals wish to become classroom teachers. They suggest that the answers provided are "inconsistent and incompatible with any sort of career in a teaching profession." Do you agree with them? If not, why not?

References

Antonek, J., McCormick, D., & Donato, R. (2011). The student teacher portfolio as autobiography: Developing a professional identity. *The Modern Language Journal, 81*(1), 15-27.

Berliner, D. (1986). In pursuit of the expert pedagogue. *Educational Researcher, 15*(7), 5-13.

Bolton, G. (2010). *Reflective practice: Writing and professional development* (3rd ed.). Los Angeles, CA: Sage.

Brookfield, S. (2000). The concept of critically reflective practice. In A. Wilson & E. Hayes (Eds.), *Handbook of adult and continuing education* (new ed.) (pp. 33-49). San Francisco, CA: Jossey-Bass.

Brookfield, S. (2005). Critically reflective practice. *Journal of Continuing Education in the Health Professions, 18*(4), 197-205.

Cadiero-Kaplan, K. (2002). Literacy ideologies: Critically engaging the language curriculum. *Language Arts, 79*(5), 371-381.

Case, C., Lanier, J., & Miskel, C. (1986). The *Holmes Group Report*: Impetus for gaining professional status for teachers. *Journal of Teacher Education, 37*(4), 36-43.

Connelly, F., & Clandinin, D. (1990). Stories of experience and narrative inquiry. *Educational Researcher, 19*(5), 2-14.

Dewey, J. (1910). *How we think*. Boston, MA: D.C. Heath.

Dewey, J. (1933). *How we think: A restatement of the relations of reflective thinking to the educative process* (2nd rev. ed.). Lexington, MA: D.C. Heath.

Dewey, J. (1938). *Logic: The theory of inquiry*. New York, NY: Henry Holt.

Dewey, J. (1976). The relationship of thought and its subject matter. Reprinted in J. Boydston (Ed.), *John Dewey: The middle works, Volume 2 (1902-1903)* (pp. 298-315). Carbondale: Southern Illinois University Press. (Original work published 1903)

Fitzgibbons, R. (1981). *Making educational decisions: An introduction to philosophy of education*. New York, NY: Harcourt Brace Jovanovich.

Floridi, L. (2004). On the logical insolvability of the Gettier Problem. *Synthese, 142*, 61-79.

Fook, J. (2006, July 3). Beyond reflective practice: Reworking the "critical" in critical reflection. Keynote address presented at the 'Professional Lifelong Learning: Beyond Reflective Practice' conference held at Trinity and All Saints College, Leeds, UK.

Fosnot, C. (1989). *Enquiring teachers, enquiring learners: A constructivist approach to teaching*. New York, NY: Teachers College Press.

Freedman, H. (2014). *The Talmud: A biography*. London, UK: Bloomsbury.

Gettier, E. (1963). Is justified true belief knowledge? *Analysis, 23*(6), 121-123.

Ghaye, T. (2010). *Teaching and learning through reflective practice: A practical guide for positive action* (2nd ed.). New York, NY: Routledge.

Giroux, H. (1988). *Escola crítica e política cultural* (2nd ed.). São Paulo, Brazil: Cortez Editora.

Giroux, H. (Ed.) (1991). *Postmodernism, feminism, and cultural politics: Redrawing educational boundaries.* Albany: State University of New York Press.

Giroux, H., & McLaren, P. (1986). Teacher education and the politics of engagement: The case for democratic schooling. *Harvard Education Review, 56*(3), 213-227.

Goodlad, J. (1994). *Educational renewal: Better teachers, better schools.* San Francisco, CA: Jossey-Bass.

Goodlad, J. (1997). *In praise of education.* New York, NY: Teachers College Press.

Goswami, D., & Stillman, P. (Eds.). (1987). *Reclaiming the classroom: Teacher research as an agency for change.* Portsmouth, NH: Heinemann.

Gutek, G. (1997). *Philosophical and ideological perspectives on education* (2nd ed.). Needham Heights, MA: Allyn & Bacon.

Hamm, C. (1989). *Philosophical issues in education: An introduction.* New York, NY: Falmer Press.

Howard, T. (2010). Culturally relevant pedagogy: Ingredients for critical teacher reflection. *Theory into Practice, 42*(3), 195-202.

Irwin, J. (1987). *What is a reflective/analytical teacher?* Unpublished manuscript, University of Connecticut, School of Education, Storrs, Connecticut.

Irwin, J. (1996). *Empowering ourselves and transforming schools: Educators making a difference.* Albany: State University of New York Press.

Jay, J., & Johnson, K. (2002). Capturing complexity: A typology of reflective practice for teacher education. *Teaching and Teacher Education, 18*(1), 73-85.

Killion, J., & Todnem, G. (1991). A process for personal theory building. *Educational Leadership, 48*(6), 14-16.

Küng, H. (1991). *Das Judentum: Die religiöse Situation der Zeit.* Zürich, Switzerland: Piper München.

Loughran, J. (1996). *Developing reflective practice: Learning about teaching and learning through modelling.* New York, NY: Routledge.

Loughran, J. (2002). Effective reflective practice: In search of meaning in learning about teaching. *Journal of Teacher Education, 53*(1), 33-43.

Lycan, W. (2006). On the Gettier Problem problem. In S. Hetherington (Ed.), *Epistemology futures* (pp. 148-168). Oxford, UK: Clarendon Press.

McDaniel, C. (2004). Critical literacy: A questioning stance and the possibility for change. *The Reading Teacher, 57*(5), 472-481.

Mulcahy, C. (2010). *Marginalized literacies: Critical literacy in the language arts classroom.* Charlotte, NC: Information Age.

Noddings, N. (1995). *Philosophy of education.* Boulder, CO: Westview Press.

Norlander-Case, K., Reagan, T., & Case, C. (1999). *The professional teacher: The preparation and nurturance of the reflective practitioner.* San Francisco, CA: Jossey-Bass.

Orland-Barak, L., & Yinon, H. (2007). When theory meets practice: What student teachers learn from guided reflection on their own classroom discourse. *Teaching and Teacher Education, 23*(3), 957-969.

Ornstein, A., Levine, D., Gutek, G., & Vocke, D. (2017). *Foundations of education* (13th ed.). Boston, MA: Cengage Learning.

Osterman, K., & Kottkamp, R. (2004). *Reflective practice for educators: Professional development to improve student learning* (2nd ed.). Thousand Oaks, CA: Corwin.

Peters, R. S. (1967). The place of philosophy in the training of teachers. *Paedagogica Europa, 3,* 152-153.

Polyani, M. (1958). *Personal knowledge: Towards a post-critical philosophy.* Chicago, IL: University of Chicago Press.

Polyani, M. (1966). *The tacit dimension.* Chicago, IL: University of Chicago Press.

Reagan, T., Case, C., & Brubacher, J. (2000). *Becoming a reflective educator: How to build a culture of inquiry in the schools* (2nd ed.). Thousand Oaks, CA: Corwin.

Reagan, T., & Osborn, T. A. (2021). *World language education as critical pedagogy: The promise of social justice.* New York, NY: Routledge.

Schön, D. (1983). *The reflective practitioner: How professionals think in action.* New York, NY: Basic Books.

Schön, D. (1987). *Educating the reflective practitioner.* San Francisco, CA: Jossey-Bass.

Shavelson, R. (1973). What is the most basic teaching skill? *Journal of Teacher Education, 24*(2), 144-151.

Shulman, L. (1987). Knowledge and teaching: Foundations of the new reform. *Harvard Educational Review, 57*(1), 1-22.

Silberman, C. (1971). *Crisis in the classroom.* New York, NY: Random House.

Sparks-Langer, G., & Colton, A. (1991). Synthesis of research on teachers' reflective thinking. *Educational Leadership, 48*, 37-44.

Steinsaltz, A. (1989). *The Talmud: The Steinsaltz edition, A reference guide.* New York, NY: Random House.

Straughan, R., & Wilson, J. (1983). *Philosophizing about education.* London, UK: Cassell.

Strike, K., Haller, E., & Soltis, J. (1988). *The ethics of school administration.* New York, NY: Teachers College Press.

Strike, K., & Soltis, J. (1992). *The ethics of teaching* (2nd ed.). New York, NY: Teachers College Press.

Sturgeon, S. (1993). The Gettier Problem. *Analysis, 53*(3), 156-164.

Teal, S., & Reagan, G. (1973). Educational goals. In J. Frymier (Ed.), *A school for tomorrow* (pp. 37-84). Berkeley, CA: McCutchan.

Turri, J. (2011). Manifest failure: The Gettier Problem solved. *Philosophers' Imprint, 11*(8), 1-11.

van Manen, J. (1977). Linking ways of knowing with ways of being practical. *Curriculum Inquiry, 6*(3), 205-208.

van Manen, M. (1995). On the epistemology of reflective practice. *Teachers and Teaching: Theory and Practice, 1*(1), 33-50.

Vélez-Rendón, G. (2008a). From student to teacher: A successful transition, *Foreign Language Annals, 39*(2), 320-333.

Vélez-Rendón, G. (2008b). Second language teacher education: A review of the literature. *Foreign Language Annals, 35*(4), 457-467.

Wilson, J. (1983). Reflections: A letter from Oxford. *Harvard Educational Review, 53*(2), 190-194.

Zeichner, K., & Liston, D. (1987). Teaching student teachers to reflect. *Harvard Educational Review, 57*(1), 23-48.

Zeichner, K., & Liston, D. (1996). *Reflective teaching: An introduction.* Mahwah, NJ: Lawrence Erlbaum.

Zubizarreta, J. (2009). *The learning portfolio: Reflective practice for improving student learning* (2nd ed.). San Francisco, CA: Jossey-Bass.

Chapter 7

Culture, Cultural Diversity, and Schooling

People need to see that, far from being an obstacle, the world's diversity of languages, religions and traditions is a great treasure, affording us precious opportunities to recognize ourselves in others. (Youssou N'Dour)

If you talk to a man in a language he understands, that goes to his head. If you talk to a man in his language, it does to his heart. (Nelson Mandela)

Throughout American history, addressing cultural diversity has been an important challenge for our society – and it has been in the schools, more than in any other social institution, that this challenge has been faced (see Banks & Nguyen, 2008; Mirel, 2010; Moses & Chang, 2006). Wave after wave of immigrants have come to the United States, driven by a host of factors – economic, political, and religious factors most common among them. Over our history, there have been three major waves of immigration. The first was that of the English settlers during the Colonial era, who in many ways provided the foundation for the 13 colonies that would become the United States. In general, these immigrants were English-speaking, Protestant, and brought with them skills needed in the colonies. The two major exceptions to these generalizations were the English Roman Catholics[1] and the Germans.[2] The second significant wave of immigration, which is commonly called the "old immigration," took place between 1830 and 1880, when large numbers of Irish and German immigrants came to the United States. Unlike earlier immigrants, many of the Irish were Gaelic-speaking (though many were also English-speaking, especially by the late-19th century), Roman Catholic, and unskilled.[3]

---

[1] Although there were small numbers of Roman Catholics in some of the colonies, in many others they were persecuted and outlawed. Furthermore, it is important to understand that during the colonial era, there was an almost universal anti-Catholic bias in the American colonies (Duncan, 2005; Farrelly, 2018; Verhoeven, 2010).

[2] There was a significant settlement of German speakers, for instance, in Pennsylvania. Benjamin Franklin held strongly anti-German biases; he argued that the Germans would "soon so outnumber us, that all the advantages we have will not in My Opinion be able to preserve our language, and even our Government will become precarious."

[3] The Irish immigration was driven by a number of factors, most of them economic, but among the more important was the Great Famine (also called the Great Hunger, or, somewhat misleadingly, the Irish Potato Famine), which took place between 1845 and 1849. This was a period of mass starvation and disease in Ireland; although directly caused by a potato blight, this was in fact only the proximate cause of the widespread poverty and mass starvation in Ireland. The situation was actually the result of a combination of British government policies, absentee landlords, and the over-dependence on a single crop (see Kinealy, 2002; Ó Gráda, 1999; Ó Gráda & O'Rourke, 1997).

When large numbers of Irish Catholics began immigrating to the United States in the 1840s, there was considerable resistance to their arrival among Anglo-Americans -- this was the time of "no Irish need apply" advertisements for jobs and the like. By the late-19th century, the Irish had been largely Americanized, and were no longer seen as the social problem that had been the case earlier in the century. The German immigrants of this second wave of immigration shared a number of characteristics with the Irish – they were being driven to the United States largely from southwestern Germany, as a result of poverty brought about by crop failures and industrialization; they arrived as non-English speakers, and many were Catholic. However, the Germans were able to settle in America considerably more successfully than the Irish and were even able to maintain their language and culture to a considerable extent.[4]

In due course, the Irish and German immigration was followed by a significant increase in immigration from other parts of Europe. The third wave of immigration to the United States, which historians call the "new immigration," took place between 1880 and the First World War, and entailed two major changes that had a huge impact on American society and culture (see Tozer, Violas, & Senese, 1993, pp. 119-122). From the mid-19th century to the first few decades of the 20th century, the number of immigrants increased dramatically. In addition, over that same period of time, the origins of the immigrants changed, from predominantly Northern and Western Europe to Southern, Central, and Eastern Europe (see Table 7.1; Mirel, 2010; Olneck, 1989).

Years	Total European Immigration to the United States	Percentage from Northern and Western Europe	Number from Northern and Western Europe	Number from Southern, Central and Eastern Europe
1866-1870	1,338,000	98	1,314,000	24,000
1871-1875	1,462,000	94	1,368,000	94,000
1876-1880	813,000	87	704,000	109,000
1881-1885	2,508,000	86	2,154,000	354,000
1886-1890	2,231,000	73	1,625,000	606,000
1891-1895	2,073,000	55	1,143,000	930,000
1896-1900	1,477,000	34	501,000	976,000
1901-1905	3,646,000	26	939,000	2,707,000
1906-1910	4,493,000	22	973,000	3,520,000
1911-1915	3,801,000	21	790,000	3,011,000
1916-1920	581,000	36	207,000	374,000

Table 7.1 Patterns of Change in American Immigration, 1866-1920 (based on Tozer et al., 1993)

---

[4] This was true until World War I, when anti-German sentiment and hysteria resulted in a radical decline in the use of the German language in schools, churches, and so on. (see Gilbert, 1971; Holian, 1998; Kloss, 1998).

It should be noted that the arrival of the predominantly Roman Catholic Irish immigrants in the early 19th century was one of the major drivers in the creation of the Common Schools (see Kaestle, 1978; Katz, 2001; Reese, 2005); later in the 19th century, the immigrants from Southern, Central and Eastern Europe provided the rationale for intensive efforts in the public schools to "Americanize" the new immigrants (see Beatty, 2000; Kraver, 1999; Mirel, 2010), as we will discuss later in this chapter.

What Is Culture?

Underlying the core focus of this chapter is the concept of culture. Many years ago, historian Carl Becker (1955) commented,

> Now, when I meet a word with which I am entirely unfamiliar, I find it a good plan to look it up in the dictionary and find out what someone thinks it means. But when I have frequently to use words with which everyone is perfectly familiar – words like "cause" and "liberty" and "progress" and "government" – when I have to use words of this sort which everyone knows perfectly well, the wise thing to do is to take a week off and think about them. (p. 328)

The word "culture" is just such a "week off" word. It is a word that we all use, and one that we use frequently and much of the time without giving much thought to what it actually refers. There are at least two quite different ways that the word is sometimes used in educational contexts. It can refer to what has been called "high culture," implying the great works from the aesthetic elements of a society, such as music, art, literature, and so on. Although one could argue that the purpose of education is indeed concerned, at least in part, with helping students become "cultured" individuals in this sense, this is not really what most educators have in mind when we talk about issues of culture and cultural diversity. Rather, we are using the term in more or less the same way that anthropologists talk about it. As Young Pai (1990) has explained, "In general terms, culture is most commonly viewed as that pattern of knowledge, skills, behaviors, attitudes and beliefs, as well as material artifacts, produced by a human society and transmitted from one generation to another" (p. 21).

Understood in an anthropological sense, "culture" includes virtually every aspect of our lives as social beings – and human beings are profoundly social beings. Since schools are social institutions, grounded in and reflecting particular societies, this means that "culture" is deeply embedded in almost every part of schooling. The culture of a society includes many different factors, including (but certainly not limited to) such things as:

- Language.
- Attitudes, values, and beliefs.
- Family and kinship patterns.
- Gender roles and expectations.
- History and mythology.
- Foods and eating.
- Sanctions and taboos.

We will now briefly discuss some of these components of culture. As we do so, it is important to keep in mind that many of these elements overlap – and that they do not constitute clear and distinct, let alone exclusive, categories much of the time. For example, we often talk about the behavioral norms in a culture, but such norms can be linguistic, religious, nutritional, familial, ritual, and so on in nature, and violations of these norms are often sanctioned or even taboo. In the same way, it is common in anthropology to talk about the "folkways and mores" of a culture, but these include virtually all of the elements that together constitute a culture. It is also extremely important to understand that when we are talking about "culture," we are doing so as a heuristic device, and that it is very important that we avoid any sort of essentialism in discussing cultures and cultural differences.

Language

Language plays a central role in social life in general, and in distinguishing different cultures from one another in particular. As Neil Smith (2002) has written,

> Language makes us human … Whatever we do, language is central to our lives, and the use of language underpins the study of every other discipline. Understanding language gives us insight into ourselves and a tool for the investigation of the rest of the universe. Proposing marriage, opposing globalization, composing a speech, all require the use of language; to buy a meal or sell a car involves communication, which is made possible by language; to be without language – as an infant, a foreigner or a stroke victim – is to be at a devastating disadvantage. Martians and dolphins, bonobos and bees, may be just as intelligent, cute, adept at social organization and morally worthwhile, but they don't share our language, they don't speak "human." (p. 3)

One of the key ways in which different cultures maintain boundaries between themselves and other cultures is through language. Most cultures are characterized, at least in part, by linguistic differentiation from other cultures. Although this linguistic differentiation usually involves different languages, this is not always the case – sometimes, cultures share a common language but utilize different varieties of the language (as is the case with British and American English).

In thinking about language and linguistic diversity, it is important to bear in mind that a language or language variety are not "better" or "worse" than some other language or language variety. Victoria Fromkin, Robert Rodman, and Nina Hyams (2014) have explained this from the perspective shared by virtually all modern linguists:

> No language or variety of language … is superior or inferior to any other in a linguistic sense. Every [language] is equally complex, logical, and capable of producing an infinite set of sentences to express any thought. If something can be expressed in one language … it can be expressed in any other language … It might involve different means and different words, but it can be expressed … All human languages … are fully expressive, complete and logical … (pp. 10-11)

Indeed, linguistics as an academic discipline is concerned with studying different languages *descriptively* rather than *prescriptively* – that is, with seeking to understand how native speakers of a language actually use the language, rather than offering rules for how the language "ought" to be used. As Ralph Fasold and Jeff Connor-Linton (2014) have commented,

> Linguists approach language in the same way that astronomers approach the study of the universe or that anthropologists approach the study of human cultural systems. It would be ridiculous for astronomers to speak about planets orbiting stars "incorrectly" and inappropriate for anthropologists to declare a culture "degenerate" simply because it differs from their own. Similarly, linguists take language as they find it, rather than attempting to regulate it in the direction of preconceived criteria. Linguists are equally curious about *all* the forms of language that they encounter, no matter what the education or social standing of their speakers might be. (p. 9, emphasis added)

It is this non-judgmental approach to the study of language that characterizes linguistics, just as such a non-judgmental approach to the study of cultures and cultural differences that characterizes anthropology. And, further, there are no "primitive" languages just as there are no "primitive" cultures.

Attitudes, Values and Beliefs

Each of us holds a variety of attitudes, values, and beliefs about the universe, the world in which we live, other human beings, different societies, the environment, knowledge and education, morality and ethics, and so on. To some extent, these attitudes, values and beliefs are personal and idiosyncratic, but most of the time they are also grounded in and reflective of those of the society in which we grew up and live. Our ideas about what is of value, what is not of value, and about what is right and wrong are determined in part by our culture. Is absolute monarchy a better system of government than democracy? For much of human history, the most common answer to this question would probably have been a resounding yes. Is premarital sex immoral? Is homosexuality sinful? The answers to these questions are not ones that human beings have universally agreed about – indeed, different cultures answer them quite differently, and even in our own society, our answers have changed dramatically over the past century. Furthermore, many of our "factual" beliefs are grounded in our culture, as are our ideas about how truth and true beliefs are determined. If one is raised in a society in which everyone knows that the earth is flat, and where all of the relevant authorities in the society agree on this matter, then it is highly likely that this is a belief that a person will not only accept, but will hold deeply. Of course, it is important to note that within a culture there may exist serious disagreements with respect to attitudes, values, and beliefs as well as commonalities.

Familial relations are another way in which cultures vary. Basically, when we talk about families and kinship, we are talking about how we think about and categorize relationships between and among individuals. Our relationships are most often by blood or marriage,[5] but such relationships differ from culture to culture, and ultimately serve social ends. There are many different kinds of kinship systems in the world, just as there are culturally determined different sorts of systems of descent. There are, broadly speaking, two different kinds of kinship systems: descriptive systems and classificatory systems. In a descriptive system, a word refers to a single, specific kind of relationship (as in "brother" in English, which indicates the son of one's parent). In a classificatory system, a term can be used to refer to multiple types of relations; for instance, in many languages the same word is used to describe not only the person English calls "brother," but also any male first cousin, including the son of your mother's brother, the son of your mother's sister, the son of your father's brothers, the son of your father's sister, and so on. In fact, since the last quarter of the 19th century, anthropologists have typically classified kinship systems into seven types (see Table 7.2).[6]

Type of Kinship System	Characteristics
Iroquois	The Iroquois kinship system has both descriptive and classificatory categories. It marks not only gender and generation, but also same-sex and cross-sex parental siblings; non-parental kinship terms are used to describe parallel cousins. This type of kinship system is also called "bifurcate merging."
Crow	The Crow kinship system is an expansion of bifurcate merging. Unlike the Iroquois kinship system, the Crow kinship system distinguishes between the individual's maternal and paternal relatives, using more descriptive terminology for the former and more classificatory terminology for the latter. Unlike most other kinship systems, the Crow kinship system does not distinguish among certain generations.

---

[5] Anthropologists also sometimes talk about "fictive kinship," which refers to kinship or social relationships that are based on *neither* blood (consanguineal) ties *nor* marriage (affinal) ties. Examples of fictive kinship – which is also called "chosen kinship" or "voluntary kinship" – include kinship based on things such as shared residence, economic ties, and nurture kinship.

[6] The kinship categorization system used in contemporary anthropology is still based, to a large part, on that proposed by Lewis Henry Morgan in the late-19th century (see Morgan, 1871). The only significant change has been the addition of the Dravidian kinship system, and that addition remains controversial.

Omaha	The Omaha kinship system is also an example of bifurcate merging, and is similar to the Crow kinship system. However, unlike the Crow system (which is generally matrilineal), the Omaha kinship system is usually patrilineal. In the Omaha kinship system, relatives are classified based on gender and descent. Cross-cousins are differentiated by generational divisions, while parallel cousins are not differentiated or distinguished.
Eskimo	The Eskimo kinship system, which is also referred to as lineal kinship, is the sort that is most common in Western societies. It is based on the nuclear family, stressing father, mother, brother, and sister. There is no distinction between matrilineal and patrilineal relatives. It employs both descriptive and classificatory terms and differentiates between gender, generation, lineal relatives, and collateral relatives.
Hawaiian	The Hawaiian kinship system, which is also called the generational system, is the simplest classificatory system. It distinguishes by gender and generation. Thus, all females in the mother's generation are "Mother," and all males in the father's generation are "Father." All siblings and cousins are "Brother" and "Sister."
Sudanese	The Sudanese kinship system, which is also called the descriptive system, is an incredibly complex kinship system. It distinguishes almost every person from oneself, based on their gender, their generation, their relationship, and their distance. For example, for what English would call a "cousin," there are 8 possible terms in the Sudanese kinship system.
Dravidian	The Dravidian kinship system is somewhat controversial, with some anthropologists arguing that it is really simply a sub-category of the Iroquois kinship system. It distinguishes relatives by marriage from blood relatives, utilizes gender as a category, and involves what is called "selective cousinhood." There is a distinction between cross cousins (or true cousins) and parallel cousins (siblings).

Table 7.2 Types of Kinship Systems

In the dominant culture in the United States, the key family unit is most often the nuclear family: father, mother, and children. We can and do expand this nuclear family to include a recognition of shared kinship with grandparents, aunts and uncles, and cousins, and ultimately, grandchildren; however, for most of us this is approaching the limits of our kinship relations. To be sure, this is by no means universally true, and sometimes we expand this to include great-grandparents, great-aunts and uncles, and so on.[7] Furthermore, many people in our culture expand this kinship structure to include second and third cousins, cousins once removed, cousins twice removed, and so on, but for the most part the nuclear family remains our normative base. Thus, we are basically an example of the Eskimo kinship system, although

---

[7] In our culture, we also, of course, recognize step- and ex- relationships, as in step-siblings, ex-spouses, and so on.

it is worth noting that this is a serious oversimplification of a very complex situation. In fact, Talcott Parsons published a fascinating article in the *American Anthropologist* in 1943 in which he utilized the tools of anthropology to analyze the kinship patterns of our own society. After noting that "it is a remarkable fact that in spite of the important interrelations between sociology and social anthropology, no attempt to describe and analyze the kinship system of the United States in the structural terms current in the literature of anthropological field studies exists" (Parsons, 1943, p. 22), he went on to argue that our system is an "open, multilineal, conjugal" one (p. 24) – a description that would seem to be still relatively valid today.

Gender Roles and Expectations

Related to family and kinship patterns, gender roles and expectations differ from culture to culture and from society to society. In our own society, these have changed dramatically over the past 50 to 75 years and continue to change in a host of different ways. Gender roles are basically the standard range of behaviors associated with and expected of males and females in a society[8] – that is, with ideas of what is appropriate or acceptable for boys and girls to do, how they should behave, play, and so on, and what is appropriate or acceptable for men and women in the society. Gender roles are normally (though not always) tied to biological gender, but what the specific gender roles in different societies are differs a great deal. It is important to understand that our gender roles in society are socially constructed – that is, they are not predetermined or in some way mandated by our biological sex, but rather, are the result of "gender socialization."[9] There are a number of different elements of gender roles and expectations: dress and clothing, professional options and expectations, educational options, social and cultural responsibilities, decision-making responsibilities, childrearing obligations, language, hobbies, and so on. In some societies, there is a great deal of freedom and integration of gender roles and responsibilities, and members of any biological gender may perform them; in other societies, there is considerable (or even total) gender segregation of roles. Gender roles and expectations are often determined, or at least strongly influenced, by other social, cultural, and religious factors.

Historically, the organization of American society has been patriarchal, which basically means that men have held most of the power and control in the society. It also, though, is reflected in social ideologies about the differences between men and women, and is grounded in what is really a belief in the superiority of men and the inferiority of women, based on claims about the "natural differences" between the two. In fact, patriarchy is a social system grounded

---

[8] In fact, this suggests that issues of gender, gender identity, and gender expression are binary in nature, and that is simply not the case. The distinctions among biological sex, gender, and gender identity are part of an incredibly complex part of personhood that goes far beyond the binary approach that has been commonly (and wrongly) assumed in the Western tradition, and in some (but not all) others. As Cydney Adams (2017) has explained, "Gender identity is an extremely personal part of who we are, and how we perceive and express ourselves in the world. It is a separate issue entirely from sex, our biological makeup; or sexual orientation, who we are attracted to."

[9] The concept of social construction of gender, race, and so on, is discussed in detail in Chapter 8.

in a particular kind of ideology that creates and maintains fundamental systemic differences between men and women in terms of the legal, political, economic, and religious structures, institutions and resources of the society. American society is not, of course, unique in being a patriarchal one – patriarchy has been a core feature of Western society and culture throughout our history.

History and Mythology

Every society has its own unique history. Every society also has its own unique way of understanding and remembering that history – and these two things are not necessarily the same. By this, we do not mean that a society (or some subset of the society) is necessarily engaged in the deliberate rewriting of history, although that certainly takes place from time to time. One of the important tasks of institutions of schooling is to pass on what the society considers to be its history – that is, what it believes that all of its members ought to believe about its history. Much of that knowledge is true, although often simplified and seen through a kind of "lens." One of the most powerful ways in which this occurs is simply in the determination of which events and facts we decide are worth teaching and passing on, and those which we do not consider important enough to emphasize. Many of the "Founding Fathers" – including both George Washington and Thomas Jefferson – were slave owners, for instance. For most of our educational history, while a great deal was taught about both Washington and Jefferson, and while they were both frequently identified as being among our greatest presidents, this particular aspect of their lives was not seen as worth mentioning. Obviously, this is no longer the case, and we now teach more about the complexity of these men's lives and the moral issues that all of this raises. There are also sometimes purposeful efforts to "slant" our history of contemporary political and ideological purposes. For example, in a manner reminiscent of Theodore Roosevelt and others in the early 20th century, President Trump:

> painted criticism of America's past as unpatriotic, and attempted to create a space where White voters can feel OK with that. That includes "restoring patriotic education" in schools "where they're trying to change everything that we've learned," Trump told reporters … "The only path to unity is to rebuild a shared national identity focused on common American values and virtues, of which we have plenty," Trump said …. In his Republican National Convention acceptance speech, Trump promised "new pride in our history" and said "Americans build their future, we don't tear down our past." He hailed America's westward settlement under Lewis and Clark, a movement that shaped the modern U.S. and ultimately led to the forced removal of Native Americans from their ancestral lands, and touted his protection of monuments to Confederate figures. (Bennett, 2020)

Regardless of one's views of President Trump, what he was actually suggesting was that the schools teach a very particular version and perspective on the past – a version for which there is virtually no support among any credible contemporary historians or scholars.

Foods and Eating

The foods that we consume are, to a great extent, determined by our material culture and setting. Basically, all that this means is that historically, different cultural groups have eaten the kinds of things that were readily available in their own physical setting. If a group of people lived in an area in which a particular food source was common and easily gathered or grown, then it was likely that that food would play an important role in their diet. More importantly, perhaps, if a food source was not common, or not present at all, in their environment, then it would not be a common food in that culture. Thus, it is hardly surprising that seafood of various sorts has long been a staple in much of Scandinavia, or that olives form a common part of most Mediterranean diets. As human societies became more complex, and as trade increased, some foods travelled from one part of the world to others, and thus spread and became common in cultures in which they had not originated. Potatoes are an excellent example of this phenomenon, as is corn – both had been common sources of food in pre-Columbian America for millennia prior to the "discovery" of the Americas.[10] Beginning in the 16th century, both were exported to Europe, where they became staples in the diets of many cultures. In addition to the availability of particular foods, of course, are food taboos that exist in various cultures. The laws of *kashrut* in Judaism, which govern not only what kinds of food may be eaten but also contain other food-related rules, are a good example of such taboos.[11] People sometimes see the taboos of other cultures as strange or odd, but one needs to keep in mind that most cultures have certain kinds of food taboos and restrictions. For example, in Anglo-American culture, although you may not have thought of it before in this way, we too have food taboos. We not only do not eat, but find it offensive to even think about eating, animals such as cats and dogs – and yet, both have been eaten in some human societies. Finally, cultures develop different rules about *how* food is to be eaten – whether one uses fingers, cutlery, chop sticks, or some other manner to move food from the plate to one's mouth, for instance.

Sanctions and Taboos

One characteristic of all cultures is that there are certain activities, behaviors, ways of speaking, relationships, and so on that are sanctioned or forbidden – that is, each culture has taboos. Although some taboos are far more common than others – most societies have taboos about cannibalism, in-group murder, and at least some kinds of incest[12] – even these prohibitions are not universal. Among the most common taboos in different societies are those

---

[10] Corn was first domesticated by indigenous people in southern Mexico at least 10,000 years ago; potatoes were domesticated in modern Peru between 7,000 and 10,000 years ago.

[11] The laws of *kashrut* are extremely complete. Basically, there are three major issues in determining whether food is *kosher*: (i) the types of animal that can be consumed and those that cannot be consumed (e.g., pork and shellfish), (ii) how any animal to be consumed has been slaughtered, and the related prohibition on eating any animal's blood, and (iii) the prohibition of mixing meat products and dairy products.

[12] Incest is an interesting example here, because while most societies do forbid incest, what *constitutes* an incestuous relationship differs. Typically, parent-child relations are forbidden, as are relationships between siblings (though there have been exceptions to both of these in particular societies).

that deal with such matters as sex and sexual relations, reproduction and parenthood, death and the dead (as well as burial places), religious practices and restrictions, and dietary codes and rules. Some taboos make a great deal of sense: for instance, the common ban on in-group murder is clearly an adaptive norm that is necessary for the long-term benefit of the group. Taboos related to incest are, whether consciously or unconsciously, efforts to prevent inbreeding and the genetic problems that can arise from such mating practices. Some dietary restrictions probably have similar underlying rationales. In the case of both Judaism and Islam, the ban on eating pork could be related to the conditions of the middle eastern life during the times when the rules of *kashrut* and *halal* were developing.[13] Other taboos may make a great deal of sense in their own cultural context. For example, in some cultures that are linguistic restrictions on a married woman's speech that reflect concerns about the supernatural power of using and misusing a person's real name (see Herbert, 1990; Zungu, 1997). Taboos related to menstruation (as in Judaism) are also common (see Wasserfall, 1999), often related to notions of ritual purity and impurity.[14]

In contemporary American society, there are of course numerous taboos, although we are often not aware of them as such – though when one of them is violated, we have negative responses. Consider the following examples of situations in which a taboo is being violated, and try to judge your own reaction:

- You go to a friend's house for dinner. As you sit down to eat, your host comments, "I think that you'll really like this tonight. We're having cat as the main course."
- A classmate invites you to her wedding, which is scheduled to take place in about a month. You ask about her fiancé, and she says, "Actually, we're the perfect couple, because we know each other so well. We've spent virtually our whole lives together. He's my brother."
- You are at home, visiting with your cousin, who is expecting her first child. She tells you that she knows that the baby is a boy, and you ask what names she is considering. She responds, "I've already decided. His name is Amy Marie."
- You are at church, in line waiting to take communion. The priest says, "This is the body of Christ" to the person in front of you, who responds, "Screw You."

---

[13] We recognize, of course, for both observant Jews and Muslims, any secular rationale for such restrictions is irrelevant. In both cases, these restrictions are believed to come from God, and any other explanation for them simply does not matter. In addition, in both cases talking about the "development" of such taboos in also inappropriate.

[14] The fact that things like *hlonipha* among the Nguni peoples and the rules related to *niddah* are grounded in cultural taboos does not mean that they are not also components of patriarchal structures that may disempower and contribute to the oppression of women, of course (see Rudwick & Shange, 2009; Steinberg, 1997).

In each of these cases, an important taboo has been violated. The chances are that your reactions will have varied from puzzlement to disgust to one of being deeply offended. One interesting aspect of taboos is that even within a particular society, taboos can change over time. In our own context, for instance, many traditional taboos have changed over the past several decades – taboos about sex and sexuality (e.g., same-sex marriage), food (e.g., sushi), gender roles (e.g., a female President of the United States), and so on. All of these things would have been almost inconceivable not that long ago, but today all are either common (same-sex marriages and sushi) or easy to imagine (a female President).

Cultural Diversity and Cultural Pluralism

Thus far, we have been discussing culture as if there is a single culture in a particular society, and while such a view does have a degree of heuristic value, it is also misleading, since in virtually every contemporary society there are multiple, and often competing, cultures present. One important distinction to keep in mind is that while virtually every society is culturally diverse, there are many different ways that a society can choose to respond to that diversity. The philosopher of education Richard Pratte has suggested that there are five "ideologies of cultural diversity": assimilation, acculturation, insular cultural pluralism, modified cultural pluralism, and what he calls the "Open Society."[15] Each of these different ideologies of cultural diversity is based on a distinctive view of cultural diversity, and each entails a variety of policy alternatives and proposals. With the exception of the "Open Society," each of the different ideologies of cultural diversity also reflects a particular approach to cultural diversity that has been reflected in American history and in our historical response to cultural diversity. Pratte's five ideologies of cultural diversity are presented in Table 7.3, along with the name by which each is most commonly known.

Description	Ideology	Common Name
$A + B + C + D = A$	Assimilation	Anglo-Conformity
$A + B + C + D = E$	Acculturation	The Melting Pot
$A + B + C + D = A + B + C + D$	Insular Cultural Pluralism	Classic Cultural Pluralism
$A + B + C + D = A_1 + B_1 + C_1 + D_1$	Modified Cultural Pluralism	Hyphenated Americanism
$A + B + C + D = O$	The "Open Society"	

Table 7.3 Ideologies of Cultural Diversity (Pratte, 1979)

Table 7.3 represents in a formulaic manner the presence of diversity in a society and the way in which that society seeks to address that diversity. The "A + B + C + D" refers simply to multiple cultural groups; in the U.S. context, we would be thinking primarily about different immigrant groups that have, over our history, come to America.[16] Thus, A might refer to those immigrants from Britain, B to those from Ireland, C to those from Germany, D to those from Italy, and so on. One possible goal would be to expect all of the different cultural groups to

---

[15] Pratte's model is actually based on an earlier one proposed by Thomas Green (see Green, 1966).

[16] It is extremely important to note that this model works reasonably well in describing the experiences of most immigrant groups. Because of the confounding variable of race, it most certainly does not explain the historical experience of African Americans, Native Americans and (some) other people of color. See Chapter 8 for a discussion of race and racism in our society.

adopt this culture, language, and so on, of one particular cultural group. In the case of the United States, one of the dominant approaches to cultural diversity has been to expect immigrants to assimilate into the dominant Anglo-American (i.e., basically British-based) culture that was the major cultural foundation at the time of the American Revolution. In our history, this is commonly referred to as Anglo-Conformity, and while it does not account for all aspects of modern American society, it does explain certain elements of contemporary America. Our language is English, and our political and economic institutions are based largely on those of Britain. To be sure, all of these have been modified in the American context, but they are built on what is fundamentally a British foundation.

Although built on a British foundation, what has been created in the United States is nevertheless a unique, and new, culture. This culture is the result of a blending of the many different cultures that have been brought here and thus called acculturation. This idea is often called the "Melting Pot" and suggests that what is "typically" American is a mixture of many different cultures. Like Anglo-Conformity, there is an element of truth in this view of the American experience, but it is also not a completely accurate picture of our history.

Cultural pluralism basically refers to the idea that not only have multiple cultures arrived in America but they have also, in one way or another, continued to coexist here side by side. The metaphor of a "salad" is sometimes used to represent cultural pluralism: there is a single salad, but within the salad, there are multiple distinct components; lettuce, tomatoes, avocados, and so on. Tied to changes that have taken place over generations, there are basically two kinds of cultural pluralism in the United States -- insular cultural pluralism and modified cultural pluralism. Insular cultural pluralism describes situations in which a cultural group chooses to remain relatively isolated from the surrounding dominant culture. In cases of this sort, groups typically maintain their language, foods, local shops, religious institutions, and social networks. In the history of the United States, for many immigrant groups insular cultural pluralism describes fairly accurately what took place in the first generation of immigrants. Modified cultural pluralism still entails distinctive cultural identities, but these identities are changed as individuals are increasingly integrated into the dominant culture – often becoming bilingual and bicultural. In our history, this describes what took place most often in the second generation, though some elements of the culture of origin may continue for several generations (e.g., in terms of food, religion, etc.). When an individual self-identifies as Irish-American, German-American, Chinese-American, Russian-American, and so on – that is, when they become what has been called "hyphenated Americans" – this is usually a weak sort of modified cultural pluralism.

The last of the ideologies of cultural diversity identified by Pratte is what he termed the "Open Society." The Open Society is perhaps best understood as aspirational in nature. The basic idea is that the Open Society is one in which one's ethnic, national, religious, linguistic, or other identity is simply irrelevant. While this may sound appealing, it in effect parallels assimilation and acculturation without claiming to do so.

Cultural Diversity and Education: Multicultural Education

This chapter began by noting that throughout American history, addressing cultural diversity has been one of the more important functions of public schooling. At the same time, at almost every point in our history our social and educational responses to diversity have been characterized by a considerable degree of tension and disagreement. This tension has been reflected in our rhetoric about unity and difference, our policies and laws, our views of newcomers and "outsiders," and the ways that we have treated the "Other." The *laissez faire* approach to immigrants of much of the colonial era was possible because the immigrants were coming with skills and backgrounds very similar to those who were already here. As the immigrants began to differ increasingly from the dominant population in the country, bigotry and discrimination became more common, and the conflict between the early immigrants and the "native" Americans[17] led to the first organized efforts to provide public schooling in the Common Schools. The Common Schools were largely successful, and the German and Irish Roman Catholic immigrants of the first part of the 19th century were, for the most part, assimilated into the dominant culture and society – only to be replaced following the Civil War by the "new immigrants" from Southern and Eastern Europe. The arrival of huge numbers of immigrants who were seen as being even more different led to active Americanization programs in public schools, the expansion of public schooling, and stronger efforts on the part of the government to control and limit immigration. During the second half of 20th century, and especially beginning in the era of the Civil Rights Movement, the public schools in general became more open and positively oriented toward at least some sorts of diversity. Beginning with multiethnic education, followed by multicultural education, the schools adopted an ideological approach that was clearly more pluralistic in nature (see Banks, 1993, 1997; Banks & Banks, 2016; Gollnick & Chinn, 2006; Nieto, 1992; Sleeter, 1991, 1996).

Multicultural education is not a unified discipline or field of study; therefore, it is not possible to list its goals or objectives, since these vary from one scholar or practitioner to another. However, there are certain general characteristics that are typically associated with multicultural education, among which are to:

- Promote social justice.
- Promote equity in society and in schools.
- Foster the student's ability to function as an autonomous person.
- Promote civic good.
- Increase the self-esteem of students from marginalized and dominated backgrounds.
- Ensure that the curriculum is inclusive and historically accurate.
- Provide all students with a culturally, racially, and linguistically diverse educational experience.
- Celebrate and preserve non-dominant cultures in the classroom.

---

[17] In this context, "native" American does not refer to Native Americans – that is, to the indigenous peoples of North America – but rather, to Anglo-Americans who had become the culturally, politically, and economically dominant group in the U.S. society.

- Ensure that all students have the skills and knowledge required to succeed in an increasingly diverse and global world.

One of the important features of multicultural education programs is that they are designed and intended to benefit all students, not just students from marginalized backgrounds. As Matthew Lynch (2016) has argued,

> In its most basic sense, multicultural education is a progressive approach for transforming education based on educational equality and social justice. The components required in educating a multicultural education are content integrations, prejudice reduction, empowering school culture and social culture. These all relate and all require attention as they relate to the efforts of conflict resolution in today's world. What kids learn in their classroom environments when it comes to interactions with those who are different from them translates into how well they will manage life in the global marketplace.

Multiculturalism in general, and multicultural education in particular, have come under attack in some corners of our society, but often this has been the case because of misunderstandings of the central concepts and concerns that they involve. An example of such concerns is a quote from Thomas Sowell, a Senior Fellow at the Hoover Institution at Stanford University, who has claimed that, "What 'multiculturalism' boils down to is that you can praise any culture in the world except Western culture – and you cannot blame any culture in the world except Western culture." The idea that multiculturalism constitutes an attack on Western culture and civilization – although a very common one -- is simply not true. Rather, multiculturalism is a call for the inclusion of ideas and perspectives from cultures other than the one culture that has historically dominated our society. Even more, though, it is about how people are treated. As Nelson Mandela commented, "My dream would be a multicultural society, one that is diverse and where every man, woman and child are treated equally. I dream of a world where all people of all races work together in harmony."

Questions for Reflection and Discussion

1. In this chapter, a number of important components of "culture" are identified and discussed. There are, though, many other significant facets of what constitutes any particular culture. What are some of these other components of culture? What do you believe that their implications for the classroom might be?

2. Consider the five "ideologies of cultural diversity" identified by Richard Pratte. What kind of public education would best meet the objectives of each of these five ideologies? Be sure to include consideration not only of the curriculum, but also teaching methods, assessment and evaluation, and other parts of schooling.

3. Review the examples of taboos that the authors provide for our own society. Do you believe that all of these are valid? Which appear especially powerful for you? Which are the least powerful for you? Are there any taboos that have special implications for the public school classroom?

4. What does the phrase "patriotic history curriculum" mean to you? Do you believe that the public schools should make a point of ensuring that the curriculum is "patriotic"? Why or why not?

5. In this chapter, the authors argue that, "there are no 'primitive' languages just as there are no 'primitive' cultures." Do you agree? If not, can you offer any counter-examples?

References

Adams, C. (2017, March 24). The new gender identity terms you need to know. *CBS News.* Retrieved from https://www.cbsnews.com/news/transgender-gender-identity-terms-glossary/.

Banks, J. (1993). Multicultural education: Historical development, dimensions, and practice. *Review of Research in Education, 19,* 3-49.

Banks, J. (1997). *Educating citizens in a multicultural society.* New York, NY: Teachers College Press.

Banks, J., & Banks, C. (Eds.). (2016). *Multicultural education: Issues and perspectives* (10th ed.). Indianapolis, IN: John Wiley.

Banks, J., & Nguyen, D. (2008). Diversity and citizenship education: Historical, theoretical, and philosophical issues. In L. Levstik & C. Tyson (Eds.), *Handbook of research in social studies education* (pp. 137-151). New York, NY: Routledge.

Beatty, B. (2000). "The letter killeth": Americanization and multicultural education in kindergartens in the United States, 1856-1920. In R. Wollons (Ed.), *Kindergartens and cultures: The global diffusion of an idea* (pp. 42-58). New Haven, CT: Yale University Press.

Becker, C. (1955). What are historical facts? *Western Political Quarterly, 7,* 327-340.

Bennett, B. (2020, September 1). "Patriotic education": Trump rejects grappling with America's racist past. *Time.* Retrieved from https://time.com/5885345/patriotic-education-trump-rejects-grappling-with-americas-racist-past/?ocid=uxbndlbing.

Duncan, J. (2005). *Citizens or papists? The politics of anti-Catholicism in New York, 1685-1821.* New York, NY: Fordham University Press.

Farrelly, M. (2018). *Anti-Catholicism in America, 1620-1860*. Cambridge, UK: Cambridge University Press.

Fasold, R., & Connor-Linton, J. (Eds.). (2014). *An introduction to language and linguistics* (2nd ed.). Cambridge, UK: Cambridge University Press.

Fromkin, V., Rodman, R., & Hyams, N. (2014). *An introduction to language* (10th ed.). Boston, MA: Wadsworth.

Gilbert, G. (Ed.). (1971). *The German language in America*. Austin: The University of Texas Press.

Gollnick, D., & Chinn, P. (2006). *Multicultural education in a pluralistic society* (7th ed.). Upper Saddle, NJ: Pearson.

Green, T. (1966). *Education and pluralism: Ideal and reality*. Syracuse, NY: Syracuse University.

Herbert, R. (1990). *Hlonipha* and the ambiguous woman. *Anthropos, 85*(4/6), 455-473.

Holian, T. (1998). *The German-Americans and World War II: An ethnic experience*. New York, NY: Peter Lang.

Kaestle, C. (1978). Social change, discipline, and the Common School in early 19th century America. *Journal of Interdisciplinary History, 9*(1), 1-17.

Katz, M. (2001). *The irony of early school reform: Educational innovation in mid-19th century Massachusetts* (new ed.). New York, NY: Teachers College Press.

Kinealy, C. (2002). *The Great Irish Famine: Impact, ideology and rebellion*. London, UK: Palgrave.

Kloss, H. (1998). *The American bilingual tradition*. Washington, DC: Center for Applied Linguistics.

Kraver, J. (1999). Restocking the melting pot: Americanization as cultural imperialism. *Race, Gender and Class, 6*(4), 61-75.

Lynch, M. (2016, November 13). The call to teach multicultural education. *The Edvocate*. Retrieved from https://www.theedadvocate.org/the-call-to-teach-multicultural-education/.

Mirel, J. (2010). *Patriotic pluralism: Americanization education and European immigrants*. Cambridge, MA: Harvard University Press.

Morgan, L. (1871). *Systems of consanguinity and affinity of the human family*. Washington, DC: Smithsonian Institution.

Moses, M., & Chang, M. (2006). Toward a deeper understanding of the diversity rationale. *Educational Researcher, 35*(1), 6-11.

Nieto, S. (1992). *Affirming diversity: The sociopolitical context of multicultural education*. White Plains, NY: Longman.

Ó Gráda, C. (1999). *Black '47 and beyond: The Great Irish Famine in history, economy, and memory*. Princeton, NJ: Princeton University Press.

Ó Gráda, C., & O'Rourke, K. (1997). Migration as disaster relief: Lessons from the Great Irish Famine. *European Review of Economic History, 1*(1), 3-25.

Olneck, M. (1989). Americanization and the education of immigrants, 1900-1925: An analysis of symbolic action. *American Journal of Education, 97*(4), 398-423.

Pai, Y. (1990). *Cultural foundations of education*. Columbus, OH: Merrill.

Parsons, T. (1943). The kinship system of the contemporary United States. *American Anthropologist, 45*(1), 22-38.

Pratte, R. (1979). *Pluralism in education: Conflict, clarity, and commitment*. Springfield, IL: Charles C. Thomas.

Reese, W. (2005). *America's public schools: From the Common School to "No Child Left Behind."* Baltimore, MD: Johns Hopkins University Press.

Rudwick, S., & Shange, M. (2009). *Hlonipha* and the rural Zulu woman. *Agenda: Empowering Woman for Gender Equality, 23*(82), 66-75.

Sleeter, C. (Ed.). (1991). *Empowerment through multicultural education*. Albany: State University of New York Press.

Sleeter, C. (1996). *Multicultural education as social activism*. Albany: State University of New York Press.

Smith, N. (2002). *Language, bananas, and bonobos: Linguistic problems, puzzles and polemics*. Oxford, UK: Blackwell.

Steinberg, J. (1997). From a "pot of filth" to a "hedge of roses" (and back): Changing theorizations of menstruation in Judaism. *Journal of Feminist Studies in Religion, 13*(2), 5-26.

Tozer, S., Violas, P., & Senese, G. (1993). *School and society: Educational practice as social expression*. New York, NY: McGraw Hill.

Verhoeven, T. (2010). *Transatlantic anti-Catholicism: France and the United States in the 19th century*. New York, NY: Palgrave Macmillan.

Wasserfall, R. (Ed.). (1999). *Women and water: Menstruation in Jewish life and law*. Hanover, NH: Brandeis University Press.

Zungu, P. (1997). Some aspects of *hlonipha* in Zulu society. *Language Matters: Studies in the Languages of Africa, 28*(1), 171-181.

Chapter 8

Race and Racism in Schooling

*I have a dream that my four little children will
one day live in a nation where they will not be
judged by the color of their skin but by the content
of their character.* (Martin Luther King, Jr.)

*Racism isn't born, folks. It's taught. I have a
2-year-old son. Know what he hates? Naps.
End of list.* (Dennis Leary)

Race has played an incredibly significant role throughout American history, and racial identify remains a pervasive and ubiquitous aspect of life in the United States. In this chapter, we will examine the concept of race in the context of American society, exploring the ways in which race has been defined historically, the idea of the social construction of race, "white privilege" and its implications, racism and different kinds of racism, the distinction between prejudice and discrimination, the legacy of racism in American society, and finally, anti-racism and the commitment to anti-racist pedagogical approaches and objectives in public education. It is important to note at the outset of this chapter that issues related to race and racism are incredibly controversial and contentious ones in our society. Discussions about these matters inevitably makes many people uncomfortable and perhaps even defensive. Our purpose here is not to place blame, nor is it to challenge any person's identity – it is, rather, to allow for and to promote an honest, open, and reflective discourse about issues that not only have incredibly important implications for our society in general but which also have huge implications for both public education policy and classroom practice.

The Social Construction of Race

We often talk about race, and different races, as if they were biological in nature, but this is not actually the case at all. This is a biological and genetic fact: Not only do any two human beings share 99.9% of their DNA, but they basically possess the same set of genes. This is the evidence for the claim that human beings not only constitute a single species, but also for the shared ancestry of our species. Furthermore, while there is indeed genetic variation within the human species, there is considerably more variation *within* any particular human population (i.e., within so-called "racial groups") than there is *between* human populations. In short, in spite of what may seem obvious (especially in a society in which race and racial divisions play a significant role, as they do in the United States), human beings cannot really be meaningfully divided into discrete racial subgroups. As Gordon Hodson (2016) has observed, "Scientists generally do not recognize races as biologically meaningful." In fact, recent work on the Human Genome Project[1] suggests that, at least for scientific purposes, the concept of race

---

[1] The Human Genome Project (HGP), which took place between 1990 and 2003, was a scientific effort to sequence and map the entirety of genes (taken together known as the genome) of members of our species, *Homo sapiens*.

has little value. As Michael Yudell has explained, "It's a concept we think is too crude to provide useful information, it's a concept that has social meaning that interferes in the scientific understanding of human genetic diversity and it's a concept that we are not the first to call upon moving away from" and, further, that race should be "understood to be a poorly defined marker of that diversity and an imprecise proxy for the relationship between ancestry and genetics" (quoted in Gannon, 2016).

Rather than reflecting any biological or genetic difference, race is in fact a *social construction*. What does this mean, though? There is a common misunderstanding that by identifying something as a social construction, we are saying that it is unimportant, or in some sense not real or meaningful – even that it should be considered to be "fake." This is not at all the case, though. When we say that something is a social construct, what we are doing is recognizing that it is a product of definitions and distinctions that have been created by human beings, but which does not have an independent basis in the reality of the natural world (see Berger & Luckmann, 1966; Searle, 1995). This does *not* mean, however, that such social constructions are unimportant. The fact of the matter is that we live in human societies and that many – perhaps even most – of the institutions, concepts, structures, patterns, and so on that we deal with on a daily basis are social constructions. Although such social constructions may not exist in the natural world (as would, say, an earthquake), we choose to act as if they are "real" by intersubjective agreement, which effectively gives them the same force as if they *were* "real." In recent years, there are many things that anthropologists, historians, psychologists, sociologists, and others have suggested might be conceptualized as being social constructions. Among these are not only race but also childhood and adolescence (Gergen, Lightfoot, & Sydow, 2004; Norozi & Moen, 2016), criminality and deviance (Rock, 1998), gender and sex (Hubbard, 1991; Lorber, 2004; Plummer, 2015),[2] health and illness (Brown, 1995; Conrad & Barker, 2010), and marriage (Aniciete & Soloski, 2011). Given this list, it should be clear that by identifying something as a social construction we are in no way seeking to minimize its relevance for individuals or for society more generally. Furthermore, it is important to understand that the distinction between something that is a social construction and something that is part of natural reality is often characterized by overlap. As Han Koehle has observed, although the "President of the United States is a social construct …. The President of the United States is also real … [there is] a real person who exists, and [their] actions *as* President of the United States have an undeniable influence on reality" (Koehle, 2017). In the same way, while a particular flower is part of natural reality, the identification of the flower as a rose, and the placing of the rose in a place that we have chosen to identify and label a garden, is a social construction.

When we talk about the social construction of race, we are actually attempting to make several important, and interconnected, points. First of all, such an identification means that we recognize that, in the society in which we live, race and racial identity are significant because of the social meanings that people attach to them. We may fully understand that a socially constructed concept such as race differs in a fairly fundamental manner from one that is

---

[2] As we pointed out in Chapter 7, the distinctions between and among biological sex, gender, and gender identity are only one piece of an incredibly complex part of personhood that goes far beyond the binary approach that has been commonly (and wrongly) assumed in the Western tradition, and in some (but not all) other traditions.

ontologically (rather than socially) constructed, but we are also indicating that we are nevertheless aware of the power of social constructs in human societies. Furthermore, we are acknowledging that racial identity is the result of how a person defines themself, and how others define them, based on perceptions of physical and social characteristics – in other words, that racial classifications are the result of how people define, label, and categorize themselves and others. Last, and perhaps most powerfully, we are recognizing that the social construction of race, racial categories, and racial identities is not a neutral process but is a coercive one that functions as an ideological tool that oppresses some people and favors others.

There is a further aspect to the social construction of race that should be considered at this point, and that is the fluidity of the concept of race. Not only is race not a biological category *per se*, but over time, from one historical period to another, and from one society to another, the concept and definition of race (and the identification of specific racial groups) changes, sometimes in quite important ways. One example of this is the way that racial groups were identified and defined in *apartheid* South Africa, where both law and tradition divided the population of the country into four distinct racial groups: Africans (also, at different points in history, "Natives" and other labels), "Coloureds" (people of historically mixed race), Asians (actually, people of Indian descent), and whites (also, at different points in history, "Europeans"; see Lever, 1982; Nengwekhulu, 1986; Szeftel, 1994).[3] In the context of American history and society, although racial categories have been reasonably stable over time with respect to some groups (for instance, African Americans and Native Americans), some immigrant groups have also been identified as "non-white" during particular periods. This was true, for example of the Irish, of many Southern and Eastern Europeans, and of Jews (see Brodkin, 2010). More recently, we have also witnessed increases in the numbers of people who identify as members of two or more racial groups. For census and affirmative action purposes, for instance, the U.S. government typically employs the following racial classification system:

White[4]
Black or African American
American Indian and Alaska Native
Asian

Native Hawaiian and Other Pacific Islander
Two or More Races
Some Other Race

Finally, there are groups that have moved from category to category; in 1977, for instance, the classification of East Asians' race changed from white to Asian (Brodkin, 2010, p. 74).

---

[3] *Apartheid* was far more complex than simply a system of racial segregation. It was a complex ideological approach to social engineering that envisioned a total territorial division among people of different "racial" groups, but most especially between black South Africans and others (see Dubow, 2014; Norval, 1996).

[4] There is usually a separate category for "Hispanic origin," which is a clear indication of the fundamental confusion here, since it demonstrates a conflation of race and ethnicity.

The History of Race and Racism in the United States

Issues of race and racism have characterized virtually every time period in the history of the United States, beginning in 1619, when the first African slaves were brought to Jamestown Colony,[5] and continuing to the present day (Roediger, 2008). Indeed, slavery has often been called the "original sin" of our society, and it has either directly or indirectly impacted virtually every social, economic, political, and education institution in the United States. Among the complaints against King George III that the colonists included in the *Declaration of Independence* were that "He has excited domestic insurrections amongst us," referring to a 1775 proclamation issues by Governor Lord Dunmore in Virginia, which promised that slaves owned by revolutionaries their freedom should they join the British army. Following the Revolution, not only did slavery continue throughout much of the country, but the *Constitution* of the newly created United States of America included the notorious "three-fifths compromise" between Northern and Southern representatives at the 1787 Constitutional Convention.

Slavery was a key economic and social institution in a large part of the United States from the 17th through the mid-19th centuries (see Drescher, 2009; Ogden, Perkins, & Donahue, 2008). Although it is not possible to provide a completely accurate number, some historians have estimated that as many as 6 to 7 million Africans were brought to North America in the 18th century alone, and in the antebellum South around one-third of the total population consisted of enslaved persons. Initially, large numbers of the enslaved population worked on tobacco, indigo, and rice plantations, but following the invention of the cotton gin in 1793, the Southern economy rapidly shifted to a reliance on cotton – a shift that resulted in an even greater reliance on enslaved labor. In the decades leading up to the Civil War, there were two parallel historical developments taking place: the growing abolition movement in the Northern states (Drescher, 2009), and the westward expansion (Woodworth, 2010). These two developments inevitably came into conflict, and in 1820 Congress admitted Missouri and Maine as new states – Missouri as a slave state, and Maine as a free state. This decision was the result of what was called the "Missouri Compromise," which dictated that any new states in the area of the Louisiana Purchase south of the 36° 30' parallel would be slave states, while any states north of the 36° 30' parallel would be free states. The "Missouri Compromise" remained in effect for only a generation, before being replaced by the *Kansas-Nebraska Act* in 1854. The *Kansas-Nebraska Act* repealed the geographic line that had been created to guide the establishment of slave and free states, and, as a way of allowing the Nebraska Territory to be admitted to the Union, split the Territory into two areas, Kansas and Nebraska, and allowed the settlers in each area to determine the status of their territory themselves.[6]

---

[5] The arrival of these "twenty and odd" enslaved people, who were brought to America on the English privateer *White Lion*, under the command of John Jope, is often recorded as the beginning of slavery in America. In fact, this is not completely accurate; the slave trade had already been established and growing for nearly a century before 1619 (see Guasco, 2014).

[6] The assumption that was made was that the settlers in Nebraska would choose to be a free state, while those in Kansas would choose to be a slave state. In the end, it turned out to make no difference,

In November 1860, Abraham Lincoln was elected the 16th President of the United States. The tensions between the Southern states and the Northern states had been increasing for decades, and Lincoln's election was the final straw that led to the secession of seven states – Alabama, Florida, Georgia, Louisiana, Mississippi, South Carolina, and Texas – and the establishment of a provision Confederate government on February 8, 1861. Arkansas, Tennessee, North Carolina, and Virginia also joined the newly created Confederate States of America after April 15, 1861. There were multiple causes that led to the secession of the Southern states from the Union.[7] These causes included ongoing differences between the Southern and Northern states about such issues as State's rights (and, specifically, the extent to which the agreement to form the United States was a binding, permanent one, or whether a state might choose to leave the Union), protectionism (Northern manufacturers sought tariffs, while Southern planters preferred free trade), sectionalism (reflected, for instance, in the very different economic structures of the agricultural Southern states and the increasing industrialized Northern states), and the territorial crises with respect to the admission of new states to the Union. Underlying all of these, though – and of far greater significance than any of the others – was the issue of slavery. On April 12 and 13, 1861, troops under the command of General P. G. T. Beauregard, following the orders of Jefferson Davis, the newly chosen President of the Confederate States of America, fired on Fort Sumter, located in the middle of the harbor in Charleston, South Carolina. It was from this specific event that the beginning of the Civil War is traditionally dated.

The Civil War, which was fought between 1861 and 1865, was without doubt one of the most destructive events in American history. Civil wars – whether in Sudan, Yugoslavia, Spain, or Somalia – are all too often incredibly brutal and vicious affairs, and the American Civil War was no exception. The cost in human lives was terrible; the Civil War accounted for more deaths than in all of the other wars in which the United States has been involved combined. The extent of this human devastation can be seen in Table 8.1.

---

since by the time that Kansas was admitted to the Union, the Southern states had already begun to secede.

[7] Not only are there debates about the causes and consequences of the Civil War, there are even ongoing debates about what it should be called – among the names that are used to identify it are not only the Civil War but also the War Between the States, the War of Northern Aggression, and sometimes "The Lost Cause."

Category	USA	CSA
Killed in Action	110,100	94,000
Died from Disease	224,580	164,000
Wounded in Action	275,154	194,026
Captured	211,411	462,634
Died as POWs	30,192	31,000

Table 8.1 Civil War Losses and Casualties

Financially, the Civil War was also devastating, and in multiple ways. In January 1863, the U.S. government estimated that the war was costing $2.5 million per day; the total cost was over $6 billion, and by 1906, nearly $3.5 billion more had been made in pensions and other benefits for veterans.[8] The economic impact of the Civil War was not only felt in terms of actual expenditures but also as a result of the inflation experienced in all parts of the country, though inflation was most severe in the Confederate states. Economically and politically, the Civil War dramatically changed the relationships between the North and the South – as James McPherson (1988) has noted, "the North and West grew rich while the once-rich South became poor for a century. The national political power of the slaveowners and rich Southerners ended" (p. 581).

For many in the North, a central focus of the Civil War was on the abolition of slavery, but it is important to note that this was not actually an articulated objective of the war at its outset. Rather, initially the war was seen as a matter of secession, and, thus, one of state's rights versus the commitment to a continuing *United* States. Abraham Lincoln, to the considerable disappointment and frustration of many radical abolitionists in the North, did not see the elimination of slavery as a goal of the war – and, in fact, was concerned about the potential effect of any effort to free the slaves, since such an action could lead the border slave states (Delaware, Kentucky, Maryland, Missouri, and West Virginia) to join the Confederacy. But in 1862, the politics of the situation had changed sufficiency to allow Lincoln to deliver the *Emancipation Proclamation*, which freed more than 3 million slaves in the Confederacy.[9] Lincoln's views on slavery clearly evolved over time, but as late as August 1862, he wrote in an editorial published in the *Daily National Intelligencer* that "My paramount object in this struggle *is* to save the Union and is *not* either to save or to destroy slavery. If I could save the Union without freeing *any* slave I would do it, and if I could save it by freeing *all* the slaves I would do it; and if I could save it by freeing some and leaving others alone I would also do that."

---

[8] Note that these are only the expenditures incurred by the United States. In addition to these amounts, the Confederacy is estimated to have spent more than $2 billion on the war.

[9] It is important to understand that the *Emancipation Proclamation* applied only to the enslaved people in the Confederate States of America – it did *not* apply those living in what was the United States, in the border states that still maintained slavery.

Following the end of the Civil War – and, importantly, the assassination of President Lincoln, after which Andrew Johnson became President of the United States[10] – the country faced the dual challenge of reintegrating the former Confederate states into the Union while at the same time incorporating more than 4 million former enslaved people into American society. For a brief period, from 1865 to 1866, with the support of the Johnson administration under what was called "Presidential Reconstruction," racist and restrictive "black codes" were introduced throughout the South. This was met with considerable anger by more radical members of the Republican Party in Congress, which led to the passage of the *Reconstruction Act* of 1867, as well as indirectly to the impeachment of Johnson by Congress (see Zorowski, 1987).

During Radical Reconstruction, between 1867 and 1877, the Fourteenth and Fifteenth Amendments to the *Constitution* were approved – the Fourteenth Amendment granting citizenship and "equal protection" to former slaves, and the Fifteenth Amendment guaranteeing that a person's right to vote would not be denied "on account of race, color, or previous condition of servitude." The states of the Confederacy were all readmitted to the Union by 1870, with new state constitutions that were the most progressive in the history of the South. During this decade, African Americans played significant roles in the politics of the Southern states, at both the state level and were even elected to the U.S. Congress. The period also saw the passage of legislation forbidding racial discrimination in public transportation and accommodations, the creation of the first tax-supported public school systems in the South, and a variety of economic development programs. These efforts were met with increasing violence on the part of many Southern whites, and the Ku Klux Klan and other white supremacist organizations fought such changes in a variety of ways. By 1877, Radical Reconstruction had largely ended throughout the South and was followed by the era of "Jim Crow" – a collection of laws that in essence legalized racial segregation and white dominance. Jim Crow legislation was about far more than simply daily discrimination that entailed separate and in fact unequal facilities for blacks and whites, though. It disempowered African Americans in a host of ways, including denying them the right to vote (as a result of voter literacy requirements, as well as implied and often manifested physical threats), restricting educational opportunities (through segregated schooling), limiting employment options (by "reserving" certain kinds of jobs for whites), and creating social, economic, and judicial institutions that were fundamentally unfair and racist. The era of Jim Crow remained in place throughout the South until it began to be challenged during the Civil Rights Movement in the mid-20th century.

For nearly a century, Jim Crow laws, coupled with a variety of informal practices, characterized the nature of the lives of African Americans throughout the South (Blackmon, 2008). The Supreme Court's 1896 decision in *Plessy versus Ferguson* established a precedent for the constitutionality of "separate but equal" facilities, and a variety of means were utilized to prevent African Americans from achieving their rights as full and equal citizens. By the 1950s and 1960s, African Americans, and many white supporters, were no longer willing to tolerate the prejudice, discrimination, and violence against them that existed in one form or another

---

[10] While Lincoln was a Republican, Andrew Johnson was Democrat (one of the so-called "War Democrats"), who had served as the military governor of Tennessee during Lincoln's first term. As a Southerner himself, he was selected as Lincoln's running mate as a way of promoting national unity.

throughout the United States,[11] and the fight for civil rights began in earnest. The history of the Civil Rights Movement in the United States is very important, and deserves considerably more attention than we can provide it here (see Chong, 1991; Isserman & Kazin, 2000; Morris, 1984). Some of the major events in the Civil Rights Movement that are especially important, though, are presented in Table 8.2.

There is no question that our society has made huge progress with respect to race, but this progress, we would suggest, needs to be put in its proper historical context. Slavery existed for some 246 years, and segregation and Jim Crow lasted an additional 89 years. The impact and legacy of that 335 years is almost unimaginable. The post-*Brown* era is still less than 70 years old in comparison, and it is certainly not the case that *Brown* instantly established a "level playing field" for all citizens. Racism is not only still very much with us, but so too is its legacy and all that that legacy entails. In thinking about public schooling, and the obligations that public schooling entails both for all students and for students from historically marginalized and oppressed groups, there is much to consider and reflect upon.

March on Washington
© Everett Collection/Shutterstock.com

---

[11] It is very important to note that the challenges of racism are not present in the Southern states or in the former Confederacy — they are not only common, but ubiquitous, *throughout* the United States. Racism in all of its many manifestations exists in every part of our country, and in every social institution. Malcom X put this quite powerfully when he said, "If you are black, you were born in jail, in the North as well as the South. Stop talking about the South. As long as you are South of the Canadian border, you are South."

Year	Event	Details
1948	Executive Order 9981	Executive Order 9981, issued by President Harry Truman on July 26, abolished discrimination "on the basis of race, color, religion or national origin" in the United States Armed Forces.
1954	*Brown vs. Board of Education of Topeka, Kansas*	U.S. Supreme Court overturned the 1896 *Plessy vs. Ferguson* decision, and ruled that laws that allowed racial discrimination and racial segregation were unconstitutional.
1955	Murder of Emmett Till	Till, a 14-year-old African American from Chicago, was visiting relatives in Money, Mississippi, for the summer. He had an interaction with a white woman in a local grocery store that was seen as violating local racial norms, and in response he was brutally murdered by the woman's husband and his half-brother. Although tried for murder, the two men were acquitted by an all-white jury.
1955-1956	Boycott of the Montgomery Bus System	A response to the arrest of Rosa Parks in December 1955, for refusing to give up her seat in a public bus to a white man. After 381 days, the boycott was ultimately successful, and the local ordinance requiring racial segregation on public buses was repealed.

Rosa Parks
© neftali/Shuterstock.com

1957	Little Rock Crisis	Nine African American students (called the "Little Rock Nine") were scheduled to enter the formerly segregated Central High School in Little Rock, Arkansas, at the beginning of the 1957-1958 school year. Governor Orval Faubus called in the Arkansas National Guard on September 4 to prevent the students from entering the school. In response, President Eisenhower federalized the Arkansas National Guard and ordered them to return to their barracks. He then deployed elements of the 101st Airborne Division to protect the students.
1957	*Civil Rights Act* of 1957	The *Civil Rights Act* of 1957 was the first civil rights legislation passed by Congress since the *Civil Rights Act* of 1875. Its focus was primarily on the voting rights of African Americans, and its impact was fairly limited as a result of the removal of several important provisions in Congress. Perhaps most notably, it did create the United States Commission on Civil Rights and the United States Department of Justice Civil Rights Division.
1958-1960	Sit-Ins	The NAACP Youth Council began a series of sit-ins to protest racially segregated lunch counters, parks, beaches, libraries, museums, and so on, throughout the South. In July 1958, there was a sit-in at a drug store lunch counter in Wichita, Kansas, followed by many others. Among the better known of these sit-ins took place in Greensboro, North Carolina, in February 1960.
1959-1960s	Voter Registration	Black voting had been suppressed in many Southern states through a combination of poll taxes, literacy tests, residency requirements, and so on. Voter registration and education projects were launched in many areas – often with the support of coalitions of civil rights organizations.
1961	Freedom Riders	The Freedom Riders were civil rights activists who sought to integrate interstate buses in the segregated South, as well as restrooms and water fountains. Although the U.S. Supreme Court had ruled in *Boynton vs. Virginia* in 1960 that such segregated busing was unconstitutional, the resistance to the Freedom Rides was intense – involving buses being firebombed, beatings and assaults (often with the acquiescence of the local police), mob violence, and arrests for "breaching the peace" and other offenses. By the end of the summer of 1961, more than 300 Freedom Riders had been arrested in Mississippi alone.

1961-1962	The Albany Campaign	Efforts in November 1961 to desegregate Albany, Georgia, were largely unsuccessful, in spite of the involvement of Martin Luther King, Jr. This campaign was a failure for two major reasons: divisions within the black community, and because of the actions of the local police chief, who was far more sophisticated in dealing with the challenges of the campaign than most Southern police. Over the next few years, however, significant civil rights victories were gained in Albany.
1963	The Birmingham Campaign	The Birmingham Campaign was far more successful than the Albany efforts had been, in part because of what had been learned in Albany. In the case of Birmingham, the campaign involved a number of different non-violent kinds of confrontation, including sit-ins, "kneel-ins" at churches, and a voter registration march. The Commissioner of Public Safety, "Bull" Connor, led a brutal response to the campaign, which included unleashing police dogs and using fire hoses against children who had gathered. The images were broadcast on the evening news, which led to widespread public outrage. The Kennedy administration intervened, and a compromise was reached that would entail the elimination of segregation in the city and the release of arrested protesters, among other things. Four months after the campaign, the Sixteenth Street Baptist Church was bombed by four members of the Ku Klux Klan, and four young girls were killed.
1963	University of Alabama and Response	On June 11, Alabama Governor George Wallace personally intervened to prevent the integration of the University of Alabama. President Kennedy sent a military force to force the Governor to step aside and allow the registration of two African American students. That evening, he addressed the country on television, making an historic speech on civil rights and calling on Congress to pass new civil rights legislation.

1963	Assassination of Medgar Evers	On June 12, the Field Secretary of the Mississippi NAACP, Medgar Evers, was assassinated by a member of the Ku Klux Klan.
1963	March on Washington	The March on Washington took place on August 28, and involved an estimated 200,00 to 300,000 demonstrators who gathered in front of the Lincoln Memorial. It was at the March on Washington that Martin Luther King, Jr., delivered his "I have a Dream" speech.
1963	Assassination of President John F. Kennedy	President Kennedy was assassinated on November 22, and Vice President Lyndon Johnson became the 36th President of the United States. Johnson used his considerable influence in Congress to support the *Civil Rights Act* of 1964, and also launched the War on Poverty.
1964	Freedom Summer to register black voters in Mississippi	More than 1,000 activists – largely white students from the North and West -- went to Mississippi to work with local activists to register African American voters, teach in "Freedom Schools," and work on related efforts. There was considerable resistance to these activists among local whites, and the activists faced arrests, attacks, and many different sorts of harassment. In June, three activists – one a young black man from Mississippi, and two Jewish activists -- went missing; four weeks later, their bodies were found. They had been murdered by local members of the Ku Klux Klan and members of the Neshoba County sheriff's department.
1964	*Civil Rights Act* of 1964	The Act banned all discrimination based on race, color, religion, sex, or national origin in employment practices, and ended unequal application of voter registration requirements. In addition, the Act prohibited racial segregation in schools, at the workplace, and in public accommodations.
1964	Martin Luther King, Jr., awarded the Nobel Peace Prize	The award was given for King's efforts to combat racial inequality through non-violent resistance.

1965	"Bloody Sunday"	In spite of efforts since 1963, voter registration efforts in Selma, Alabama, had not been terribly successful, due in large part to the opposition of the sheriff, Jim Clark. Finally, in response to the resistance, Martin Luther King, Jr. came to Selma to lead a protest. King was arrested, along with about 250 other demonstrators. The marchers met violent resistance from the police, and one man was killed on February 17.
		A decision was made to march from Selma to Montgomery, the capital of Alabama. Led by Hosea Williams and john Lewis, some 600 people began the roughly 55-mile walk to Montgomery. Only six blocks into the walk, on the Edmund Pettus Bridge, as they left the city and entered the county, state troopers and local country law enforcement attacked the marchers. The police used tear gas to chase away the marchers and beat them with rubber tubes wrapped in barbed wire, whips, and so on. The marchers were driven back into Selma and dispersed.
		Once again, the coverage of these events on national television shocked the nation, and resulted in outrage as whites around the country witnessed the face of Southern resistance.
1965	*Voting Rights Act* of 1965	Guaranteed the voting rights for members of minority groups by authorizing federal oversight of registration and elections in areas with historical under-representation of minorities as voters.
1965	Assassination of Malcom X	Malcom X has been the national representative of the Nation of Islam, but he broke with the organization in March 1964 and began collaborating with any group that agreed to the right to self-defense for black people and a commitment to Black Nationalism. On February 21, Malcom X was assassinated.
1965 to 1975	Black Power Movement	Challenged the established leadership of the African American community for what was seen as its conservative and cooperative approach to challenging racism and discrimination through legalistic and non-violent means.

1967	The "Long, Hot Summer"	During the summer of 1967, there were some 159 riots around the country. During the riots, 83 people were killed, thousands were injured, and tens of millions of dollars in property were destroyed. In June there were riots in Atlanta, Boston, Buffalo, Cincinnati, and Tampa, and in July, riots again erupted in Birmingham, Chicago, Detroit, Milwaukee, Minneapolis, New York, Newark, Rochester, and Toledo. In the aftermath of the riots, the Kerner Commission, established by President Johnson, determined that the riots had been sparked by longstanding racial inequalities in America's urban ghettos.
1968	Assassination of Martin Luther King, Jr.	On April 4, Martin Luther King, Jr., who had in many ways become the face of the Civil Rights Movement, was assassinated in Memphis, Tennessee. His death triggered riots in more than 100 cities across the United States, including in Baltimore, Washington, DC, and Chicago.
1968	*Fair Housing Act* of 1968	Banned racial discrimination in the sale and renting of housing.

Table 8.2 Key Events in the Civil Rights Movement

Toward a Typology of Racism

Although often racism is discussed as if it were a single thing, with common elements and characteristics as well as shared challenges and outcomes, this is actually an oversimplification of a very complex social and ideological phenomenon (see Zamudio & Rios, 2006). In fact, there are a number of different *kinds* of racism – that is, different ways in which racism takes place on both a personal, individual level and on a broader, societal and institutional level. There have been a number of models proposed to address this complexity, but the most popular approach is to talk about four major kinds of racism: internalized racism, interpersonal racism, institutional racism, and structural racism. The first two of these – internalized racism and interpersonal racism – take place at the level of the individual, while the latter two – institutional racism and structural racism – are manifested at the systemic level. All have important implications for public education, as we will see.

Internalized racism rests *within* the individual. This sort of racism refers to personal beliefs, ideas, biases, and attitudes about race, racial differences, and racial identity. It is the result of one's upbringing in large part, but it also reflects the surrounding culture, and is arguably most problematic because it can (and often does) result in the emergence of stereotypes and racial prejudice. Internalized racism can entail either positive or negative beliefs and views of different groups of people, and both sorts of beliefs and ideas are obviously deeply problematic. In addition, internalized racism can be manifested both in individuals from the dominant social group and from marginalized groups. Interpersonal racism is closely related to internalized racism and depends on the presence of internalized racism. It is found when the attitudes and beliefs found in internalized racism are manifested in actions between people -- that is, when individuals are interacting with others, and their personal racial beliefs impact their public interactions. Examples of interpersonal racism include the use of racial slurs and insults, bigotry, hate crimes, and other kinds of racial violence. In terms of seeking to address and challenge racism, there is no question that interpersonal racism is easier to address than internalized racism because it is behavioral in nature, and thus "public" in a way in which internalized racism is often not.

Institutional racism, unlike internalized racism and interpersonal racism, takes place not at the individual level but rather within institutions and other "systems of power" (Bourne, 2001; Williams, 1985). One important characteristic of institutional racism is that it is possible to identify institutional racism *in the absence of internalized or interpersonal racism* (Massey, Scott, & Dornbusch, 1975). To be sure, some individuals within any particular social institution may very well hold biased or racist views, but this is not actually a necessary condition for institutional racism to exist. Rather, institutional racism is produced by policies, practices, and procedures that result in inequitable outcomes related to race. For instance, if a social institution (a school, a workplace, etc.) produces outcomes that are fundamentally and unfairly different for people from different racial groups, then this would constitute evidence of institutional racism. This is true even if there are no instances of internalized or interpersonal racism. In the context of public schooling, we can often see institutional racism in such factors as the concentration of students of color in overcrowded schools or in less challenging classes, or in classrooms with the least qualified classroom teachers. We also see institutional racism in disproportionate dropout rates, school suspension and expulsion data, and so on.

Structural racism, like institutional racism, is not necessarily grounded in or even dependent on internalized or interpersonal racism, although it *is* dependent on the existence of institutional racism. Basically, structural racism exists when there is racial bias among and between a variety of different institutions in a society, which results in a compounding and cumulative racist impact on people of color. Structural racism is the result of a number of factors, including the history, ideology, and interactions of social institutions that systematically privilege members of the dominant group. In our society, there is clear evidence of structural racism related to the health care system, law enforcement, the judicial system (including prison incarceration rates), in employment, in housing and residential patterns, and so on (Griffith et al., 2007).

I Stand Against Racism
© Maria Symchych/Shutterstock.com

Understanding Prejudice and Discrimination

Prejudice and discrimination are both closely related to each other and closely related to the phenomenon of racism. Indeed, Stuart Oskamp (2000) has gone so far as to argue that, "finding ways to *reduce* prejudice and discrimination is *the* central issue in attacking racism in our society" (p. vii). While we might argue about whether simply reducing prejudice and discrimination are sufficient – in fact, we believe that reduction is *not* sufficient, and that our goal as educators must be the elimination of prejudice and discrimination – we agree with Oskamp's central point. In order to address both prejudice and discrimination, whether in society at large or merely in the school and classroom, it is first necessary for us to be clear about what exactly we mean by these terms, and how they are related to racism. One useful way to begin to answer this question is to think about prejudice and discrimination not as a duality at all but rather as part of a triad that consists of prejudice, discrimination, and stereotypes. Prejudice is essentially affective in nature and is concerned first and foremost with a person's feelings and emotions. Discrimination is concerned with behavior and is therefore concerned with actions.

Stereotypes obviously overlap both prejudice and discrimination; they play a role in both, but are also distinctive (Hamilton & Sherman, 1994; Macrae, Stangor, & Hewstone, 1996). They are actually cognitive in nature, and deal with questions of knowledge and belief.[12] There are certain characteristics that *all* members of a particular group might share – indeed, these characteristics might be definitional in nature. Thus, it would be true to suggest that professional chefs know a fair amount about food and cooking. This is what sociologists call a *sociotype,* and it can be quite useful. When a belief or set of beliefs about a group of people are over-generalized, however, and a claim that may (or may not) be true of some members of the group is asserted to be true of *all* members of the group, then we are dealing with a stereotype. Stereotypes are closely tied to prejudices, and, like prejudices, they can be positive or negative

---

[12] This does not mean that the beliefs that they represent are necessarily true, however. Many stereotypes are in fact demonstrably false, regardless of how widely or deeply they might be held.

194

in nature. Regardless of whether they are positive or negative, though, they are problematic precisely because they are misleading, and based on over-generalizations that simply do not apply to all members of the group. The relationships between and among stereotypes, prejudice and discrimination are laid out in Table 8.3.

Category	Function	Definition
Stereotype	Cognitive	Overgeneralized beliefs about individuals and groups that can lead to prejudice. May be positive or negative in nature.
Prejudice	Affective	Feelings and emotional reactions to other people and groups, typically based on stereotypes and group membership, that can lead to discrimination. May be positive or negative in nature.
Discrimination	Behavioral	Treating people differently based on their membership in a particular group. Can include exclusion, avoidance, inappropriate judging, as well as demonstrating favoritism. May be positive or negative in nature.

Table 8.3 Stereotypes, Prejudice and Discrimination

In 1949, the sociologist Robert Merton proposed a model for conceptualizing the relationship between prejudice and discrimination that is still widely used (see Farley, 1988). Basically, Merton suggested that there are four categories of people, based on whether or not the individual is prejudiced and whether or not they discriminate. Merton's model is presented in Table 8.4.

	Not Prejudiced	Prejudiced
Does Not Discriminate	All-Weather Liberals	Timid Bigots
Discriminates	Fair-Weather Liberals	Active Bigots

Table 8.4 Relationship Between Prejudice and Discrimination (based on Merton, 1949)

This model is useful as an overarching way of conceptualizing the relationship between prejudice and discrimination, but it also inevitably oversimplifies a very complex relationship. In addition, of course, human beings do not behave consistently much of the time – it is hardly unreasonable to imagine a person holding certain prejudices who clearly discriminates sometimes but does not do so other times.

The Concept and Reality of White Privilege

The idea of "white privilege" in American society is a controversial one that is on occasion understood by some whites as an attack on them personally – but in fact it is nothing of the sort (see Rothenberg, 2008). It is not a claim about any single individual, nor is it concerned with the actions, beliefs, biases, and so on of any single person (Solomona, Portelli, Daniel, & Campbell, 2005). Rather, it is merely the recognition that in our society members of certain groups are the beneficiaries of assumptions, institutions, and freedoms that are not automatically available to members of other groups (see Bonnett, 1996). This is true, for instance, in the case of gender: Males in our society have historically had, and continue to have, privileges and opportunities that women have simply not had. Some of the barriers that women face are legal or institutional ones, but others are personal or interpersonal in nature, and many are grounded in assumptions about what is "normal" or "natural" (Case, 2007; Dolan-Del Vecchio, 1998). In the case of race, "white privilege" refers to societal privileges that benefit white people and which do not accrue to non-whites in the same way or to the same extent. Peggy McIntosh (1998) has described this phenomenon as the advantages that whites in our society possess that constitute "an invisible package of unearned assets" (p. 31). Included in this "invisible package of unearned assets" are such assumptions as:

1. I can expect that the curricular materials that my children will receive in school will include the inclusion of people of their race – and that their role in the history of our society will be accurately, fairly and appropriately represented.
2. When I go into a store, I will be able to find foods, goods, and services that fit into my cultural traditions and needs.
3. People will not expect me to speak about what people of my group believe or think about a topic – that is, I will not be asked to speak for my entire group.
4. I can criticize the government and its actions without being seen as an outsider or a radical.
5. When I get a new job or position, I do not need to worry that some of my colleagues or fellow workers will suspect that I got the position on grounds other than my merits.
6. When I go to a school or other institution, I can expect to be treated politely and not mistreated in any way. I can assume that my concerns will be taken seriously, and that they will be addressed appropriately.
7. If while I am driving I am pulled over by a police officer, I do not have to wonder if I was pulled over only because of my race.
8. If I am not satisfied in a business situation and ask to speak with the manager or person in charge, I can expect that there is a good likelihood that the person I will be facing will be a person of my own group. (Based on McIntosh, 1998, pp. 31-33)

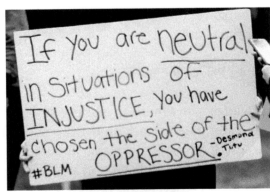

Desmond Tutu Quote
© Branson Stivers/Shutterstock.com

The idea of white privilege overlaps many of the core ideas in the interdisciplinary approach of critical race theory, which is essentially an effort to understand society and culture as they relate to and overlap the categories of race, law, power, and so on (Crenshaw, Gotanda, Peller, & Thomas, 1995; Delgado & Stefancic, 2017; Dixson & Rousseau, 2006). Originally developed in the context of legal studies, critical race theory entails two key features, one that is explanatory, and one that is concerned with advocacy and the promotion of change. Critical race theory is grounded in the recognition that white supremacy and domination are both processes and realities that are maintained over time and that are supported by legal and other social institutions, including most notably schools. As the UCLA School of Public Affairs (2009) has argued,

> [Critical race theory] recognizes that racism is engrained in the fabric and system of the American society. The individual racist need not exist to note that institutional racism in pervasive in the dominant culture. This is the analytical lens that [critical race theory] uses in examining existing power structures. [Critical race theory] identifies that these power structures are based on white privilege and white supremacy, which perpetuates the marginalization of people of color.

In addition, advocates for critical race theory assert that the reality of white supremacy and domination can be successfully challenged and that it is possible not only to eliminate racism but also to achieve racial emancipation in society – a more proactive outcome than merely the elimination of racism.

Anti-Racist Education and Public Schooling

The focus of this chapter has been on race and racism. The point of including such a topic in a book of this sort is not its general importance in our society, or that race and racism continue unabated and are systematically perpetuated across the globe that we all need to examine and reflect upon race and racism as conscientious human beings and citizens. All of this is true, but there is a more compelling reason for making race and racism the central point of this chapter, which is that issues of race and racism – as well as the related concepts of stereotypes, prejudice, discrimination, white privilege, and the other topics that we have explored here – matter a great deal for children and affect them the most. They have profound impacts on almost every aspect of the teaching and learning process. Understanding and reflecting on race and racism, however, are not sufficient in our view. It is necessary for educators to be willing to take on the role of advocates for all of their students, and this means that we must accept responsibility for both the institutional barriers that our students face and any biases, assumptions, prejudices, or stereotypes that we may personally hold that can impact them.

There are many phenomena that arise in the context of the public school about which multiple opinions and perspectives are both reasonable and valuable. We have discussed many of those things thus far in *The Art and Science of Teaching*: the school and its role as a political and ideological institution, the purposes of public schooling, the legal and organizational foundations of public schooling, issues of epistemology and questions about the nature of learning, the distinction between schooling and education, the ideal of the "educated person," issues related to curriculum and instruction, the idea of reflective practice and its implications for the classroom teacher, and so on. For all of these things, there can be legitimate differences of opinion that can be raised, discussed, and debated. However, teaching – and teaching in the context of a public school in particular – is a particular type of profession, and as such there are certain dispositions, beliefs, and behaviors related to the way that the teacher treats and responds to each and every one of their students that constitute fundamentally non-debatable matters (see Reagan, 2009). In Chapter 6, we briefly discussed examples of student comments that we indicated that we believe are problematic in those who wish to become classroom educators. Here, we would take that idea one step further, and suggest that while there are certainly many issues related to issues of race and racism about which discussion and debate are appropriate, there are also some bedrock principles and commitments that the classroom teacher should accept. Furthermore, we would point out that the same is true with respect to many other issues: gender, LGBTQIA+ issues, how one views and treats children who are differently abled, children whose native language is not English, and so on. *All* children deserve our full support, and all should be accepted and valued as unique, and as uniquely gifted, human beings. This means that it is not enough merely to reject racism but that we need to go further than this – to support and implement *anti-racism* in the schools. As Dena Simmons has argued, "educators have an obligation to confront the harm of racism. That is why we must commit to becoming antiracist educators and to preparing our young people to be antiracist, too" (Simmons, 2019). Furthermore, anti-racist education should be understood to be part of a much broader agenda. As Audrey Thompson (1997) pointed out, "democratic education in a racist society *requires* anti-racist pedagogy" (p. 7, emphasis added). Furthermore,

> traditional approaches to democratic education conceive racism in terms of personal prejudice [so] they cannot adequately address the problems that racism actually poses. Racism is structural and institutional as well as embodied and ideational; if education is to do more than refine social expressions of and responses to racism, it must take on racism as a way of framing meaning and value … this cannot be accomplished, however, if anti-racist education is conceived in terms of reactive or corrective argumentation. This is because a reactive or even a corrective response to racist arguments accepts the terms of racism even in arguing against them. To avoid invoking the very assumptions and framework we mean to discredit, we must shift out of the racist framework altogether. (Thompson, 1997, p. 7)

What, then, is "anti-racist education"? A good place to begin answering this question is to discuss briefly some of the criticisms that have emerged of multicultural education, not only in the United States, but also in other predominantly anglophone societies in which such programs have been popular in recent years, including Australia, Canada, and the United Kingdom. Perhaps the most common critique of multicultural education programs has been that such efforts are little more than window-dressing that "operate beneath a veneer of professed tolerance and diversity" (Gillborn, 2006, p. 11) while not actually addressing either the real structural issues related to racism and oppression or the actual concerns of marginalized and oppressed groups (Karumanchery, 2005; Troyna, 1987). While multicultural education does on some accounts minimize the role of institutional processes and structures, anti-racist education "questions power relations in the school and society, recognizes the importance of personal experience and lived realities as a source of knowledge, and explores the perspectives of different social groups in society" (Dei, 1993, p. 36).

Fundamental to anti-racist education is the recognition that the opposite of racism is not "non-racism" but, rather, is "anti-racism" (see Kendi, 2019). The difference is an important one – in a racist society, there is really no such thing as neutrality about race and racism. Anti-racism entails a conscious commitment to challenge racism and to engage in resistance to the various structures and institutions in our society that perpetuate racism (Patterson, 2019). It also involves a basic shift in our thinking; as Robert Patterson has pointed out, "If your default thinking is 'I'm not racist," a more informed point of view would be recognizing how you're informed and influenced by the embeddedness of race and institutionalized racism" (quoted in Hoffower, 2020).

Questions for Reflection and Discussion

1. In this chapter, the idea of the social construction of race is explored. Given the arguments presented here, how do you believe that the authors might respond to Juliet in Shakespeare's *Romeo and Juliet* when she says, "What's in a name? That which we call a rose ... By any other name would smell as sweet?"

2. How would you explain the concept of "white privilege" in your own words? What examples can you give of the operation of white privilege in contemporary American society? In contemporary American public schools?

3. In their discussion of the social construction of race, the authors argue that while something may not exist in the natural world, by effectively choosing to act as if they are "real" by intersubjective agreement, we give them the same force as if they *were* "real." Do you agree with this claim? What would be the implications of such a position for classroom practice?

4. Do you believe that educators in American public schools have an obligation to deal with issues of racism and white privilege in the school and classroom? How can educators working in the context of public schools work to challenge institutional and structural racism in our society? How can they address white privilege?

5. Angela Davis has argued that "In a racist society, it is not enough to be non-racist, we must be anti-racist. What do you believe that she meant by this? What are the implications of this for American public schooling?

References

Aniciete, D., & Soloski, K. (2011). The social construction of marriage and a narrative approach to treatment of intra-relationship diversity. *Journal of Feminist Family Therapy, 23*(2), 103-126.

Berger, P., & Luckmann, T. (1966). *The social construction of reality: A treatise in the sociology of knowledge*. London, UK: Penguin.

Blackmon, D. (2008). *Slavery by another name: The re-enslavement of Black Americans from the Civil War to World War II*. New York, NY: Anchor.

Bonnett, A. (1996). Anti-racism and the critique of 'white' identities. *Journal of Ethnic and Migration Studies, 22*(1), 97-110.

Bourne, J. (2001). The life and times of institutional racism. *Race and Class, 43*(2), 7-22.

Brodkin, K. (2010). *How Jews became white folks, and what that says about race in America*. New Brunswick, NJ: Rutgers University Press.

Brown, P. (1995). Naming and framing: The social construction of diagnosis and illness. *Journal of Health and Social Behavior (Extra Issue)*, 34-52.

Case, K. (2007). Raising male privilege awareness and reducing sexism: An evaluation of diversity courses. *Psychology of Women Quarterly, 31*(4), 426-435.

Chong, D. (1991). *Collective action and the Civil Rights Movement*. Chicago, IL: University of Chicago Press.

Conrad, P., & Barker, K. (2010). The social construction of illness: Key insights and policy implications. *Journal of Health and Social Behavior, 51*(1), S67-S79.

Crenshaw, K., Gotanda, N., Peller, C., & Thomas, K. (Eds.). (1995). *Critical race theory: The key writings that formed the movement*. New York, NY: The New Press.

Dei, G. (1993). The challenges of anti-racist education in Canada. *Journal of Canadian Ethnic Studies, 25*(2), 36-51.

Delgado, R., & Stefancic, J. (2017). *Critical race theory: An introduction* (3rd ed.). New York, NY: New York University Press.

Dixson, A., & Rousseau, C. (Eds.). (2006). *Critical race theory in education: All God's children got a song*. New York, NY: Routledge.

Dolan-Del Vecchio, K. (1998). Dismantling white male privilege within family therapy. In M. McGoldrick (Ed.), *Re-visioning family therapy: Race, culture, and gender in clinical practice* (pp. 159-175). New York, NY: Guilford.

Drescher, S. (2009). *Abolition: A history of slavery and anti-slavery.* Cambridge, UK: Cambridge University Press.

Dubow, S. (2014). *Apartheid, 1948-1994.* Oxford, UK: Oxford University Press.

Farley, J. (1988). *Majority-minority relations* (2nd ed.). Upper Saddle River, NJ: Prentice Hall.

Gannon, M. (2016, February 4). Race is a social construct, scientists argue. *Live Science.* Retrieved from https://www.livescience.com/53613-race-is-social-construct-not-scientific.html.

Gergen, K., Lightfoot, C., & Sydow, L. (2004). Social construction: Vistas in clinical child and adolescent psychology. *Journal of Clinical Child and Adolescent Psychology, 33*(2), 389-399.

Gillborn, D. (2006). Critical race theory and education: Racism and anti-racism in educational theory and praxis. *Discourse: Studies in the Cultural Politics of Education, 27*(1), 11-32.

Griffith, D., Mason, M., Yonas, M., Eng, E., Jeffries, V., Plihcik, S., & Parks, B. (2007). Dismantaling institutional racism: Theory and action. *American Journal of Community Psychology, 39*, 381-392.

Guasco, M. (2014). *Slaves and Englishmen: Human bondage in the early modern Atlantic world.* Philadelphia: University of Pennsylvania Press.

Hamilton, D., & Sherman, J. (1994). Stereotypes. In R. Wyer & T. Srull (Eds.), *Handbook of social cognition, Volume 2: Applications* (2nd ed.) (pp. 1-68). New York, NY: Psychology Press.

Hodson, G. (2016, December 5). Race as a social construction. *Psychology Today.* Retrieved from https://www.psychologytoday.com/us/blog/without-prejudice/201612/race-social-construction.

Hoffower, H. (2020, June 8). What it really means to be an anti-racist, and why it's not the same as being an ally. *Business Insider.* Retrieved from https://www.businessinsider.com/what-is-anti-racism-how-to-be-anti-racist-2020-6.

Hubbard, R. (1991). *The politics of women's biology.* New Brunswick, NJ: Rutgers University Press.

Isserman, M., & Kazin, M. (2000). *America divided: The Civil War of the 1960s.* New York, NY: Oxford University Press.

Karumanchery, L. (Ed.). (2005). *Engaging equity: New perspectives on anti-racist education*. Edmonton, Alberta, Canada: Brush Education.

Kendi, I. (2019). *How to be an antiracist*. New York, NY: Random House.

Koehle, H. (2017, April 10). What's the opposite of "socially constructed"? *Radical Reference*. Retrieved from https://medium.com/the-radical-arcanist/whats-the-opposite-of-socially-constructed-a04ec446bd32.

Lever, H. (1982). Ethnicity in South African society. *Humboldt Journal of Social Relations, 10*(1), 239-253.

Lorber, J. (2004). "Night to his day": The social construction of gender. In R. Rothenberg (Ed.), *Race, class and gender in the United States: An integrated study* (6th ed.) (pp. 54-65). New York, NY: Worth Publishers.

Macrae, C., Stangor, C., & Hewstone, M. (Eds.) (1996). *Stereotypes and stereotyping*. New York, NY: Guilford.

Massey, G., Scott, M., & Dornbusch, S. (1975). Racism without racists: Institutional racism in urban schools. *The Black Scholar: Journal of Black Studies and Research, 7*(3), 10-19.

McIntosh, P. (1988). White privilege: Unpacking the invisible knapsack. In A. Filor (Ed.), *Multiculturalism* (pp. 30-36). Schenectady: New York State Council of Educational Associations.

McPherson, J. (1988). *Battle cry of freedom: The Civil War era*. New York, NY: Oxford University Press.

Merton, J. (1949). Discrimination and the American creed. In R. MacIver (Ed.), *Discrimination and national welfare* (pp. 99-126). New York, NY: Institute for Religious Studies.

Morris, A. (1984). *The origins of the Civil Rights Movement: Black communities organizing for change*. New York, NY: The Free Press.

Nengwekhulu, R. (1986). Race, class and ethnicity in South Africa. *African Journal of Political Economy, 1*(1), 29-39.

Norozi, S., & Moen, T. (2016). Childhood as a social construction. *Journal of Social and Educational Research, 6*(2), 75-80.

Norval, A. (1996). *Deconstructing apartheid discourse*. London, UK: Verso.

Ogden, N., Perkins, C., & Donahue, D. (2008). Not a peculiar institution: Challenging students' assumptions about slavery in U.S. history. *The History Teacher, 41*(4), 469-488.

Oskamp, S. (2000). Preface. In S. Oskamp (Ed.), *Reducing prejudice and discrimination* (pp. vii-ix). Mahwah, NJ: Lawrence Erlbaum.

Patterson, R. (2019). *Destructive desires: Rhythm and blues cultural and the politics of racial equality*. New Brunswick, NJ: Rutgers University Press.

Plummer, K. (2015). *Cosmopolitan sexualities: Hope and the humanist imagination*. Cambridge, UK: Polity.

Reagan, T. (2009). The professional status of teachers. In R. Bailey, D. Carr, R. Barrow, & C. McCarthy (Eds.), *The Sage handbook of philosophy of education* (pp. 209-221). London, UK: Sage.

Rock, P. (1998). Murderers, victims and "survivors": The social construction of deviance. *The British Journal of Criminology, 38*(2), 185-200.

Roediger, D. (2008). *How race survived U.S. history: From settlement and slavery to the eclipse of post-racialism*. London, UK: Verso.

Rothenberg, P. (2008). *White privilege: Essential readings on the other side of racism* (3rd ed.). New York, NY: Worth Publishers.

Searle, J. (1995). *The construction of social reality*. New York, NY: The Free Press.

Simmons, D. (2019, October). How to be an antiracist educator. *ASCD Education Update, 61*(10). Retrieved from http://www.ascd.org/publications/newsletters/education-update/oct19/vol61/num10/How-to-Be-an-Antiracist-Educator.aspx.

Solomona, R., Porttelli, J., Daniel, B-J., & Campbell, A. (2005). The discourse of denial: How white teacher candidates construct race, racism and "white privilege." *Race, Ethnicity and Education, 8*(2), 147-169.

Szeftel, M. (1994). Ethnicity and democratization in South Africa. *Review of African Political Economy, 21*(60), 185-199.

Thompson, A. (1997). For: Anti-racist education. *Curriculum Inquiry, 27*(1), 7-44.

Troyna, B. (1987). Beyond multiculturalism: Towards the enactment of anti-racist education in policy, provision and pedagogy. *Oxford Review of Education, 13*(3), 307-320.

UCLA School of Public Affairs. (2009, November 4). UCLA School of Public Affairs: Critical Race Studies. Retrieved from https://spacrs.wordpress.com/what-is-critical-race-theory/.

Williams, J. (1985). Redefining institutional racism. *Ethnic and Racial Studies, 8*(3), 323-348.

Woodworth, S. (2010). *Manifest destinies: America's westward expansion and the road to the Civil War*. New York, NY: Alfred A. Knopf.

Zorowski, R. (1987). To begin the nation anew: Congress, citizenship, and civil rights after the Civil War. *The American Historical Review, 92*(1), 45-68.

Zumudio, M., & Rios, F. (2006). From traditional to liberal racism: Living racism in the everyday. *Sociological Perspectives, 49*(4), 483-501.

Chapter 9

Religion and Religious Diversity in the United States

As long as there are math tests, there will be prayer in the schools. (Anonymous)

In America our public schools are intended to be religiously neutral. Our teachers and schools are neither to endorse nor inhibit religion. I believe this is a very good thing. (Rev. Adam Hamilton)

The United States is among the most religiously diverse nations in the world – there are members of almost every faith on earth found in the U.S., as well as those of no faith. When the new Republic was first established in the late-18th century, the approach to religion of the Founders – and the guarantees of religious freedom embedded in the *Constitution* – were radical for their time. Europe, following centuries of wars and persecutions as Roman Catholics and Protestants fought for dominance in different countries, had generally followed the principle of *cuius regio, eius religio* – "the state follows the religion of the ruler" since the Peace of Augsburg in 1555. This meant, in other words, that a country with a Roman Catholic monarch would be Roman Catholic, and the Roman Catholic Church would be the official state religion, while in a country with a Protestant ruler, the ruler's particular variety of Protestant Christianity would predominate. It was for this reason that Henry VIII's break with the Roman Catholic Church in 1534 was so significant, and why the different religions of the monarchs who followed him on the British throne led to such terrible conflicts (Edward VI, who ruled under a regency, was Protestant, Mary was Roman Catholic, while Elizabeth I was Protestant). In the Muslim world, Islam universally functioned as the official state religion, although non-Muslims who were considered to be "People of the Book" (*'Ahl al-Kitāb*) – that is, Jews and Christians – while not having all of the rights of Muslims in society, were generally granted a number of protections. The religious toleration that has characterized the United States, while far from complete or without blemish, was nevertheless remarkable for the principles upon which it was based. A product of Enlightenment thought, the approach to religion and religious freedom found in the Bill of Rights was unlike that found anywhere in Europe in the 18th century.

The Religious Diversity of the United States

There are no questions on the U.S. Census about religious identity or membership in a particular faith organization, and so it is somewhat difficult to get precise numbers about the size of different religious communities in the country. However, in its 2014 *Religious Landscape Study*, the Pew Research Center, based on telephone interviews with more than 35,000 Americans in all 50 states, documented the religious diversity of the United States as follows:

Religious Affiliation	Percentage of Total Population
CHRISTIAN	70.6%
Evangelical Protestant	25.4%
Mainline Protestant	14.7%
Historically Black Protestant	6.5%
Roman Catholic	20.8%
Mormon (LDS)	1.6%
Orthodox Christian	.5%
Jehovah's Witness	.8%
Other Christian	.4%
NON-CHRISTIAN FAITHS	5.9%
Jewish	1.9%
Muslim	.9%
Buddhist	.7%
Hindu	.7%
OTHER WORLD RELIGIONS	.3%
OTHER FAITHS	1.5%
Unaffiliated (None)	22.8%
Atheist	3.1%
Agnostic	4.0%
Nothing in Particular	15.8%
DON'T KNOW	.6%

Table 9.1 Religious Groups in the United States (Pew Research Center, 2014; Statista, 2020)

Teaching About Religion in Public Schools

As we saw in Chapters 1 and 2, the First Amendment to the U.S. *Constitution* guarantees the of freedom of religion, through both the Establishment Clause and the Free Exercise Clause. Unfortunately, legitimate concerns about the inappropriate teaching of religion have often led to an avoidance of teaching about religion altogether – which is most certainly neither required by the *Constitution* nor educationally sound practice. This has led to a situation in which "most Americans are woefully ignorant of the importance of religion in American and world history" (Moore, 2006, p. 280). As James Moore (2006) has noted,

> Courses about religion – not indoctrinating students into any religion but teaching about major religions and their critical roles in world and American history, jurisprudence, contemporary global affairs, and the humanities – constitutes a very small part of the curriculum in American public schools and universities … Public educational institutions, including colleges and schools of education – reflecting the secularization of America's dominant political, economic, and social institutions and the remarkable success of science in explaining human existence – have removed religion from the curriculum … The removal of religion from the curriculum has occurred because some educators

have misinterpreted the "separation of church and state" doctrine to mean that any discussion of religion in schools is prohibited. (p. 280)

In fact, teaching about religion is extremely important. As Supreme Court Justice William Brennan argued, "It would be impossible to teach meaningfully many subjects in the social sciences or the humanities without some mention of religion" (quoted in Stopsky & Lees, 1994, p. 42).

Christianity

Given that the overwhelming majority of people in the United States self-identify as Christians, and that even non-Christians are likely to be extensively exposed to Christianity in a variety of settings and ways, it may seem strange for us to begin by discussing the history of Christianity and its core beliefs. Surely, you might think, this is material with which virtually everyone in our society is familiar. And yet, in our experience this does not appear to be the case much of the time. To some extent, this is due to the diversity of Christianit*ies* in the United States, but may it also be the result of poor religious education programs in many religious and secular institutions. In any event, we believe that it is essential for teachers to be broadly familiar with the central beliefs of Christianity, the historical development of Christianity, and denominational differences among Christians in the United States.

Christianity is one of the world's three great monotheistic, Abrahamic religious traditions,[1] which means that it is historically linked to both Judaism and Islam. It is based on the life and teachings of Jesus Christ, and initially emerged in 1st century CE Judea as a distinct branch of Judaism. Christians believe that Jesus was the Messiah prophesied in the Jewish Scriptures and that he is the Son of God. The central religious text for Christianity is the Bible, which consists of both the *Old Testament*[2] and the *New Testament*. Christianity is the world's largest religion in terms of numbers of adherents, with nearly 2.5 billion believers around the world.

It is important to understand that Christianity did not emerge as we know it today – it has evolved historically as doctrines, dogmas, organization, and institutional structures, and

---

[1] The Abrahamic religions – Judaism, Christianity, and Islam – all trace their origins to Abraham and his sons (Jews and Christians trace their religions back to Isaac, while Muslims trace Islam back to Ishmael). The single most important shared characteristic of the Abrahamic religions is that all are monotheistic. As a result of the adoption of Christianity as its official state religion by the Roman Empire in the 4th century CE, and the spread of the Islam beginning in the 7th century CE, the Abrahamic religions constitute the single largest grouping of religions by population in the world (see Feiler, 2002; Peters, 2006).

[2] The labels given to the core scriptural texts in the Judeo-Christian tradition are actually somewhat problematic. What Christians refer to as the "Old Testament" includes a number of different Jewish texts: the *Torah* itself, which consists of the five "Books of Moses" (Genesis, Exodus, Leviticus, Numbers, and Deuteronomy), the Prophets (*Nevi'im*) and the Writings (*Ketuvim*). All of these texts taken together are called the *Tanakh*. For Jews, it is obviously misleading to talk about the *Tanakh* as the "Old" Testament, since they do not recognize the *New Testament*.

both internal and external challenges have changed. For example, the *New Testament* itself, originally written in Greek and Aramaic, was not codified until the late-4th century CE, and there is considerable debate about when each of the four gospels was written. In the first few centuries after the death of Jesus, there were numerous Church councils that sought to determine and articulate orthodox Christian beliefs, condemn various heresies, establish acceptable and unacceptable practices in the Church, and so on – and sometimes with one Council overturning the decisions of another Council.[3] Furthermore, Christianity is by no means a uniform or unitary faith. Most Christians and Christian denominations (but by no means all) accept some version of the Nicene Creed,[4] which includes the following as essential parts of the Christian faith:

- Belief in God the Father, Jesus Christ as the Son of God, and the Holy Spirit (i.e., the Trinity).
- The crucifixion, death, and resurrection and ascension of Christ.
- The holiness of the Church and the communion of saints.
- The Second Coming of Jesus, the Day of Judgment, and the salvation of the faithful.

There are, broadly speaking, four different "branches" of Christian churches: the Roman Catholic Church, the Protestant churches, the Eastern Orthodox Churches, and the Oriental Orthodox Churches. Each of these "branches" of Christianity is the result of historical events and theological differences tied to particular times, places, and issues (see Chadwick, 1995; Dowley, 2013; Green, 1996). Even in the early centuries of Christianity, there was a diversity of Christians who believed somewhat different things, practiced their faith in different ways, had different organizational structures for their local communities, and accepted different scriptures. We know, for instance, that in the Ante-Nicene period (prior to 325 CE), there were

---

[3] Between 325 CE and 787 CE, there were a total of seven generally accepted "ecumenical councils," all summoned by the Byzantine Emperor, to attempt to reach a consensus on a variety of theological and practical matters. These Councils dealt with such matters as the nature of the Trinity, the divinity and humanity of Christ, the nature of Christ's will, condemnations of specific heresies (such as Arianism, Nestorianism, Monophysitism, and Monothelitism), and the rejection of iconoclasm, as well as the date for the celebration of Easter, ordination, disputes about bishops and sees, and a host of other issues. The Roman Catholic and Eastern Orthodox Churches accept the legitimacy of all seven of these Ecumenical Councils, while the Oriental Orthodox Churches (including the Armenian Apostolic Church, the Coptic Orthodox Church, and the Ethiopian Orthodox Tewahedo Church) accept only the first three. Most Protestant Christians accept the *outcomes* of the first seven Councils (though they maintain that the teachings of the Councils were not new doctrines but only explanations of existing ones); the Roman Catholic Church has had multiple church councils since 787 that it also considers valid, and the Eastern Orthodox Church maintains that there is the possibility of other ecumenical councils.

[4] The Nicene Creed is a commonly used statement of Christian belief. Originally developed at the Council of Nicaea in 325 CE, and amended at the First Council of Constantinople in 381 CE, it is widely accepted by the Roman Catholic Church, the Eastern Orthodox Churches, the Oriental Orthodox Churches, the Church of the East, and many Protestant dominations, including the Anglican Communion.

Orthodox Priest
© Svetlana Lazarenka/Shutterstock.com

a wide array of different Christian sects and movements, many with quite distinct views about what constituted the Christian Scripture, how Scripture should be interpreted, the nature of Jesus and the Trinity, and a host of other factors (see Bauer, 1971; Ehrman, 2003; Hengel, 1983; Pagels, 1979). Although most of these early non-Orthodox groups no longer exist, the Christian Church has historically been more divided in terms of practices, structures, and beliefs that many of its believers may claim. One of the consequences on the internal diversity of Christianity has been the existence, since the very early periods of Christian history right up to the present, of debates about who "counts" as *Christian* and who does not. The answer to this question, on the one hand, is quite simple: Jews, Muslims, Buddhists, and so on, are not considered to be Christians, either by the broad Christian community or by their own communities of faith. The problem comes from primarily within the Christian community: Some groups maintain, for instance, that Roman Catholics are not Christian, while others would argue that members of the Church of Jesus Christ of Latter Day Saints or Jehovah's Witnesses should not be considered Christian. Although we do not wish to minimize the significance of these questions, which are grounded in deeply held and debated theological positions and in important historical contexts, they are really matters for members within the larger Christian community to decide and are really beyond our concerns here.

Church with Martin Luther Banner
© Mirko Kuzmanovic/Shutterstock.com

For the most part, since Christianity is normative in the United States, there are not major issues in which there are tensions related to *most* Christian students in public school contexts. However, this is not universally true, and there are a number of Christian denominations with beliefs and practices that *do* require awareness and sensitivity on the part of educators. Examples of such issues include:

- Jehovah's Witnesses do not observe holidays and customs that they consider to have pagan origins (which include Christmas, Easter, and birthdays). They also do not participate in reciting the Pledge of Allegiance or singing the national anthem.
- Seventh Day Adventists often follow very healthy, but also extremely strict, diets, including not eating any food identified as "unclean" in the Bible. More than one-third of Seventh Day Adventists are vegetarians.
- Christian Scientists are best known for their view that disease is best treated through prayer, by Christian Science Practitioners. Although the Church does not require its members to reject all medical care, it does teach that Christian Science prayer is most effective when not combined with medical treatment. Some Christian Scientists will allow their children to be vaccinated, but others do not do so. There have been a number of court cases about the medical treatment of children of Christian Scientists; the American Academy of Pediatrics has indicated that in its view the failure to seek appropriate medical care for children is "child neglect, regardless of the motivation."
- Some Mennonites will not participate in the singing of the national anthem because they believe it to be militaristic.
- Although there is not any formal, institutional position on the matter, many Quakers (Friends) will not say the Pledge of Allegiance.
- Some conservative Christians find any literature, games, or other materials dealing with witchcraft, magic, sorcery, and so on extremely objectionable, and even Satanic. This can include literature that is otherwise widely accepted in American society, such as the Harry Potter novels.
- Some Christians believe that the teachings of the school in certain areas, such as evolutionary theory, are inherently hostile to Christians and Christianity, due to perceived conflicts with the teachings of the Bible.

It is obviously – and emphatically – not the task of the public school to teach children what they should believe with respect to religion. It is our task, however, to do our very best to accommodate the needs of, and show respect to, all religious minorities, whether Christian or non-Christian, within reason and insofar as it is practicable.[5]

---

[5] The issue of practicality is an important one. Some religious accommodations are absolutely essential (e.g., not requiring students to recite the Pledge of Allegiance or permitting students to wear a head covering), while others are context-dependent. In a school with a single Jewish student, for instance, a request for the school to provide kosher lunches would not be a reasonable accommodation (though it would be inappropriate to expect the child to eat non-kosher foods; alternatives should be possible). In a school with a relatively significant Jewish population, not holding school during major Jewish holidays might make sense, while in a community in which there are very few Jews, appropriate accommodation would not require closing the schools altogether.

Is the United States a "Christian Nation"?

It is sometimes claimed that the United States is, and was founded as, a Christian nation. For example, President George W. Bush once commented that "The United States is a Christian nation founded on Christian principles and beliefs," and former Senator and Attorney General Jeff Sessions has been quoted as asserting that "Separation of church and state is unconstitutional."[6] In fact, answering this question is difficult, since the question itself can mean different things. If the intent of saying that the United States is a Christian nation is to indicate that a majority of citizens in the country identify themselves as Christians, then it is obviously true. Similarly, if the intent of saying that the United States is a Christian nation is to indicate that many of its founding principles were grounded in an historical context that had developed in and out of the Judeo-Christian tradition,[7] then it is also (though somewhat less clearly) true. However, if the intent of saying that the United States is a Christian nation is to indicate that it is a country in which Christianity is in some sense its "official" or "national" religion, then the claim is true neither historically nor constitutionally. One powerful articulation of this point was provided by President Jimmy Carter, arguably one of the most religious of modern U.S. Presidents:

> Last year I was on Pat Robertson's show, and we discussed our basic Christian faith – for instance, separation of church and state. It's contrary to my beliefs to try to exalt Christianity as having some sort of preferential status in the United States. That violates the *Constitution*. I'm not in favor of mandatory prayer in school or of using public funds to finance religious education.

Are There Anti-Christian Biases in American Society?

There is a final point that we wish to raise here, and it is an important one in any serious discussion about the role of religion in American society in general, and in U.S. public schools in particular. As we have noted, roughly 75% of the population of the United States self-identifies as Christian – and while for many, such identification is incredibly important, even central to their core beliefs and way of life, for many others the identification as Christian may mean a good deal less. For many, perhaps even most, Americans, Christianity is, as we have seen, normative – a kind of "default" religious identity. In fact, to a considerable extent our society is

---

[6] As Daniel Patrick Moynihan once commented, "Everyone is entitled to his own opinion, but not his own facts." In spite of their respective exalted positions, both President Bush and Senator Sessions were simply wrong about this matter, as the Supreme Court has consistently ruled. Nor, we would note, is this a change from even the earliest years of the Republic. John Adams, arguably one of the most religious of the Founders, wrote about the *Treat of Tripoli* in 1797 that "The United States is not a Christian nation any more than it is a Jewish or Mohammedan nation."

[7] The idea that there is a single, monolithic Judeo-Christian tradition is one that is widely held, and certainly makes sense insofar as one wishes to point out that Christianity is historically grounded in the Judaism of the 1st century CE and that they share many scriptural texts, doctrinal tenets and beliefs. However, it is also important to note that for most of the past two millennia, Judaism and Christianity have developed quite differently, often oppositionally, and, further, that even the concept of the Judeo-Christian tradition is largely a quite recent one (see Gatson, 2019).

a secular one in which religion plays a fairly minor role in many people's lives. It is when we take this into account that claims that Christians are in some sense being persecuted by non-Christians need to be understood. Such claims focus not on persecution by other religious traditions, for the most part, but rather on the belief that "secular humanism" – essentially, non-religious (or, on some accounts, anti-religious) ideologies -- is challenging the belief systems and practices of believers. One may question such assertions, of course, but it is probably not appropriate to question the sincerity of those who make such claims. It is also the case, of course, that whether or not Christians in general are persecuted, there is no doubt at all that particular *groups* of Christians certainly have been discriminated against in American history – as the cases of the Quakers, Roman Catholics, Mormons, and many other Christian groups make abundantly clear.

Judaism

Of the three great Abrahamic religions in the United States – Judaism, Christianity, and Islam – Judaism is by far the oldest, with a history going back thousands of years. The religious literature dates it back at least as far as 1,500 BCE; the earliest external documentation of the Jews dates to the Merneptah Stele, which has been dated to between 1,200 and 1,213 BCE. In contemporary American society, Jews constitute the second largest religious community, after Christianity, but even so they are less than 2% of the total population of the country. Jews also constitute a relatively small part of the world's population, around .2% of the total population, concentrated primarily in the United States (43%) and Israel (43%).

Any discussion about Jews and Judaism will be extremely complex because, unlike Christianity and Islam, Jews are an *ethnoreligious* group rather than simply a religion. In other words, being Jewish does not require that one accept any particular set of beliefs or practices – Jews are most typically Jews by birth.[8] During most of the history of the Jewish people, conversion to Judaism has not been encouraged; indeed, in some times and places, it has essentially been forbidden.[9] The concern with and commitment to proselytism that characterizes both Christianity and Islam has not been a general feature of Judaism. This does not mean that Judaism is not a religion, though – it most certainly is. It simply means that while Judaism is a religious faith, it is far more than that definition because in essence, it is an ethnic civilization that encompasses cultural, religious, linguistic, and legal elements dating back millennia. These facets help to explain why the Jews are sometimes called an ethnic group, a

---

[8] In Judaism, one's status as a Jew is determined matrilineally. If you have a Jewish mother, you are considered Jewish; if your mother is not Jewish, then you are not Jewish. The status of one's father, at least in traditional Judaism, is irrelevant. In recent years, the Reform Movement has modified this rule to some extent, recognizing patrilineal descent in cases where a child is raised Jewish – but this status is not recognized by the other religious movements in Judaism.

[9] During the Middle Ages, for instance, in many places conversion to Judaism meant that both the convert and members of the Jewish community might be executed. Under such circumstances, a tradition developed to discourage or forbid conversion. Even today, individuals are commonly discouraged from conversion, although the extent to which this is true varies among the different Jewish movements.

national group, a religious group, and so on.[10] The most commonly accepted terminology is to talk about the "Jewish people." It also helps to explain why the question, "Who is a Jew?" is an incredibly complex and controversial one within the Jewish community.[11]

Menorah
© Fevziie/Shutterstock.com

Jews have, for most of their history, been a diasporic community – in other words, they have lived in a diaspora rather than in their own country (Küng, 1991). The Babylonian exile, which took place in three waves, beginning in 597 BCE, saw the destruction of the First Temple and the political and religious élite of the society taken from the Kingdom of Judah to Babylon. The more significant exile, though, took place in the 1st and 2nd centuries CE, after the Great Revolt and the Bar Kokhba revolt, when the Second Temple was destroyed by the Romans and large numbers of Jews were dispersed throughout the Roman Empire. The religious Judaism of the 1st century was temple-based and sacrificial, and the destruction of the Temple led to major changes in Judaism, most notably the development of what is called Rabbinic Judaism.[12] Basically, Rabbinic Judaism has traditionally been built on the idea that Moses received the *Torah* (both the Written *Torah* and the "Oral *Torah*") from God at Mt. Sinai, and transmitted it in its full and complete form to the Jewish people. The role of the rabbis has been to interpret the *Torah* and to offer legal (*halakhic*) decisions based on the *Torah*. Jews migrated to many different parts of the Roman Empire, and then to other parts of the world, bringing Rabbinic Judaism with them. Each new locale, though, also provided new ideas, insights, experiences, and languages, and so the Jewish experience over time became an extremely multilingual,

---

[10] The Jewish people can be legitimately conceptualized in a number of different ways. However, what they are *not* is a racial group.

[11] There is a simple, *halakhically* sound answer to this question, which is that a Jew is anyone whose mother was Jewish, or who has undergone an appropriate conversion. However, in practice this definition turns out to be extremely problematic.

[12] It is commonly suggested that Christianity grew out of Judaism, but this is somewhat misleading. Both early Christianity and Rabbinic Judaism co-existed in the 1st century CE as competing kinds of Judaism – and there were a number of other sorts of Judaism at that point in time as well.

multiethnic, and multicultural one. Jews thus had both a Jewish identity and an identity grounded in the society in which they lived.

In an examination of the religious aspects of Judaism, we can start by discussing the key religious texts of the Jewish faith. A central feature of Judaism is its textual tradition, and this tradition has at its core the *Torah* (the "Five Books of Moses" – Genesis, Exodus, Leviticus, Numbers, and Deuteronomy).[13] The *Torah* is just one part of the Jewish scriptural tradition, however – in addition to the *Torah* itself, the *Tanakh* (the Hebrew "Bible"), includes not only the *Torah* but also the *Nevi'im* (Prophets) and *Ketuvim* (Writings). The *Tanakh* is basically what Christians called the *Old Testament*.[14] As important as these fundamental religious texts are, though, the focus of Jewish scholarship and learning for centuries has been a large body of work called the *Talmud*, which has been the central text of teaching and study in Rabbinic Judaism. The *Talmud* is a collection of writings about Jewish religious law, theology, and interpretation; there are actually two distinct *Talmuds*, the *Babylonian Talmud* (compiled in the 3rd to 6th centuries) and the *Jerusalem Talmud* (compiled in the 4th century), but it is the former that is most often meant when we talk about "the" *Talmud*.

Challah, Candles and Wine
© tomertu/Shutterstock.com

In most religions, there is some sort of document that presents the core, necessary beliefs of the religion – for instance, in Christianity this would, for most Christians, be the "Apostle's Creed" or the "Nicene Creed." Although there have been many attempts to create such a list of core beliefs for Judaism, none has been universally accepted. Probably the closest to achieve such status in Judaism were the "Thirteen Principles of Faith" produced by the great Jewish thinker Maimonides in the 12th century, but even that effort was never completely accepted (see Kraemer, 2008). In fact, throughout history, Judaism has tended to focus more on practices and observances than it has on specific statements of belief.

---

[13] In a synagogue, it is the handwritten *Torah* scroll (the *Sefer Torah*) that is kept in the Ark, that is read from during synagogue services.

[14] From a Jewish perspective, it is inappropriate to refer to the *Tanakh* as the "Old Testament" – this makes no sense, since for Judaism there is no "new" testament.

Torah
© John Theodor/Shutterstock.com

Among the most important set of practices and observances in Judaism historically have been those dealing with *halakha*, or Jewish law. *Halakha* is concerned not just with religious practices but also with virtually all aspects of everyday life. Traditionally, *halakha* was viewed as divine law, commanded by God in the *Torah* and reinforced by rabbinic laws and decrees, customs, traditions, and so on. One of the most obvious examples of *halakha* are the laws governing *kashrut*. Basically, these are the dietary laws that have been traditionally observed in Judaism. The rules of *kashrut* are quite complex, but they are grounded in the following broad principles:

- Only certain kinds of animals and birds can be eaten; others (such as pork and shellfish) cannot be consumed.
- Kosher animals and birds must be slaughtered in a particular way, intended to minimize any pain that the animal might experience.
- No blood from any animal may be consumed (blood is removed from meat by a process of salting and soaking in water).
- Meat and dairy products cannot be eaten together, or even prepared using the same instruments.

It is important to note here that *halakha* applies only to Jews; non-Jews are bound only by what are called the Noahide (or Noachian) Laws, which were the seven biblical laws given to Adam, and then Noah, before the revelation to Moses on Mt. Sinai. The Noahide Laws are believed to be binding on all of humanity.

What we have said thus far is about historic Judaism, but it does not represent the daily practice of most Jews in North America (or, for that matter, in Israel) today. Actual religious observance varies significantly from one person to another and is also tied in part to the particular Jewish "denomination" with which one is affiliated. There are three major Jewish religious movements in the United States, though individual congregations and individuals inevitably vary with respect to observance. The three major movements in Judaism are

Orthodox Judaism, Conservative Judaism, and Reform Judaism.[15] In addition to the formal, institutional Jewish religious movements, it should be noted that a majority of American Jews are actually secular — that is, they are unaffiliated with any of the institutional movements in contemporary Judaism and as a general rule do not observe any of the traditions associated with religious Judaism.[16] However, for the most part they still identify as Jewish and are identified by other Jews as Jewish.

Jews in the United States are often thought of as an ethnic group, and while this is true to some extent, it is also somewhat misleading — it assumes that the largest group of American Jews (who are Ashkenazi Jews, from Europe and typically from Yiddish-speaking backgrounds) represent "Jews" in the country. This is simply not true; *within* the Jewish community, there is also considerable ethnic diversity. It is possible to categorize Jews into three major groups based on their backgrounds: the Ashkenazi Jews, the Sephardic Jews, and the Mizrahi Jews.[17] The largest single group of Jews in the United States are the Ashkenazim, whose ancestors were the part of the Jewish diaspora that settled initially in France and Germany, and over several centuries moved east into Central Europe and Poland, as well as into Belarus, Estonia, Latvia, Lithuania, Russia, and the Ukraine. Ashkenazi Jews in Western Europe benefited in the 18th and 19th centuries from the liberalization and secularization of their societies,[18] and began assimilating into the dominant cultures in which they lived. In Eastern Europe, and especially in the part of the Russian Empire known as the "Pale of Settlement,"[19] such assimilation and

---

[15] There are other Jewish movements, including Reconstructionist and Humanistic Judaism. It is extremely important to understand that from a Jewish perspective, while members of all of these movements — as well as secular Jews with no religious affiliation, including agnostics and even atheists -- are considered to be Jewish, this is *not* the case with Messianic Jews, such as the "Jews for Jesus." Such individuals and groups are seen as Christians. Regardless of whether they employ Jewish ceremonial objects, observe Jewish religious holidays, and so on, they are nevertheless not considered to be Jewish.

[16] This varies by individual, of course. Many otherwise non-observant Jews do attend services on Rosh Hashanah and Yom Kippur, and many maintain family traditions grounded in Judaism (for instance, not eating pork).

[17] There are a number of other groups that self-identify as Jewish, but about whom mainstream Judaism has had some concerns. The status of Beta Israel (the Ethiopian Jews), for instance, is a case in point. In 1973, the Ministry of Absorption in Israel ruled that the Beta Israel population was "foreign in all aspects to the Jewish nation," and thus not eligible to make *aliyah* to Israel. Shortly after this ruling, the Sephardic Chief Rabbi of Israel, Rabbi Ovadia Yosef, ruled that Beta Israel were indeed descendants of Israelites, and further, that providing them with a Jewish education and granting them the right to make *aliyah* was a *mitzvah*. In 1977, the Israeli government determined that the Israeli "Law of Return" applied to Beta Israel, and several major transport actions (Operation Moses, Operation Joshua and Operation Solomon) brought large numbers of Beta Israel to Israel.

[18] This period, called the Enlightenment and began in the 1770s, is known as the *Haskalah* in Judaism.

[19] In tsarist Russia, from 1791 to 1917 Jews were restricted to a particular part of the Russian Empire — called the Черта оседлости in Russian, the "Pale of Settlement." This "Pale of Settlement" included much of contemporary Ukraine, Belarus, Latvia, Lithuania, Moldova, and parts of western Russia. It was only in the "Pale of Settlement" that the overwhelming majority of Jews were allowed to reside, and even within the Pale of Settlement there were a number of cities in which they were not allowed to live.

emancipation was for the most part not possible, and the Jews remained a distinctive ethnic, cultural, linguistic, and religious civilization. The language of this community was Yiddish, which is related to German but which also has many elements drawn from Hebrew and Aramaic, as well as both the Romance and Slavic languages. The second major group of Jews are the Sephardim, who are the descendants of the Jews expelled from Spain and Portugal in the late-15th century as part of the *Reconquista*. The Sephardim settled in North Africa, Southeastern and Southern Europe, Anatolia, the Levant, and the Americas. The third group of Jews are the Mizrahim. Prior to the establishment of the state of Israel, the Mizrahim typically identified themselves as Sephardim rather than as a distinctive subgroup, and even today there is some ambiguity about the use of the two terms.[20] Generally speaking, the Mizrahim are Jews from North Africa and the Middle East; they are the descendants of Babylonian Jews and were concentrated in Iran, Iraq, Kurdistan, Syria, Yemen, and so on. They constitute a small minority of the Jews in the United States, and are often overlooked by those who focus only on the Ashkenazim-Sephardim distinction (see Dromi, 2020). These divisions are internal divisions, brought about by a number of factors, but members of all of these groups see themselves, and are seen by others, as being Jewish.

As a future educator, there are a number of things that you should be familiar with in terms of Judaism and having Jewish students in your classes. In general, many of these points – while presented here with respect to the specific case of Judaism – are actually good pedagogical points that would be relevant in dealing with any student or group of students. In addition, we would argue that in the cases of both Judaism and Islam, some degree of knowledge about our fellow Americans would be valuable not only for any teacher, but indeed, for any citizen.

Shofar
© John Theodor/Shutterstock.com

First, there are a number of major holidays that are celebrated or observed during the year.[21] As is true in all religions, of course, some of these are of considerably more importance than others. The major Jewish holidays include:

---

[20] For example, in contemporary Israel there are two Chief Rabbis -- one for Ashkenazi Jews and one for Sephardic Jews. The Mizrahim fall under the authority of the Sephardic Chief Rabbi.

[21] The Jewish calendar is lunar, unlike the secular one, which is solar. This explains why most Jewish holidays do not take place at the same time (i.e., according to the solar calendar) each year.

Rosh Hashanah.
Yom Kippur.
Sukkot.
Hanukkah.
Purim.
Pesach (Passover).

Of the holidays listed here, by far the most significant from a Jewish perspective are *Rosh Hashanah* (the New Year) and *Yom Kippur* (the Day of Atonement). These take place during the fall, and are the two occasions on which Jews are most likely to attend services at a synagogue – regardless of whether they normally attend services or not. Together, *Rosh Hashanah* and *Yom Kippur* (as well as the period between the two) are called the "High Holidays." These are days when most Jews are unlikely to engage in work, attend school, and so on. In school districts in which there is a large Jewish population, schools are often closed on these days. *Sukkot* (the "Feast of Tabernacles") is a reminder of the three pilgrimages that the Israelites were required to make to the Temple when it still existed. Today, it is perhaps best known as the holiday when a *sukkah* is constructed. The celebration of *Hanukkah* in the contemporary United States is especially interesting because, while it is indeed a traditional Jewish holiday, its relative significance has increased as a way of countering the role of Christmas in the more general society. This has led some people to consider *Hanukkah* to be the "Jewish Christmas," and even to the mixing of the two holidays – Christmas trees with Stars of David on them, nativity scenes next to menorahs, and so on, but this is inaccurate both in terms of the Jewish meaning of *Hanukkah* and the Christian meaning and importance of Christmas. *Purim* is a holiday that is based on the account in the *Book of Esther* of the efforts of Haman to destroy the Jews in the Persian Empire, and of how Haman was defeated by Mordecai and his adopted daughter Esther, who had become the Queen. *Purim* is a celebratory occasion, and sometimes involves activities that might seem to be a bit like Halloween to outsiders, though for very different reasons (masquerades are a common part of celebrations of *Purim*, for instance). Finally, *Pesach* (or Passover) recounts the exodus of the Jews from Egypt. The Passover Seder, or meal, is a central feature of the celebration of *Pesach*.

In addition to simply being aware of the major Jewish holidays, there are a number of other things that are relevant for the classroom teacher to be aware of in dealing with Judaism and the needs of Jewish students. It is important, though, that you keep in mind that these are generalizations that will apply to some students, parents, community members, and so on, and not at all to others – just as would be true with respect to any other group.

- Although most Jews no longer observe the laws of *kashrut*, some do. Public schools are *not* required to provide fully kosher meals for students, but they should be sure that there are reasonable options available to such students. Vegetarian meals, for instance, are generally perfectly acceptable. If you have any question about dietary restrictions (kosher issues, halal issues in Islam, food issues for Hindu students, medical issues such as nut allergies, etc.), the best thing to do is to simply ask parents about restrictions and concerns and about how these can be accommodated.

- As is true with many other groups, more observant Jews may be concerned with ensuring that modesty can be maintained. This does not refer to what others can or should wear — but it does mean that the school should be aware of the fact that certain kinds of clothing (and activities) may not be acceptable to some families. Public schools are not expected to provide same-sex or gender-segregated classrooms as a general rule, for instance, but do need to recognize and accommodate the fact that co-educational swimming or physical education classes may be problematic, and should offer reasonable accommodations.

- Many public schools have dress codes that have been created for a variety of reasons, including as a result of worries about safety, concerns about maintaining a particular kind of school climate and environment, minimizing distractions that might interfere with the academic tasks of the school, and so on. For example, as a general rule it is quite common for a school to have a "no hats or caps" rule. For most students, this is not a problem, and the rule is a very reasonable one. However, for some students this conflicts with religious obligations — Jewish students wearing *kippot*, Muslim girls wearing the *hijab*, Sikh students wearing turbans, and so on. In cases such as these, the student's constitutional right to the free exercise of religion takes precedence over any other rationale that the school might offer.

- In the modern world, many of us deliberately seek to be religiously inclusive. This is not an intrinsically bad thing, but it can sometimes lead to oversimplifications and distortions of important differences among students. For example, it is inaccurate to think of Christianity as simply "Judaism with Christ." Such a view is a distortion of both Judaism and Christianity. Although they do share a common historical tradition up to a certain point, and while some scriptural texts are the same, they should be seen as distinct, independent religions. Certainly from a Jewish perspective, Judaism is in no way "incomplete," nor is Christianity simply a "finished" or "complete" form of Judaism.

- When we are dealing with a child from a "minority" group in the school – whether an ethnic or racial group, a linguistic group, or a religious group – it is important to remember that they are first and foremost an individual. Do not assume that any person -- a child, colleague, or parent -- can or does speak for their entire group or community. Although no harm or offense may be intended, a question directed to a Jewish student such as, "Richard, what do Jews believe about *x*?" is deeply problematic, and is troubling for several reasons. First, it is unfair to ask a child (or any person) to speak an entire group of which they may be a member. Even more, though, such a question can have no answer. Within every group, on almost any question, different individuals will have different answers. Indeed, there is an old Yiddish saying specifically about this: "If there are two Jews in a room, there are three opinions." And, the more important or more controversial a matter might be, the more impossible an answer to a question such as "What do *x* believe?" becomes.

Anti-Semitism in American Society

Just as the American response to immigration has been ambiguous over our history, so too has been the response of parts of the dominant society to religious minorities. There has been ongoing anti-Roman Catholic sentiment in many parts of the nation, and smaller Christian religious groups – including the Quakers, the Jehovah's Witnesses, Christian Scientists, and certainly the Church of Jesus Christ of Latter Day Saints (the Mormons) – have been persecuted. In recent years, as the Muslim population of the United States has increased, we have also witnessed the rise of considerable Islamophobia, as we will discuss in the next part of this chapter. The situation with respect to Jewish Americans and anti-Semitism[22] is both similar to and different from these other kinds of religious bias.

Although the term "anti-Semitism" was first coined in 1879, the phenomenon of anti-Jewish persecutions dates back millennia (see Nirenberg, 2013). In the Byzantine Empire, the *Theodosian Code* and the *Code of Justinian* both restricted the legal status of Jews; more violent examples of anti-Semitism included the Rhineland massacres of 1896, the Edict of Expulsion in England in 1290, the ongoing persecutions of Jews in Europe during the Black Death, the massacres of Spanish Jews in 1391, the expulsion of the Jews from Spain in 1492 and from Portugal in 1496, the massacres in the Ukraine from 1648 to 1657, various pogroms in the Russian Empire throughout the 19th and early 20th centuries, the Dreyfus affair in France in the late 19th and early 20th centuries, the Holocaust during the Nazi period, and Soviet anti-Jewish policies especially under Stalin. Given this historical background, the situation in America has been a remarkable one for Jews. From the earliest days of the history of the United States, there have been small Jewish communities in parts of the United States, and for the most part

---

[22] The term "anti-Semitism" is misleading because it seems to suggest that the biases involved target all Semitic people – which would include Arabs, Assyrians, and so on. In fact, it historically refers only to anti-Jewish sentiment. It was a late-19th century German term that was used to replace *Judenhass* ("Jew-hatred") and is virtually universally used solely with reference to Jews.

there has not been widespread anti-Semitism in the country. It is useful to distinguish between anti-Semitic attitudes, beliefs, and even some behaviors from specific anti-Semitic incidents that threaten the safety or security of individuals. Although the former have always been present in North America, the latter have been fairly unusual, though not altogether absent. Interestingly, over the past 15 years two different trends have been occurring in the United States with respect to attitudes toward Jewish Americans. The Anti-Defamation League (ADL) has documented a significant decline in anti-Semitic attitudes in recent years, with individuals with anti-Semitic views and beliefs dropping from almost 30% in the early 1960s to only about 15% today. To put this in a broader context, according to an ABC News poll in 2007, almost 35% of all Americans reported having "some racist feelings," and although 6% reported prejudice against Jews, 25% indicated that they felt prejudice against Arab Americans and 10% reported feeling prejudice against *latinx* people (ABC News, 2007) At the same time, though, data from the Federal Bureau of Investigation indicate that Jews have been the most commonly targeted group for religiously-motivated hate crimes since 1991 (Anti-Defamation League, 2019). Anti-Semitic attacks against synagogues, especially since 2016, are powerful reminders of this phenomenon.

Anti-Semitism is actually a very complex matter, because it can take a variety of different forms and is grounded in many different sets of claims. In a powerful three-volume study of anti-Semitism, Louis Harap (1987) has pointed out that "anti-Semitism is an apparently simple term which, on further scrutiny, reveals considerable complexity" (p. 24). He goes on to suggest different varieties or types of anti-Semitism, including:

- Religious anti-Semitism.
- Economic anti-Semitism.
- Racist anti-Semitism.
- Ideological anti-Semitism.
- Social and cultural anti-Semitism.

These kinds of anti-Semitism and the broader claims and assertions that they support can and frequently do overlap. What is most important here is to understand precisely what these claims really are – unsubstantiated claims that are in fact simply not true. Christ was not in fact killed by the Jews (a proposition that the Roman Catholic Church has now denounced), Jews do not secretly control the economy (claims about individuals like George Soros – a common target of anti-Semites – notwithstanding), they are not an inferior race (because, first, there is no such thing as an "inferior" or "superior" race, and second, because they do not constitute a racial group in any case), they do not share a common ideology (there are right-wing, left-wing, revolutionary, counter-revolutionary, reactionary, political and apolitical Jews), and they are not a threat to the culture and society in which they live (indeed, they are most often active and supportive members of their societies).

In contemporary American society, blatantly anti-Semitic beliefs and claims are rare and unusual. What are far more common, and perhaps more dangerous, is that there are also what might be called anti-Semitic "tropes" or "dog whistles" – themes or particular terminology that will appeal to anti-Semites while at the same time not sounding clearly anti-Semitic to others. Among the more common of these "tropes" are messages about divided loyalties, perceived power (especially economic power and control of the media), and assumptions about in-group clannishness. Perhaps one of the more dangerous and offensive elements of contemporary anti-Semitism are various efforts at Holocaust denial – that is, arguments and claims that the Holocaust itself is simply a created fiction. Such claims have been powerfully repudiated both by historians and in the courts, but they nevertheless do continue to appear on occasion – though more often in some other countries than in the United States (see Lipstadt, 1993; Shermer & Grobman, 2000).

Islam[23]

More than two decades ago, John Esposito (1994) argued that "a basic knowledge of Islam is becoming essential for every American today …. Islam, like Judaism and Christianity, is an *American* religion" (p. 243, emphasis added). The recognition of this fact has been, and continues to be, problematic in many settings in the United States. The conflation of Islam with what has been labelled "militant Islam" coupled with perceived ties of Islam to terrorism (especially in the post-9/11 era), all contribute to the challenges that are faced by Muslim children in public schools, as does the more general politicization of the discourse about Islam.

Islam is a relatively recent part of the religious diversity that characterizes American society. Although there were small numbers of Muslims in the country as early as the late-19th century CE (and in fact far earlier),[24] it was not really until after the Second World War that a robust Muslim community began to develop (see Haniff, 2003, pp. 303-304). By the 1990s, both the number of Muslims in the United States and their visibility had grown substantially – according to the Council on American-Islamic Relations (CAIR), between 1994 and 2000 the number of mosques in the country increased by 25% (from 962 to 1209), while the total number of mosque-goers had increased by 300% (from .5 million to over 2 million; Council on American-Islamic Relations, 2001). Reliable data on religious affiliation are not easy to come by in the United States, but the most reliable estimates suggest that there are between 4 and 5 million Muslims in the country, which means that Muslims constitute the third largest religious group in the nation after Christians and Jews.[25] Demographically, there are five significant facets of the Muslim population in the United States:

- Muslims are extremely diverse ethnically and linguistically, including groups from some 80 different countries.

---

[23] Much of this section of the chapter is based on Reagan (2020), used here with permission.

[24] In fact, the earliest Muslims in North America were undoubtedly enslaved Africans – a fascinating and important historical point that was largely ignored until the 1998 publication of Sylviane Diouf (see Diouf, 2013).

[25] According to the Pew Research Center, "Muslims in the U.S. are *not* as numerous as the number of Americans who identify as Jewish … but projections suggest that the U.S. Muslim population will grow much faster than the country's Jewish population. By 2040, Muslims will replace Jews as the nation's second-largest religious group after Christians. And by 2050, the U.S. Muslim population is projected to reach 8.1 million, or 2.1% of the nation's total population -- nearly twice the share of today" (Mohamed, 2018).

- The Muslim population is disproportionately composed of immigrants (some 64% of U.S. Muslims are foreign-born), although this is changing as increasing numbers of American Muslims are native-born.
- The Muslim population is young (47% of Muslims in the United States are 35 years of age or younger, and 61% are under the age of 49).
- Both the number and percentage of Muslims in the United States are growing rapidly, and by 2050 Muslims will constitute the second largest religious group in the United States.
- The Muslim population it is concentrated in specific parts of the United States, including parts of California, Florida, Illinois, Michigan, New Jersey, New York, and Ohio.[26] (Council on American-Islamic Relations, 2001)

The Muslim population in the United States is also distinctive in several other significant ways. Unlike the situation in Western Europe, for instance, Muslims in America are better educated than the general population of the country (58% of Muslims have college degrees, while only 37% of the general population are college-educated), they are economically prosperous (28% of the Muslim population have incomes of $75,000 or more, in comparison with just 17% of the general population), and while formal religious affiliation is declining among many young Americans, about 47% of Muslims under the age of 35 attend mosques regularly (see Haniff, 2003, pp. 308-309).This overview makes evident the importance of education (and public schooling in particular) in the United States in meeting the needs of Muslim students – and of their non-Muslim classmates as well.

Girl Reading the *Qur'ān*
© Asada Nami/Shutterstock.com

---

[26] We do not mean to suggest, however, that it is only in these areas that non-Muslim students need to learn about Islam. In fact, quite the opposite is true – we would argue that *all* students in the United States need to know about Islam.

There is an unfortunate tendency in the West to attempt to deal with Islam and the Islamic world as if the two were both synonymous and monolithic. Karim H. Karim (2000), in a study of the treatment of Islam by Western media, has argued that, "the terms 'Muslim world' or 'Islamic world' … reinforce the false impression of a monolithic global Muslim entity, the self-image of a unified Muslim *ummah* (community) notwithstanding" (p. 7). This is a significant point that has been made repeatedly by any number of informed writers about Islam, and yet it is also one that has often failed to be understood:

> Islam is … Islam is … Islam is … Islam is many things. Just as there is no single America or Europe or the West, a seamless caption etching diverse groups and persons with the same values and meanings, so there is no single place or uniform culture called Islam. There is no monolithic Islam. There is a Muslim world spanning Africa and Asia. It is as pluralistic as the West, outstripping both Europe and America in the numerous regions, races, languages, and cultures that it encompasses. The Afro-Asian Muslim world is also internally pluralistic, containing multiple groups who might be said to represent Islamic norms in each Muslim country. (Lawrence, 1998, p. 4)

Islam is not monolithic, any more than Christianity or Judaism are monolithic. Islam constitutes a faith community of some 1.3 billion human beings, spread throughout not only some 55 nations that are predominantly Muslim, but also throughout the West. Such a community is inevitably highly diverse. However, just as Christians share certain common beliefs and practices, and just as Jews share a number of fundamental beliefs and practices, in spite of their differences, so too are Muslims united both with respect to core beliefs and common religious practices. What is essential in this regard is to understand both the diversity and the unity that are present in the Islamic world, and among individual Muslims.

Just as there are different denominations in Christianity and Judaism, so too are there different denominations in Islam. The most well-recognized distinction in Islam is that between Sunni Muslims and Shi'a Muslims, although each of these groups has multiple divisions within it. Sunni Muslims constitute the overwhelming majority of Muslims in the world, somewhere between 87% and 90%, while Shi'a constitute around 10 to 13% of the Muslim populations globally (Pew Forum on Religion and Public Life, 2012, p. 21).[27] The distinction between Sunni and Shi'a Muslims has been explained as follows:

---

[27] This is in fact an oversimplification of the complexity of the make-up of the Islamic faith. There are a number of other groups of Muslims in the world, including the Ahmadiyya movement, the Ibadi sect, the Mahdavia sect, and so on, as well as groups such as the Nation of Islam.

Sunni Muslims and Shia Muslims … comprise the two main sects within Islam. Sunni and Shia identities first formed around a dispute over leadership succession soon after the death of the Prophet Muhammad in 632 A.D. Over time, however, the political divide between the two groups broadened to include theological distinctions and differences in religious practices as well. While the two sects are similar in many ways, they differ over conceptions of religious authority and interpretation as well as the role of the Prophet Muhammad's descendants … (Pew Forum on Religion and Public Life, 2009)

Mosque in Dearborn, Michigan
© James R. Martin/shutterstock.com

Discussions of Islam intended for non-Muslims often begin with Muhammad, but this is perhaps misleading. The word *Islam* actually means "submission," as in "submission to the will of God," and the focus of Islam is not Muhammad, but rather, *Allāh* (God) (Abdalati, 1975, p. 1).[28] Muhammad is important in his role as *Allāh*'s Prophet, as the messenger bringing the word of *Allāh* to humanity, and as a perfect example of how a Muslim should seek to lead their life. As Mary Pat Fisher (1994) has explained, "Muhammad's life story is important to Muslims, for his example is considered a key that opens the door to the Divine Presence" (p. 298). Nevertheless, Muhammad was a human being, the last of a long series of prophets sent by *Allāh* to reveal His will -- a series of prophets that included Adam, Abraham, Noah, Moses and Jesus, among others. Before Muhammad, each prophet was sent to renew the message of *Allāh*'s Oneness and unity to a particular people (Haneef, 1985, pp. 20–21). Only Muhammad, though, "was entrusted with the final and complete statement of *Allāh*'s guidance for the whole of humanity for all time to come" (Haneef, 1985, p. 20). Because of his unique role, Muhammad is called the "Seal of the Prophets" (*khātam an-nabīyīn*) in the *Qur'ān* and is believed by Muslims to be the last and final authority in this prophetic tradition (Fisher, 1994, p. 309). Islam, though, is far more than its messenger.

The core beliefs of Islam are identified in the *Qur'ān* itself: "The Prophet believes in what has been revealed to him from his Lord, and so do the Believers. They all believe in God,

---

[28] This is a very important point and helps to explain why the term "Mohammedan," which implies (falsely) that Muslims worship Muhammad, is deeply offensive to Muslims (see Jameelah, 1986, pp. 20–21).

His angels, His scriptures and His messengers, making no distinction among His prophets. And they say, 'We hear and we obey. Grant us Thy forgiveness, our Lord, and unto Thee is the journeying'" (Sura 2: 285). At the same time, it is important to bear in mind that "the principles on which the Islamic systems are based are constant, unalterable and universal ones originating in Divine revelation. However, the details of their application may certainly be adjusted as necessary within the Islamic framework to fit existing needs and circumstances" (Haneef, 1985, p. 93). In other words, although the core beliefs may be the same, the ways in which they will be manifested in practice may differ in various social and cultural contexts (Amdouni, 1992).

The most fundamental belief of Islam is in the unity and Oneness of *Allāh*. From a Muslim point of view, "the Oneness of God is the primordial religion taught by all prophets of all faiths. Muhammad merely served to remind people of it" (Fisher, 1994, p. 308). In Arabic, the concept of the unity of *Allāh* is expressed in the term *tawḥīd*, which Khurshid Ahmad has suggested is "a revolutionary concept and constitutes the essence of the teachings of Islam. It means that there is only One Supreme Lord of the universe. He is Omnipotent, Omnipresent and the Sustainer of the world and of mankind" (Ahmad, 1980, p. 29). *Tawḥīd* is commonly translated as "monotheism," but this is somewhat misleading. To be sure, *tawḥīd* does refer to a monotheistic conception of the universe, but to a far more vibrant and powerful monotheism than is that found, for instance, in Christianity.[29]

Although there is a great deal of diversity in the Islamic world with respect to religious practice, there is a core of practices shared by all Muslims. Specifically, there are five essential practices, commonly called the "five pillars of Islam" (*arkān al-Islām*), which are universally accepted throughout the Islamic world (Riddell & Cotterell, 2003, pp. 45-57). The "five pillars of Islam" include:

- The profession of faith (*shahādah*).
- Prayer (*salāt*).
- Almsgiving (*zakat*).
- Fasting (*sawm*).
- The pilgrimage to Mecca (*haj*).

The *profession of faith* (or *shahādah*, literally "witness" or "testimony") refers to the obligation of the Muslim to declare their faith that "There is no god but Allah, and Muhammad is His Prophet" (*La ilaha illa Allah, Muhammadu Rasul Allah,* in Arabic; Fluehr-Lobban, 1994, pp. 23–24; Hamidullah, 1981, pp. 51–53; Haneef, 1985, pp. 11–15, 42–43). In other words, the believer accepts the absolute monotheism of Islam, the oneness and unity (*tawḥīd*) of *Allāh*,

---

[29] We do not mean to suggest that Christians are in any way insincere about their belief in a single God. However, for non-Christians (not simply Muslims, but also Jews), the Trinitarian view of God (i.e., that God is three consubstantial "persons" [*hypostasis*, ὑπόστασις] having a single divine nature) is not an acceptable articulation of monotheism. It is worth mentioning here that the development of Trinitarianism in Christianity was one that took considerable time, dialogue and debate to emerge in orthodox Christianity and was historically far from universally acceptable to (let alone accepted by) all early Christians (see Holmes, 2012; Kaiser, 1976; McGrath, 2012).

and accepts Muhammad as *Allāh*'s final messenger to humanity. Furthermore, this implies that one accepts the obligation to inform others of the faith, although the *Qur'ān* explicitly rejects the use of coercion in such efforts: "Let there be no compulsion in religion; truth stands out clear from error: whoever rejects evil and believes in God has grasped the most trustworthy handle, that never breaks" (Sura 2: 256).

The second pillar of Islam is prayer (*salāt*). Muslims pray five times a day, at daybreak, noon, midafternoon, sunset, and evening (see Abdalati, 1975, pp. 55–86; Fluehr-Lobban, 1994, pp. 25–28; Haneef, 1985, pp. 43–46). Prayer is preceded by ritual ablutions (*wuḍū'*), normally done with water, which help to prepare the individual for worship. The Muslim then faces Mecca and recites a series of prayers and *Qur'ānic* passages. On Fridays, the noon prayer is a congregational one, led by a religious leader (called an *imām*). Prayer is thus both an individual and a communal obligation for the Muslim:

> For the Muslim, prayer is not simply a mental or spiritual attitude or even just a matter of thanksgiving of the mind and heart. It involves a total bodily response, not simply sitting but putting oneself through a series of complete prostrations. For that reason, mosques do not have chairs or pews. Each of the five daily prayers consists of a series of ritual bowings and bendings (each called a *raka'*) accompanied by the appropriate prayers and invocations. Standing shoulder to shoulder, feet to feet, the worshippers are lined in rows facing the imam, or leader, of the prayer ... Together they perform several sets of prayer prostrations, which include standing, bowing at the waist with hands placed near the knees, and kneeling and placing one's forehead on the carpet in full supplication. "When you are in that position of complete vulnerability," explains the imam, "you really get a feel for what it means to submit yourself fully to God." (Smith, 1999, pp. 1-2)

Almsgiving (*zakāt*) "is an act both of worship or thanksgiving to God and of service to the community" (Esposito, 1998, p. 92). Although the basic goal of almsgiving is to redress economic inequities and to support the poor, it is not simply charity, in that it is obligatory rather than voluntary (Esposito, 1998, p. 92). Muslims are expected to donate at least 2.5% of their income in this manner (Fisher, 1994, p. 321), and the funds are used both for the poor (including widows and orphans) and for the spread of the faith (which includes support for religious and educational institutions). This emphasis on the obligation to help those in need is one that occurs repeatedly in the *Qur'ān*: "Who denies religion? It is the person who repulses the orphan and does not promote feeding the poor. Woe to those who worship but are neglectful, those who want to be noticed but who withhold assistance from those in need" (Sura 107: 1–7).

Once each year, during the entire month of Ramadan,[30] all adult Muslims who are able are required to fast (*sawm*) from sunrise to sunset (Haneef, 1985, pp. 46–48; Sarwar, 1989, pp. 76–78). During the fast, Muslims must abstain from food, drink, smoking, and sexual activity.

---

[30] Islam, like Judaism, uses a lunar calendar, which means that the date of Ramadan (on the solar calendar) changes from year to year.

This is a time for reflection and self-discipline and "a time to thank God for His blessings, repent and atone for one's sins, discipline the body and strengthen moral character, remember one's ultimate dependence upon God, and respond to the needs of the poor and hungry" (Esposito, 1994, p. 249).

The fifth and final pillar of Islam is the pilgrimage (*hajj*) to Mecca (Peters, 1994). All Muslims who can possibly do so are expected to make the pilgrimage at least once in their lifetime. The *hajj*:

> constitutes a form of worship with the totality of the Muslim's being: with his body, mind and soul, with his time, possessions and the temporary sacrifice of all ordinary comforts, conveniences and tokens of status and individuality which human beings normally enjoy, to assume for a few days the condition of a pilgrim totally at God's service and disposal, His slave who seeks only His pleasure. (Haneef, 1985, p. 51)

Great Mosque of Mecca
© Mohamed Reedi/Shutterstock.com

Underlying all five of the pillars of Islam is the unity of belief and practice, as well as the idea that Islam is not simply a body of religious beliefs, but is, rather, a unified and consistent way of life for both the individual and the community (van Nieuwenhuijze, 1985, pp. 93–132).

An understanding of Islam is possible only with an understanding of the *Qur'ān,* which holds a unique place in Islam. While both Judaism and Christianity have scriptural traditions that include sacred texts (and are, therefore, as already noted, *ahl al-kitāb* – that is, "people of the Book"),[31] these texts are viewed by most believers in a way quite different from the dominant view of the *Qur'ān* in Islamic thought. The *Qur'ān* is not the *inspired* Word of God, nor is it a record of what was reported to have been told to Muhammad. Rather, for the Muslim, the *Qur'ān* is the exact, literal transcription of the words of *Allāh* Himself, precisely as

---

[31] "People of the Book" is a phrase with different meanings in Judaism and Islam. In Judaism, the phrase refers specifically to the Jewish people and the *Torah*, while in Islam it refers to those who belong to the Abrahamic religions that predate Islam (i.e., Judaism and Christianity). In Islam, "people of the book" are granted a certain degree of tolerance and autonomy under *Sharī'a*, since they recognize the God of Abraham and practice religious faiths based on divine law.

they were given to Muhammad (Sahadat, 1996).[32] In other words, the *Qur'ān* is "the unadulterated word of God, which has become audible through Muhammad" (Arkoun, 1994, pp. 35–39; Guillaume, 1956, p. 55). As Suzanne Haneef (1985) explains, "The Holy *Qur'ān* is the only divinely-revealed scripture in the history of mankind which has been preserved to the present time in its exact original form" (p. 18). This means, of course, that since the *Qur'ān* was revealed in Arabic, it was spoken by *Allāh* (through the angel Gabriel) in Arabic, and should therefore only be read and recited in that language: "To recite the *Qur'ān* is the most sublime and edifying occupation for the Muslim, even when [they do] not intellectually understand its words, as is the case with most non-Arab believers. Because the *Qur'ān* is the Divine Word *par excellence*, Muslims consider it inconceivable to 'translate' it into any language" (Haneef, 1985, p. 18).

It is for this reason, at least in part, that in Islam the status of the *Qur'ān* is so different from that of the *Torah* in Judaism or the Bible in Christianity:

> The inherent sacredness of the *Qur'ān* has historically created an unusual problem for many Muslims. Since the end of the 7th century CE, when its verses were collected into a single, authoritative canon, the *Qur'ān* has remained fixed in Arabic, the language in which it was originally revealed. It was believed that translating the *Qur'ān* into any other language would violate the divine nature of the text. Translations were done, of course. But to this day, non-Arabic versions of the *Qur'ān* are considered *interpretations* of the *Qur'ān*. Unless the original Arabic verses are embedded on the page, it cannot technically be called a *Qur'ān*. (Aslan, 2008)

Although there is a growth in both the numbers and the percentage of Muslim students enrolled in private Islamic schools, such schools serve only about one-third of the total population of Muslim children, which means that nearly three-quarters of Muslim children attend public schools (Al-Romi, 2000, p. 634). Muslims in K-12 public schools face numerous challenges, some social and interpersonal, some academic, and some religious. Roughly 53% of Muslim children report having been bullied, in contrast with around one-quarter of Jewish students and 10% of the general public (Dupuy, 2017; Mogahed & Chouhoud, 2017, p. 3; Tahseen, 2019). Perhaps most depressing, such bullying of Muslim students is not limited to peers:

> teachers and school officials have participated in one in four bullying incidents involving Muslim students .... the American Civil Liberties Union (ACLU) filed letters of complaint with the U.S. Department of Justice and U.S. Department of Education on behalf of an 11-year-old Muslim Somali refugee student who was repeatedly discriminated against by his teacher in Arizona. "I can't wait until Trump is elected. He's going to deport all you Muslims," the teacher exclaimed, according to the ACLU letter of complaint. "Muslims shouldn't be given visas.

---

[32] The Muslim view of the nature and status of the *Qur'ān* is, simultaneously, both fairly straightforward and quite complex (see Abu-Hamdiyyah, 2000; Ali, 1992; Esack, 2002; Haleen, 2001; Kahn, 1981).

They'll probably take away your visa and deport you. You're going to be the next terrorist, I bet." Soon after, the boy's classmates followed the teacher's lead and called him a terrorist, according to the complaint. They also accused him of planning to blow up the school bus on the ride home. When the boy's mother complained to the school, administrators encouraged him to withdraw. (Ochieng, 2017)

There is a growing recognition about the extremely harmful nature and potential outcomes of bullying for *all* children (see Salmivalli, Kaukiainen, & Voeten, 2010; Sullivan, 2011; Ttofi & Farrington, 2009), but these dangers are significantly greater for students who are members of marginalized groups. Farha Abbasi, an associate professor of psychiatry at Michigan State University, has noted that with respect to Muslim children in U.S. schools that:

> racism and discrimination can cause a cycle of "defensiveness, dissociation, disconnection, dissonance and, finally, distress or desperation" ... [and] the increase in bullying among Muslim schoolchildren is a life-or-death matter. People who are bullied are more susceptible to suicide. "Think of trauma and toxic stress as putting brick over brick on someone's shoulder ... Right now, many Muslim children are carrying a very heavy burden and one more brick can be the breaking point." (Quoted in Ochieng, 2017)

Academically, Muslim students are often faced with curricula that either overlook or ignore the significant contributions of Muslims or which distort or misrepresent Islamic history and civilization across different subject areas. The inclusion of content about Islam in the curriculum needs to take into account a number of issues and factors. First, students need to understand that Islam is part of the Western tradition – or, more accurately, of the Judeo-Christian-Islamic tradition (see Taylor & Omar, 2012). It is *not* an alien cultural, historical and religious tradition in any sense but, rather, is closely tied to the history and development of the civilization in which we live.[33] Nor are the contributions of Islam and of Muslims to the world in which we live merely historical ones; Muslims *continue to make* very significant contributions to the world and in virtually every domain of life. One of the interesting aspects of an exercise to identify Islamic contributions to different areas of study (especially in the sciences) is that there is a tendency to focus on the "Golden Age of Islam" (roughly, the 8th to 14th centuries CE). This implicitly suggests that Muslims have not made significant scientific and intellectual contributions since then, which is demonstrably false.[34] There is a similar problem found in many of the textbooks used to teach about Islam more generally; as Susan Douglass and Ross Dunn have pointed out, "The textbooks disconnect Islam from the Judeo-Christian tradition

---

[33] One powerful example of this is that much of what is generally considered to be the basis for the Western tradition from the period of classical antiquity was preserved not in the West, but rather by Islamic scholars in the Middle Ages (see Fakhry, 2004; Rosenthal, 1965; Tolan, Veinstein, & Laurens, 2013).

[34] In addition to what might be considered more mainstream contributions to different disciplines, during the past three decades there has also been an increasing focus on what has been termed the "Islamization of knowledge" (see Ahsan, Shahed, & Ahmad, 2013; Dzilo, 2012).

even as they emphasize how Islam borrowed from Jewish and Christian scriptures. Textbook writers portrayed Islam in light of the Arab nomadic society and the life of the Prophet of Islam while deliberately downplaying the Abrahamic legacy in Islam" (Douglass & Dunn, 2003, p. 52). The study of the Islamic world, as part of the examination of contemporary world events, is an incredibly important aspect of such teaching and learning. Many contemporary issues that directly impact the lives of Americans are related, either directly or indirectly, to events in the Islamic world, and it is important for students, both as educated persons and as future citizens, to understand the contexts and backgrounds of such events.

Perhaps even more important than what is taught about Islam is what is *not* taught. Throughout the corpus of his work, Edward Said warned of the dangers of Orientalism (Said, 1978, 1993, 1994; see also Ashcroft & Ahluwalia, 2001; Hussein, 2002; Kennedy, 2000). Orientalism not just colors, but indeed permeates, much of the current teaching about Islam in the public schools.[35] One especially unfortunate example of the results of such teaching took place when President George W. Bush used the term "Crusade" to describe the U.S. "War on Terrorism" (see Buzbee, 2001; McSmith, 2001; Waldman & Pope, 2001). Soheib Bensheikh, the Grand Mufti of the mosque in Marseille, France, indicated that this choice of words "was most unfortunate," since "it recalled the barbarous and unjust military operations against the Muslim world" by Christians over a period of several centuries (quoted in Ford, 2001). The inappropriate use of the term "Crusade" by an American President, problematic though it was, is far less significant than the on-going discourse found in contemporary media and, even more relevant for our purposes here, in national educational standards, textbooks, and the like (see Jackson, 2011).

Finally, Muslim students in public schools face a number of challenges that are, to a significant degree, religious in nature. Understandably, students from more conservative homes are more likely to face challenges in this regard, but most Muslim students are affected to a greater or lesser extent. As Iftikhar Ahmad and Michelle Szpara (2003) have argued,

> Awareness among school officials about issues including clothing (especially for physical education and swimming), provision of *halal* food, music, sex education, and the separation of sexes is crucial. Although it may be impractical for schools to be completely accommodating, small changes can be made easily. As an example, one mother said, "The teacher knows the Jewish children don't eat pork, but they don't know about Muslims. There should be a non-pork option in school lunches" ... school officials also need to facilitate Muslim children's needs for observing prayers and religious festivals such as Ramadan and Eid holidays, without penalty. (pp. 299-300)

---

[35] As Craig Considine (2017) has noted, the "constructions of Orientalism and Islamophobia (incivility, inferiority, and incompatibility) are key tools of contemporary racism in the United States. Following Carr and Haynes (2015), American Muslims appear to be caught in a 'clash of racializations' between exclusionary notions of American national identity and racialized 'Muslimness', both of which operate to expose Muslims to racist activity while concomitantly excluding them from the protection of the state ... While Muslims are not a 'race', they are examined through a racial process that is demarcated by physical features and racial underpinnings" (p. 6).

One important way of recognizing and responding to the needs of Muslim students is to know something about the major religious holidays in Islam. The most important of these holidays are Eid al-Fitr, which marks the end of Ramadan, and Eid al-Adha, which is observed on the tenth day of Dhu al-Hijah, when the Hajj takes place, and which lasts for four days.

Islamophobia in the United States

The rise in bullying of Muslim students in the public schools is one manifestation of a much larger problem in American society: the increase in Islamophobia in the West generally. Although there is certainly a popular understanding of the word, the term "Islamophobia" lacks a generally agreed-upon definition (see Allen, 2010b; Bleich, 2011; Shryock, 2010). However, the lack of a precise definition does not mean that a "rough and ready" definition of the term is not possible.[36] As Craig Considine (2017) has noted,

> There is a cluster of terms and phrases referring to hostility towards American Muslims. The most widely known term is Islamophobia. One of the first uses of Islamophobia in English appears in an article by Said (1985); he initially brought into focus the stigmatized identity of Muslims in his work *Orientalism*, which unpacked the Western perspectives that create dehumanizing representations of the "exotic" and "barbarous" countries of the Middle East, Africa, and Asia. (p. 5)

Many elements of Islamophobia are grounded in fear, but the real concerns about Islamophobia are the responses to that fear (see Beydoun, 2018; Cook, 2015; Ekman, 2015; Tibi, 2010). The rise of both explicit and implicit anti-Muslim attitudes and policies, coupled with discrimination and discriminatory practices in various settings, are one aspect of Islamophobia, as are examples of bigotry directed toward individuals and groups because they are Muslim (see Allen, 2010a, 2010b; Gottschalk & Greenberg, 2008; Lean, 2012; Shryock, 2010; Werbner, 2005).

A foundational effort in attempting to define Islamophobia was provided in the late 1990s with the publication of *Islamophobia: A Challenge for Us All* by the Runnymede Trust in the United Kingdom (Bogacki, Jaap de Ruiter, & Sèze, 2018; Runnymede Trust, 1997, 2017). The original *Runnymede Trust Report* contrasted "open" views of Islam with "closed" views of Islam.[37] Open views of Islam, it should be noted, are not synonymous with *positive* views of Islam. Rather, while presupposing an overall respect for Islam, such views allow for legitimate

---

[36] As Abdul Rashid Moten has commented, "Much debate has surrounded the use of the term, questioning its adequacy as an appropriate and meaningful descriptor. However, since Islamophobia has broadly entered the social and political lexicon, arguments about the appropriateness of the term now seem outdated" (Moten, 2014, p. 618).

[37] The first Runnymede Trust report on Islamophobia, which was a seminal contribution to the field in spite of its limitations, was published in 1997 under the title *Islamophobia: A Challenge for Us All*. Twenty years later, in 2017, a second Runnymede Trust report on Islamophobia, entitled *Islamophobia: Still a Challenge for Us All*, was published.

discussion, dialogue, debate and disagreement about various aspects of Islam (see Benn & Jawad, 2003, p. 178). Closed beliefs about Islam, on the other hand, are part of a broader hostility toward Islam (and Muslims more generally) that has become increasingly common and acceptable in many circles in the West. While well-intentioned, the *Runnymede Trust Report* was flawed in several important ways (see Green, 2019, pp. 11-31). Not only was it overly simplistic, the *Runnymede Trust Report* has essentialized Islam and also -- perhaps most importantly -- failed to recognize the fact that Islamophobia is basically a form of discrimination that can be thought of along the same lines as racism (see Frost, 2008; Green, 2019; Kazi, 2019; Kundnani, 2007; Love, 2017).

In recent years in the United States, there have been a number of attacks on Islam both from the political right and from religious conservatives, who generally provide considerable support to conservative politicians. Rev. Jerry Vines provides an excellent example of this phenomenon.[38] Vines argued that,

> [They] would have us to believe that Islam is just as good as Christianity, but I'm here to tell you, ladies and gentlemen, that Islam is not just as good as Christianity ... Islam was founded by Muhammad, a demon-possessed pedophile who had 12 wives -- and his last one was a 9-year-old girl. And I will tell you Allah is not Jehovah either. Jehovah's not going to turn you into a terrorist that'll try to bomb people and take the lives of thousands and thousands of people. (Quoted in Cooperman, 2002)

Nor has Vines been alone in his attacks on Islam; the Rev. Franklin Graham described Islam as a "very evil and wicked religion" (quoted in Alberts, 2015) and claimed that the *Qur'ān* "teaches its followers to hate" (quoted in Williams, 2016), while the Rev. Pat Robertson has asserted that "Islam is a political system that is intent on world domination ... It isn't a ... religion as such. It is a political system masquerading as a religion" (quoted in Hanson, 2015) and has described Muslims as "are fanatics ... motivated by demonic power" (quoted in Joyner, 2006).

Our concern here is not for the accuracy (or, more properly, the inaccuracy) of such claims; rather, it is on the implications of such beliefs and the actions that they inspire on Muslims in the United States in general, and on Muslim children – and Muslim children in public schools – in particular. Although our focus here is on the case of the United States, it is important to bear in mind that this is part of a much larger issue in many parts of the world. Although most Muslim children are educated in societies that are predominantly Muslim, increasing numbers are found in settings in which Muslims constitute a minority population, and sometimes a relatively small minority population (Musharraf & Nabeel, 2015; Shah, 2012). In some cases, Muslims have had a significance presence for centuries, while in others they are relative newcomers. Many of these countries are predominantly Christian, while others follow Hindu, Buddhist or some other religious tradition (although it might be more accurate, in many

---

[38] It is important to note that Vines is by no means a "fringe" figure. He is a past President of the Southern Baptist Convention, the largest single Protestant denomination in the United States, with roughly 50,000 congregations and more than 15 million members.

cases, to identify many of these countries, as in Western Europe, as basically secular in nature). In such settings, the challenges of Islamophobia present problems not typically encountered in the education of Muslim children in Muslim societies.

Teaching about Islam, as we have seen, is not only permissible in the context of the public school, but is arguably essential, especially in today's world. Furthermore, many educational curricula that are designed to provide students with an introduction to the study of Islam also contain curricular components that are anti-Islamophobic in nature. Such curricular developments, meaningful and positive as they certainly are, do not in and of themselves constitute solutions to the challenges of Islamophobia in public education, however. Todd Green (2020), in writing about the differences between the first and second editions of his book *The Fear of Islam: An Introduction to Islamophobia in the West*, writes:

> [My] own thinking on Islamophobia had evolved somewhat since the first edition … *It … involved a greater concern for how the most conventional explanation of Islamophobia – the notion that Islamophobia is driven by ignorance of Islam – was not up to the task of explaining why hostility toward Islam and Muslims seemed only to be getting worse.* The dominant paradigm for understanding Islamophobia since 9/11 has been through the lens of ignorance. The assumption is that those who harbor negative opinions toward Muslims do so because they do not know enough about Islam. If they were better educated on the basics of Islamic practice and beliefs -- if they knew the five pillars of Islam, if they understood what sharia really means, if they understood the nuanced meanings of *jihad* in Islamic history – then there would be less prejudice against Muslims …. there is an ongoing need to correct misunderstandings about Islam that are prevalent in public discourse. I also recognize that ignorant stereotypes frequently serve a more insidious political function: distracting Western nations and their majority populations from their own moral failings on issues such as violence or gender inequality. (emphasis added)

In short, although ignorance about Islam (and, concomitantly, about Muslims) certainly can contribute to Islamophobia, addressing that ignorance – while incredibly important -- does not on its own eliminate the problem.

One excellent curricular package designed to provide students with an introduction to Islam was *Access Islam*, which was produced by PBS/WNET in New York with financial support from the U.S. Department of Education.[39] *Access Islam* is part of a larger undertaking, *Access World Religions*, "which is designed to help students gain awareness and understanding of the diversity of religions and religious experiences, and the reasons for particular expressions of religious beliefs within a society or culture." The series included units on Buddhism, Christianity, Hinduism, and Judaism as well as Islam. The *Access Islam* unit includes not only ten videotape

---

[39] The financial support from the U.S. Department of Education was $166,000 in fiscal year 2005 and $8,000 in fiscal year 2006 – both, incidentally, provided during the administration of President George W. Bush.

lessons but also lesson plans, a glossary, and other resources to assist teachers in utilizing the program. The content of *Access Islam* is not dissimilar to what one would find in any standard academic introduction to Islam:

Lesson 1	Religion and the First Amendment
Lesson 2	The Five Pillars of Islam
Lesson 3	Salat: Prayer in Muslim Life
Lesson 4	Ramadan Observance
Lesson 5	Qur'an: Sacred Scripture of Islam
Lesson 6	The Hajj: Journey to Mecca
Lesson 7	Scholarship and Learning in Islam
Lesson 8	Islam in America
Lesson 9	Women in Islam
Lesson 10	Art in the Muslim World

Access Islam, like other parts of the *Access World Religions* series, sought to provide teachers with a well-constructed, well-researched, pedagogically sound curriculum to assist them in introducing students to different aspects of Islam.

The voluntary use of *Access Islam* in some school districts – it was never a state-mandated curriculum anywhere in the United States -- quickly led to a powerful backlash. The Christian Action Network denounced it, claiming that it was an "outright Islamic indoctrination program" aimed at the conversion of American schoolchildren to Islam. The position of the Christian Action Network (CAN), which was widely circulated in conservative Christian political circles, was that:

> By giving students a one-sided view of Islamic beliefs ... this is nothing more than an attempt to convert our children into Islam and not only that, but in some cases an attempt to turn our children into evangelists for Islam ... When children are asked to draw the Five Pillars of Islam to be displayed in the classroom or posted up-and-down the school hallway, this is an attempt to use children to spread the message of Islam ... Clearly, having children engaged in such activity goes well beyond any argument that students are simply learning the basic facts about Islamic beliefs" (Mawyer, 2017).

The Christian Action Network denunciation of *Access Islam* went beyond public objections; a petition was sent to Department of Education Secretary Betsy DeVos, asserting that the program "is outrageous and HIGHLY unconstitutional," claiming that "no similar program is offered for Christian [sic], Jews or any other major religion," and demanding that the Department of Education end its support for the program (Mawyer, 2019). The fact that the position of the Christian Action Network is full of misleading claims and outright factual errors notwithstanding,[40] objections to *Access Islam* have continued not only to spread but have

---

[40] The objections raised by the Christian Action Network merit a full-length rebuttal, but that is not our purpose here. However, the claims that have made been about *Access Islam* are important and powerful ones and deserve at least some degree of response. The curriculum is simply not designed to convert anyone to Islam; learning the Five Pillars of Islam does not entail accepting them, but merely learning

become a widely used talking point in attacks by conservative Christians on public education. Typical of such attacks was Marisha Dowdell's (2017) polemic, which appeared in the *Conservative Daily Post*, which asserted that *Access Islam* "is a major threat not only to our children but to our communities and our country. With the rise of homegrown terrorists and suicide bombers, it is appalling and dangerous to allow this religious ideology [to] be taught to our innocent children."

At the request of the Poynter Institute, the *Access Islam* curriculum was carefully reviewed by a number of prominent educators, including Linda Wertheimer, Mark Fowler, Charles Haynes, and Diane Moore (see Sherman, 2017).[41] Their evaluative comments offer a very different perspective on the *Access Islam* curriculum:

> Nothing in these lessons crosses the constitutional line dividing education and indoctrination. Students learn the basic tenets and practices of Muslims and then are assessed on what they have learned. *Students are not asked to affirm or reject any religious teachings. Nor are students required to participate in any religious or devotional activities.* (Charles Haynes, quoted in Sherman, 2017, emphasis added)

---

about their significance for Muslims. The same is true with respect to learning about the name for God (Allah) and learning about the historic ties among Judaism, Christianity, and Islam. A curriculum can only be considered to be indoctrination if students are not allowed to develop alternative viewpoints or to challenge the content being taught (see Snook, 1970, 1972a, 1972b); there is no evidence that this is in any way part of the *Access Islam* curriculum (and, since the *Access Islam* curriculum is almost always taught by non-Muslim teachers, it seems highly unlikely that these teachers would be attempting to indoctrinate their students into a religion that they themselves do not accept). Claims that *Access Islam* is unique and that no other religions are studied in a comparable fashion is simply factually wrong – although historically true, in recent years we routinely teach students about Buddhism, Hinduism, Judaism, and other faiths as part of the public school curriculum. It may be the case that formal instruction about Christianity is less extensive than that devoted to other religions, but that would be because the vast majority of students in the classroom come from Christian backgrounds, and virtually all students in American society – whether or not they are Christian – are exposed to a great deal of information about Christianity in the general society and outside of the school environment. Concerns about the constitutionality of teaching about Islam (or of any other religion, for that matter) are misguided, and demonstrate a lack of understanding of a very consistent series of Supreme Court decisions on the matter. Finally, it is important to note that the situation – constitutionally, pedagogically, culturally, socially, and interpersonally – between the majority religion in our society (Christianity) and other religions (including Islam) is simply not comparable. Non-Christians find themselves in a very different position in a host of ways than do members of the majority religion.

[41] Linda Wertheimer is a senior national correspondent for National Public Radio and the author of *Faith Ed: Teaching about Religion in an Age of Intolerance* (2015); Mark Fowler is the Chief Executive Officer of the Tannenbaum Center for Interreligious Understanding; Charles Haynes is Senior Fellow at the Religious Freedom Center; and Diane Moore is the Director of the Harvard Divinity School's Religious Literacy Project, a Senior Fellow at the Center for the Study of World Religions, and a Faculty Affiliate of the Middle East Initiative at Harvard Kennedy School.

[*Access Islam*] *is not preaching or promoting Islam over other faiths*. In fact, the lesson plans include questions about comparing and contrasting beliefs and practices of Islam to those of other faiths. (Wertheimer, quoted in Sherman, 2017, emphasis added)

When any religious tradition is only represented in its positive light, it can feel like indoctrination to those who don't believe the tradition has merit or has equal credibility to one's own faith. This is why it is so important to make the distinction between teaching about a religion and teaching religion, and the *Access Islam* site makes this distinction in its first lesson on the First Amendment. (Moore, quoted in Sherman, 2017)

Indoctrination has as its motivation having children choose a faith over another … [but the lessons in *Access Islam*] [do not] ask students to choose a religion or rank them. (Fowler, quoted in Sherman, 2017)

The Christian Action Network, although providing an important outlet for misleading information about education concerning Islam, is far from alone in such efforts. The National Coalition Against Censorship has documented more than 30 examples of protests and challenges that were raised between 2013 and 2017 to educational materials about Islam (see National Coalition Against Censorship, 2019), and this appears to be just the tip of the iceberg (for an especially egregious example of attacks on educational materials designed to teach about Islam, see Sewall, 2008). Such resistance is grounded not so much in what curricula teach about Islam as in the fact that such curricula do not teach the superiority of Christianity over Islam and other religions. This is, in fact, simply a reflection and manifestation of the growing power of Islamophobia in the U.S. society and political life.

Finally, a number of related stories have recently appeared on Facebook and in other social media recently claiming "that the Supreme Court recently ruled that public schools cannot teach Islam"– and, further, that the deciding vote in this landmark but split Supreme Court decision was cast by Justice Neil Gorsuch, who also wrote the majority opinion (Spencer, 2018). In fact, none of this is true. There was no such Supreme Court ruling on the teaching about Islam, nor is there any reason at all to believe that such instruction could be considered unconstitutional. Furthermore, as Saranac Spencer (2018) noted, "when that story began circulating, Gorsuch had yet to hear his first case as a member of the court – let alone author an opinion."

Given the presence of Islamophobia and anti-Muslim bias in American society, as well as its politicization and ties to right-wing populism, it is hardly surprising that efforts to incorporate accurate and appropriate information about Islam into the curriculum of American public schools have been met with considerable resistance. The case of *Access Islam* provides one clear example of this sort of backlash, but it is far from the only one. The challenge, then, is how to engage in efforts to address both Islamophobia and the need for greater knowledge and understanding of Islam by American students while at the same time dealing with the backlash from those who see virtually any inclusion of curricular content about Islam as threatening.

Islamophobia is without any question a serious and increasing problem in the United States, as well as in much of Europe (Ahmed, 2017; Bayrakli & Hafez, 2020; Massoumi, 2020), and the growth of Islamophobia and anti-Muslim bias presents significant challenges for any democratic, pluralistic society. These developments are especially important with respect to their implications in the educational domain (see Ahmad & Szpara, 2003; Isik-Ercan, 2015; Peek, 2003; Sabry & Bruna, 2007). We have already seen how difficult it can be to challenge Islamophobia in the context of the public schools, and yet that is precisely where such challenges are most urgently needed.

Challenging Islamophobia in the context of public schooling does not take place in a vacuum. Such teaching is best understood as part of broader initiatives that are already underway in multicultural education, anti-racist education, and social justice education. In addressing Islamophobia, it is obviously important that we include discussions of the nature of Islamophobia, the evidence for the presence of Islamophobia in the U.S. society, and explanations for why it is important that Islamophobia be challenged. It is also important that students learn about Islam and the complexities of the Muslim world. While all of these things are significant – indeed, essential – they are not, however, sufficient. In addition to such instruction, students must also learn to critique the narratives of Islamophobia. Critiques of the narratives of Islamophobia would include:

- Correcting factual mistakes about the nature and teachings of Islam.
- Challenging the conflation of Islam with violence and terrorism.
- Pointing out that Islam is not, and has really never been, "un-American" in any meaningful sense.
- Explaining how the U.S. *Constitution*'s First Amendment protections have been misunderstood and misinterpreted in the debates about Islam and Islamophobia.
- Demonstrating the role of religious and national exceptionalism in critiques of Islam.

Not only do students need to be able to challenge and critique the narratives of Islamophobia, they must also be able to offer compelling counter-narratives, which are grounded in accurate knowledge and understanding of Islam, familiarity with Muslims, and the more general components of multicultural, anti-racist, and social justice education.

The need for better education about Islam, and for education that not only teaches about Islam but which leads to challenges to Islamophobia, is one of growing concern. It is also, it should be noted, a matter that applies not only to students in K-12 settings but also to the case of teacher education. Although a far more detailed rationale for this could be easily provided, Amina Easat-Daas (2019) provided what is perhaps the clearest justification for such education when she argued that "The ultimate goal in countering Islamophobia should be to create a fair and just society for all, one that values and safeguards the citizenship of its members."

Other Faiths and Public Schooling in the United States

Up to this point, we have focused our attention on the three "Abrahamic" religions, Judaism, Christianity, and Islam. There are a number of other major world religions that are present in the United States, including Buddhism, Hinduism, Sikhism, the Bahá'í faith,[42] and many others. Children from each of these religious groups are found in the public schools, and it is important to understand that the same protections and rights that apply to Christian, Jewish, and Muslim children necessarily apply to children from these other groups. It is the very presence of this religious diversity, incidentally, that helps to provide the rationale for the importance — indeed, the necessity — of teaching about different religions and religious traditions in the public schools.

Shrine of the Bab and Lower Terraces at the Bahá'í World Center in Haifa, Israel
© Leonid Andronov/Shutterstock.com

Questions for Reflection and Discussion

1. In a growing number of schools, we teach about different religions, most often taking a kind of comparative religious studies approach. If a teacher is engaged in teaching such a unit, and they have a Muslim student in their class, would it be appropriate for them to ask the student to share about their religion? Why or why not?

2. Religion has historically had an important influence on public education in the United States and in many ways continues to do so. In what ways is this compatible with the constitutional protections of the First Amendment? In what ways are there potentials for conflicts between religious beliefs and practices in public schools and the protections of the First Amendment?

---

[42] The Bahá'í faith originated in Persia and was established by Bahá'u'lláh in 1863. It currently has between 5 and 8 million followers around the world, known as Bahá'ís, including a growing community in the United States. Since the Bahá'í faith emerged out of Islam, it would technically also be one of the Abrahamic religions (see Hatcher & Martin, 2002; Momen, 1997; Worthington, 2012).

3. What, in your view, is the difference between teaching about a religion and proselytizing for a religion? Are the times in public schools in which proselytization is permitted or appropriate? If you believe that there are such times, what limitations or restrictions might exist?

4. In this chapter, the authors suggest that Christianity is normative in American society. What do you think that they mean by this? What are the implications of this idea for classroom practice?

5. Do you believe that anti-Semitism and Islamophobia are antithetical to education in a democratic society? Would it be appropriate for a teacher to allow anti-Semitic or Islamophobic comments to take place for purposes of promoting classroom discussion and debate? Why or why not?

References

ABC News. (2007, October 8). Aquí se habla español – and two-thirds don't mind. ABC News *Good Morning America* poll: Immigration. Retrieved from https://abcnews.go.com/images/US/1048a1Hispanics.pdf.

Abdalati, H. (1975). *Islam in focus.* Indianapolis, IN: American Trust Publications.

Abu-Hamdiyyah, M. (2000). *The Qur'ān: An introduction.* London, UK: Routledge.

Ahmad, I., & Szpara, M. (2003). Muslim children in urban America: The New York City schools experience. *Journal of Muslim Minority Affairs, 23*(2), 295-230.

Ahmad, K. (Ed.). (1980). *Islam: Its meaning and message.* London, UK: Islamic Foundation.

Ahmed, S. (2017, March 14). Europe has started to enshrine Islamophobia into law: History tells us this can't end well. *Independent.* Retrieved from https://www.independent.co.uk/voices/europe-islamophobia-headscarf-eu-court-ruling-hijab-a7629531.html.

Ahsan, M., Shahed, A., & Ahmad, A. (2013). Islamization of knowledge: An agenda for Muslim intellectuals. *Global Journal of Management and Business Research Administration and Management, 13*(10), 33-42.

Alberts, W. (2015, March 2). Rev. Franklin Graham: Apostle of hatred. *CounterPunch.* Retrieved from https://www.counterpunch.org/2015/03/02/rev-franklin-graham-apostle-of-hatred/.

Ali, M. (1992). *Introduction to the study of the holy Qur'ān.* Columbus, OH: Ahmadiyya Anjuman Ishaat Islam.

Allen, C. (2010a). Fear and loathing: The political discourse in relation to Muslims and Islam in the British contemporary setting. *Politics and Religion, 2*(2), 221-236.

Allen, C. (2010b). *Islamophobia.* Farnham, Surrey, UK: Ashgate.

Al-Romi, N. (2000). Muslims as a minority in the United States. *International Journal of Educational Research, 33*, 631-638.

Amdouni, H. (1992). *La famille musulmane: Relations familiales et éducations.* Paris, France: Al Qalam.

Anti-Defamation League. (2019, November 12). ADL urges action after FBI reports Jews were target of most religion-based hate crimes in 2018. Retrieved from https://www.adl.org/news/press-releases/adl-urges-action-after-fbi-reports-jews-were-target-of-most-religion-based-hate.

Arkoun, M. (1994). *Rethinking Islam: Common questions, uncommon answers.* Boulder, CO: Westview Press.

Ashcroft, B., & Ahluwalia, P. (2001). *Edward Said* (2nd ed.). London, UK: Routledge.

Aslan, R. (2008, November 20). How to read the Quran: A new translation captures the confusion. *Slate.* Retrieved from http://www.slate.com/articles/arts/books/2008/11/how_to_read_the_quran.html.

Bauer, W. (1971). *Orthodoxy and heresy in earliest Christianity.* Philadelphia, PA: Fortress Press.

Bayrakli, E., & Hafez, F. (Eds.). (2020). *European Islamophobia report: 2019.* Istanbul, Turkey: Foundation for Political, Economic and Social Research.

Benn, T., & Jawad, H. (2003). *Muslim women in the United Kingdom and beyond: Experiences and images.* Leiden, The Netherlands: Brill Publishers.

Beydoun, K. (2018). *American Islamophobia: Understanding the roots and rise of fear.* Oakland, CA: University of California Press.

Bleich, E. (2011). What Is Islamophobia and how much is there? Theorizing and measuring an emerging comparative concept. *American Behavioral Scientist, 55*(12), 1581–1600.

Bogacki, M., Jaap de Ruiter, J., & Sèze, R. (2018). The Charlie Hebdo attacks in Paris: Defining Islamophobia and its socio-political applications. *Rozenberg Quarterly.* Retrieved from http://rozenbergquarterly.com/the-charlie-hebdo-attacks-in-paris-defining-islamophobia-and-its-socio-political-applications/.

Buzbee, S. (2001, September 17). Bush's use of word "Crusade" a red flag: Muslims link it with invasion by Europeans. *Seattle PI.* Retrieved from https://www.seattlepi.com/news/article/Bush-s-use-of-word-crusade-a-red-flag-1066045.php.

Carr, J., & Haynes, A. (2015). A clash of racializations: The policing of "race" and of anti-Muslim racism in Ireland. *Critical Sociology, 41*(1), 21-40.

Chadwick, O. (1995). *A history of Christianity.* New York, NY: St. Martin's Press.

Considine, C. (2017). The racialization of Islam in the United States: Islamophobia, hate crimes, and "flying while brown." *Religions, 8*(165), 1-19.

Cook, L. (2015, November 20). Data show links between fear of attacks, anti-Muslim bias. *US News and World Report.* Retrieved from http://www.usnews.com/news/blogs/data-mine/2015/11/20/data-show-links-between-fear-of-terrorist-attacks-anti-muslim-bias.

Cooperman, A. (2002, June 20). Anti-Muslim remarks stir tempest. *The Washington Post.* Retrieved from https://www.washingtonpost.com/archive/politics/2002/06/20/anti-muslim-remarks-stir-tempest/4577462f-cd70-458c-9fef-133b5143e144/.

Council on American-Islamic Relations (CAIR). (2001). *The Mosque in America: A national portrait.* Washington DC: Council on American–Islamic Relations.

Diouf, S. (2013). *Servants of Allah: African Muslims enslaved in the Americas* (15th anniversary ed.). New York, NY: New York University Press. (Original publication 1998)

Douglass, S., & Dunn, R. (2003). Interpreting Islam in American schools. *Annals of the American Academy of Political and Social Science, 588*(1), 52-72.

Dowdell, M. (2017, May 2). Access Islam: U.S. Dept. of Education lesson plans move towards outright indoctrination. *Conservative Daily Post.* Retrieved from https://conservativedailypost.com/democrat-shoots-foot-announcing-run-exposing-non-profit-scam/.

Dowley, T. (Ed.). (2013). *Introduction to the history of Christianity* (2nd ed.). Minneapolis, MN: Fortress Press.

Dromi, N. (2020, September 2). American Jewry's blind spot regarding Mizrahi Jews. *Jewish News Syndicate.* Retrieved from https://www.jns.org/writers/nave-dromi/.

Dupuy, B. (2017, October 31). Muslim children twice as likely to be bullied, new report finds. *Newsweek.* Retrieved from https://www.newsweek.com/more-half-muslim-students-are-bullied-new-report-finds-698023.

Dzilo, H. (2012). The concept of "Islamization of knowledge" and its philosophical implications. *Islam and Christian-Muslim Relations, 23*(3), 247-256.

Easat-Daas, A. (2019, February 21). How to tackle Islamophobia: The best strategies from around Europe. *The Conversation.* Retrieved from https://theconversation.com/how-to-tackle-islamophobia-the-best-strategies-from-around-europe-106092.

Ehrman, B. (2003). *Lost Christianities: The battles for Scripture and the faiths we never knew.* New York, NY: Oxford University Press.

Ekman, M. (2015). Online Islamophobia and the politics of fear: Manufacturing the green scare. *Ethnic and Racial Studies, 38*(11), 1986-2002.

Esack, F. (2002). *The Qurʾān: A short introduction.* Oxford, UK: OneWorld.

Esposito, J. (1994). Islam in the world and in America. In J. Neusner (Ed.), *World religions in America: An introduction* (pp. 243-258). Louisville, KY: Westminster/John Knox.

Esposito, J. (1998). *Islam: The straight path.* Oxford, UK: Oxford University Press.

Fakhry, M. (2004). *A history of Islamic philosophy* (3rd ed.). New York, NY: Columbia University Press.

Feiler, B. (2002). *Abraham: A journey to the heart of three faiths.* New York, NY: William Morrow.

Fisher, M. (1994). *Living religions* (2nd ed.). Englewood Cliffs, NJ: Prentice Hall.

Fluehr-Lobban, C. (1994). *Islamic society in practice.* Gainesville, FL: University of Florida Press.

Ford, P. (2001, September 19). Europe cringes at Bush "crusade" against terrorists. *The Christian Science Monitor.* Retrieved from https://www.csmonitor.com/2001/0919/p12s2-woeu.html.

Frost, D. (2008). Islamophobia: Examining causal links between the media and "race hate" from "below." *International Journal of Sociology and Social Policy, 28*(11/12), 564–578.

Gatson, K. (2019). *Imagining Judeo-Christian America: Religion, secularism, and the redefinition of democracy.* Chicago, IL: University of Chicago Press.

Gottschalk, P., & Greenberg, G. (2008). *Islamophobia: Making Muslims the enemy.* Washington, DC: Roman & Littlefield.

Green, V. (1996). *A new history of Christianity.* New York, NY: Continuum.

Green, T. (2019). *The fear of Islam: An introduction to Islamophobia in the West* (2nd ed.). Minneapolis, MN: Fortress Press.

Green, T. (2020, January 14). Revisiting Islamophobia: The mainstreaming of anti-Muslim racism in the age of Trump and Brexit. *Mayden: Politics and Society.* Retrieved from https://themaydan.com/2020/01/revisiting-islamophobia-the-mainstreaming-of-anti-muslim-racism-in-the-age-of-trump-and-brexit/.

Guillaume, A. (1956). *Islam.* Harmondsworth, UK: Penguin.

Haleen, M. (2001). *Understanding the Qur'ān: Themes and style.* London, UK: I. B. Tauris.

Hamidullah, M. (1981). *Introduction to Islam.* Chicago, IL: Kazi.

Haneef, S. (1985). *What everyone should know about Islam and Muslims.* Des Plaines, IL: Library of Islam.

Haniff, G. (2003) The Muslim community in America: A brief profile. *Journal of Muslim Minority Affairs, 23*(2), 303-311.

Hanson, H. (2015, December 8). Befuddled Pat Robertson declares Islam is not a religion, again. *HuffPost.* Retrieved from https://www.huffpost.com/entry/pat-robertson-islam-not-religion_n_56671841e4b08e945ff111a9.

Harap, L. (1987). *Creative awakening: The Jewish presence in 20ᵗʰ century American literature, 1900-1940s.* New York, NY: Greenwood.

Hatcher, W., & Martin, J. (2002). *The Bahá'í faith: The emerging global religion* (new ed.). Wilmette, IL: Bahá'í Publishing.

Hengel, M. (1983). *Between Jesus and Paul: Studies in the earliest history of Christianity.* London, UK: SCM.

Holmes, S. (2012). *The quest for the trinity: The doctrine of God in scripture, history and modernity.* Downers Grove, IL: IVP Academic.

Hussein, A. (2002). *Edward Said: Criticism and society.* London, UK: Verso.

Isik-Ercan, Z. (2015) Being Muslim and American: Turkish-American children negotiating their religious identities in school settings. *Race Ethnicity and Education, 18*(2), 225-250.

Jackson, L. (2011). Islam and Muslims in U.S. public schools since September 11, 2001. *Religious Education, 106*(2), 162-180.

Jameelah, M. (1986). *Islam in theory and practice.* Lahore: Mohammad Yusuf Khan & Sons.

Joyner, J. (2006, March 14). Pat Robertson: Muslims Satanic. Outside the Beltway. Retrieved from https://www.outsidethebeltway.com/pat_robertson_muslims_satanic/.

Kahn, M. (Ed.). (1981). *Education and society in the Muslim world.* Jeddah, Saudi Arabia: King Abdulaziz University.

Kaiser, C. (1976). The ontological trinity in the context of historical religions. *Scottish Journal of Theology, 29*(4), 301-310.

Karim, K. (2000). *Islamic peril: Media and global violence.* Montréal, Canada: Black Rose Books.

Kazi, N. (2019). *Islamophobia, race, and global politics.* Lanham, MD: Rowman & Littlefield.

Kennedy, V. (2000). *Edward Said: A critical introduction.* Cambridge, UK: Polity.

Kraemer, J. (2008). *Maimonides: The life and world of one of civilization's greatest minds.* New York, NY: Doubleday.

Küng, H. (1991). *Das Judentum: Die religiose Situation der Zeit.* Zürich, Switzerland: Piper München.

Kundnani, A. (2007). Integrationism: The politics of anti-Muslim racism. *Race and Class, 48*(4), 24-44.

Lawrence, B. (1998). *Shattering the myth: Islam beyond violence.* Princeton, NJ: Princeton University Press.

Lean, N. (2012). *The Islamophobia industry: How the right manufactures fear of Muslims.* London, UK: Pluto Press.

Lipstadt, D. (1993). *Denying the Holocaust: The growing assault on truth and memory.* New York, NY: The Free Press.

Love, E. (2017). *Islamophobia and racism in America.* New York, NY: New York University Press.

Massoumi, N. (2020, March 6). Why is Europe so Islamophobic? The attacks don't come from nowhere. *The New York Times.* Retrieved from https://www.nytimes.com/2020/03/06/opinion/europe-islamophobia-attacks.html.

McGrath, A. (2012). *Historical theology: An introduction to the history of Christian thought.* Hoboken, NJ: John Wiley.

Mawyer, M. (2017, October 29). Education or indoctrination? Islam in our schools. *Clarion Project.* Retrieved from https://clarionproject.org/education-indoctrination-islam-schools/.

Mawyer, M. (2019, October 4). Dump Access Islam petition. *Christian Action Network.* Retrieved from https://christianaction.org/petitions/dump-access-islam-petition/.

McSmith, A. (2001, September 21). Short attacks Bush for "crusade" quote. *The Telegraph.* Retrieved from https://www.telegraph.co.uk/news/worldnews/northamerica/usa/1341188/Short-attacks-Bush-for-crusade-quote.html.

Mogahed, D., & Chouhoud, Y. (2017). *American Muslim Poll 2017: Muslims at the crossroads.* Dearborn, MI: Institute for Social Policy and Understanding.

Mohamed, B. (2018, January 3). New estimates show U.S. Muslim population continues to grow. *FactTank: News in the Numbers.* Retrieved from https://www.pewresearch.org/fact-tank/2018/01/03/new-estimates-show-u-s-muslim-population-continues-to-grow/.

Momen, M. (1997). *A short introduction to the Bahá'í faith.* Oxford, UK: OneWorld.

Moore, J. (2006). Teaching about Islam in secondary schools: Curricular and pedagogical considerations. *Equity and Excellence in Education, 39*(3), 279-286.

Moten, A. (2014). Islamophobia. In E. Shahin (Ed.), *The Oxford encyclopedia of Islam and politics, Volume 1* (pp. 618-620). Oxford, UK: Oxford University Press.

Musharraf, M., & Nabeel, F. (2015). Schooling options for Muslim children living in Muslim-minority countries: A thematic review. *International Journal of Social Science and Humanities Research, 3*(4), 29-62.

National Coalition Against Censorship. (2019). Islam: Indoctrination or education? A timeline. Retrieved from https://ncac.org/resource/islam-indoctrination-or-education-a-timeline.

Nirenberg, D. (2013). *Anti-Judaism: The history of a way of thinking.* New York, NY: W. W. Norton.

Ochieng, A. (2017, March 29). Muslim schoolchildren bullied by fellow students and teachers. *Codesw!tch.* Retrieved from https://www.npr.org/sections/codeswitch/2017/03/29/515451746/muslim-schoolchildren-bullied-by-fellow-students-and-teachers.

Pagels, E. (1979). *The Gnostic Gospels.* New York, NY: Vintage.

Peek, L. (2003) Reactions and response: Muslim students' experiences on New York City campuses post 9/11. *Journal of Muslim Minority Affairs, 23*(2), 271-283.

Peters, F. (1994). *The Hajj: The Muslim pilgrimage to Mecca and the holy places.* Princeton, NJ: Princeton University Press.

Peters, F. (2006). *The children of Abraham: Judaism, Christianity, Islam* (new ed.). Princeton, NJ: Princeton University Press.

Pew Forum on Religion and Public Life. (2009, October 7). Mapping the global Muslim population. Pew Research Center. Retrieved from https://www.pewforum.org/2009/10/07/ mapping-the-global-muslim-population/.

Pew Forum on Religion and Public Life. (2012). *The global religious landscape: A report on the size and distribution of the world's major religious groups as of 2010*. Washington, DC: Pew Research Center.

Pew Research Center. (2014). *Religious landscape study*. Retrieved from https://www. pewforum.org/religious-landscape-study/#religions.

Reagan, T. (2020). Islam in the United States: Addressing Islamophobia in the public schools. *Journal of Education in Muslim Societies, 2*(1), 58-80.

Riddell, P., & Cotterell, P. (2003). *Islam in context: Past, present and future*. Grand Rapids, MI: Baker Academic.

Rosenthal, F. (1965). *Das Fortleben der Antike im Islam*. Zürich, Switzerland: Artemis Verlags-AG.

Runnymede Trust. (1997). *Islamophobia: A challenge for us all*. London, UK: Author.

Runnymede Trust. (2017). *Islamophobia: Still a challenge for us all*. London, UK: Author.

Sabry, N., & Bruna, K. (2007) Learning from the experience of Muslim students in American schools: Towards a proactive model of school-community cooperation. *Multicultural Perspectives, 9(*3), 44-50.

Sahadat, J. (1996). Divine revelation and the status of the *Qur'ān. Muslim Education Quarterly, 13*(4), 4-17.

Said, E. (1978). *Orientalism*. New York, NY: Vintage.

Said, E. (1985). Orientalism reconsidered. *Race & Class 27*(2), 1-15.

Said, E. (1993). *Culture and imperialism*. New York, NY: Alfred A. Knopf.

Said, E. (1994). *Representations of the intellectual: The 1993 Reith Lectures*. New York, NY: Vintage.

Salmivalli, C., Kaukiainen, A., & Voeten, M. (2010). Anti-bullying intervention: Implementation and outcome. *British Journal of Educational Psychology, 75*(3), 465-487.

Sarwar, G. (1989). *Islam: Beliefs and teaching*. London, UK: Muslim Educational Trust.

Sewall, G. (2008). *Islam in the classroom: What the textbooks tell us*. New York, NY: American Textbook Council.

Shah, S. (2012). Muslim schools in secular societies: Persistence or resistance! *British Journal of Religious Education, 34*(1), 51-65.

Sherman, A. (2017, April 5). Did the U.S. Education Department introduce an Islamic indoctrination program for public schools? *Politifact Florida*. Retrieved from https://www. politifact.com/florida/statements/2017/apr/05/volusia-county-republican-party/did-us-department-education-introduce-isl.

Shermer, M., & Grobman, A. (2000). *Denying history: Who says the Holocaust never happened and why do they say it?* Berkeley: University of California Press.

Shryock, A. (Ed.). (2010). *Islamophobia / Islamophilia: Beyond the politics of enemy and friend*. Bloomington: University of Indiana Press.

Smith, J. (1999). *Islam in America*. New York, NY: Columbia University Press.

Snook. I. (1970). The concept of indoctrination. *Studies in Philosophy and Education, 7*, 65-108.

Snook. I. (Ed.). (1972a). *Concepts of indoctrination: Philosophical essays*. London, UK: Routledge.

Snook, I. (1972b). *Indoctrination and education*. London, UK: Routledge & Kegan Paul.

Spencer, S. (2018, January 29). Teaching about Islam hasn't been banned. FactCheck.Org. Retrieved from https://www.factcheck.org/2018/01/teaching-islam-hasnt-banned/.

Statista. (2020). Self-described religious identification of the adult population in the United States in 2019. Retrieved from https://www.statista.com/statistics/183817/religious-identification-of-adult-population/.

Stopsky, F., & Lee, S. (1994). *Social studies in a global society*. New York, NY: Delmar.

Sullivan, K. (2011). *The anti-bullying handbook* (2nd ed.). Los Angeles, CA: Sage.

Tahseen, M. (2019, October 2). Bullying of Muslim youth. *Whyislam.org*. Retrieved from https://www.whyislam.org/americanmuslims/bullying/.

Taylor, R., & Omar, I. (Eds.). (2012). *The Judeo-Christian-Islamic heritage: Philosophical and theological perspectives*. Milwaukee, WI: Marquette University Press.

Tibi, B. (2010). Ethnicity of fear? Islamic migration and the ethnicization of Islam in Europe. *Studies in Ethnicity and Nationalism, 10*(1), 126-157.

Tolan, J., Veinstein, G., & Laurens, H. (2013). *Europe and the Islamic world: A history*. Princeton, NJ: Princeton University Press.

Ttofi, M., & Farrington, D. (2009). What works in preventing bullying: Effective elements of anti-bullying programmes. *Journal of Aggression, Conflict and Peace Research, 1*(1), 13-24.

van Nieuwenhuijze, C. (1985). *The lifestyles of Islam: Recourse to classicism, need of realism*. Leiden, The Netherlands: Brill.

Waldman, P., & Pope, H. (2001, September 21). "Crusade" reference reinforces fears war on terrorism is against Muslims. *The Wall Street Journal*. Retrieved from https://www.wsj.com/ articles/SB1001020294332922160.

Werbner, P. (2005). Islamophobia: Incitement to religious hatred -- Legislating for a new fear? *Anthropology Today, 21*(1), 5-9.

Williams, T. (2016, March 25). Franklin Graham: "Quran teaches its followers to hate." *Breitbart*. Retrieved from https://www.breitbart.com/national-security/2016/03/25/franklin-graham-quran-teaches-its-followers-to-hate/.

Worthington, F. (2012). *Bahá'í basics: A guide to the beliefs, practices, and history of the Bahá'í faith*. Wilmette, IL: Bahá'í Publishing.

Chapter 10

Politics, Ideology, and Schooling:
The Ideals of Democratic Education

> *Never doubt that a small group of thoughtful,
> committed citizens can change the world;
> indeed, it is the only thing that ever
> has.* (Margaret Mead)

> *Every educated person is a future
> enemy.* (Martin Bormann)

In his book *Critical Pedagogy*, Joe Kincheloe (2008) argued that, "education in political" (p. 8), by which he meant that *all* education is political and ideological in nature. What does it mean to suggest that "all education is political," though? Does the claim mean the same thing everywhere, or does its meaning perhaps vary from time to time and from place to place? And, if it *is* true, is this necessarily a bad thing, or might it sometimes actually be seen in positive terms? These are just a few of the questions that we have tried to raise and address in this book, which is concerned explicitly with public schooling in contemporary American society. One of the explicit assumptions in *The Art and Science of Teaching* is that there is a nexus – not just a connection, but a special kind of overlap – among such issues as politics, ideology, demography, economics, and institutional approaches to schooling – and that this nexus exists in every society. Certainly in this sense, at the very least, Kincheloe's claim makes a degree of sense.

We are very much aware that the initial reaction to a claim that all education is political is likely to be a negative one – indeed, most classroom teachers (and most citizens) in the United States would probably argue that the public schools are *supposed* to be politically neutral, and that if we must deal with controversial issues in the classroom, we should at the very least make every effort to do so in a fair and balanced way. There is a powerful sense in which this view of the politicization of schooling makes sense, and that is when "political" is used as a synonym for "partisan." We do not have, and for the most part would not wish to have, public schools that are clearly tied to particular political parties in our country. Indeed, the very idea that there should be Democratic[1] and Republican public schools would strike most Americans as every bit as absurd as having different schools for children with blond hair and children with brown hair – and this is a position that we would fully share. There are also many contemporary political issues – such as climate change and energy policy, terrorism and state violence, and gun control and the right to bear arms, about which it would be inappropriate for

---

[1] We are referring here to schools that would be affiliated in some manner with the Democratic political party. There is obviously another way in which this could be read, with a significantly different reading: as referring to schools concerned with creating a democratic society, promoting democracy, or operating in a democratic manner – concerns that we will discuss later in this chapter.

the teacher or the school to take or dictate a specific position.[2] These are matters for public discussion and debate, and the role of the school is to provide students with certain kinds of background information, the skills needed to evaluate and assess both arguments and evidence in different disciplines, and finally, the help they need to develop the ability to articulate and present cogent policy positions.

At the same time, there are issues that directly impact the education and lives of students that the school has – and each of us as educators have -- a moral obligation to address in a democratic society. We have already identified some of these issues in *The Art and Science of Teaching*. Among the matters that the public school should *not* be neutral are child abuse and the obligation for mandated reporting, a commitment to equity and the appropriate treatment of all children, the concern with ensuring that all students have the necessary knowledge and skills not simply to survive but to thrive in society as adults, and the creation of learning environments in which children are safe physically, psychologically and emotionally (including being free from bullying of different sorts). Further, in a society such as our own, it is essential that we consider the relationship between the institutions of public education and the nature of life in a democratic society – and we now turn to a discussion of that topic.

Education and Democracy

The way in which education and democracy are related is, perhaps surprisingly, not at all a simple one. There are many different systems of public education around the world, and many different kinds of democracies. To be sure, some national systems of education are more effective than others, some are better organized than others, some are more compatible with commitments to such matters as equity and social justice than others, some serve larger or smaller percentages of the eligible school age population, and so on, but virtually every country in the modern world offers some sort of state-supported or governmental schooling. There are also many different sorts of democratic political systems in countries around the world – some of which we would probably see as extremely democratic and representative of the country's population, and others less so. We would, in fact, even find countries that claim to be democratic, but which have constitutional, legal, political, and economic systems that from our perspective might seem to be profoundly *un*democratic. The result of this diversity is that the relationship between public schooling and democracy is conceptualized in very different ways. In this chapter, we would like to begin by discussing three ways in which public education and democracy are, or can be understood to be, related in our own society.

---

[2] This does not mean, of course, that it would be inappropriate for the teacher to play the role of "devil's advocate" in classroom discussions of such topics as a means of promoting student thinking and reflection.

Education in Democracy

The first, and most obvious, way in which education and democracy can be related is when we simply focus on the schooling that exists in a society that we accept as a democratic one. In other words, "education in democracy" refers to the ways in which schooling is manifested in a particular kind of society. Thus, there can be a variety of quite different examples of "education in democracy": there is the system of public education in the United States with which you are already quite familiar, but there are also schooling systems in other democratic societies: Canada, Denmark, Finland, France, German, Ireland, and the UK are places that might come to mind here, but there are also public education systems in places such as Argentina, Australia, Botswana, Brazil, Chile, Costa Rica, Ecuador, Japan, Mexico, New Zealand, Peru, South Africa, and a very long list of other countries. In all of these cases, there is a general consensus in the United States that these are what we would consider to be countries that are fundamentally democratic in nature, and thus, in each case, the education provided for young people in the society can be considered to be "education in democracy." We believe that it is important to note here that there are many other countries in which the government and the citizenry might very well consider their political system to be a democratic one, but where such claims are sometimes rejected -- for a variety of reasons -- in the United States. In most cases, these nations do indeed have constitutions, elections, political parties, and so on, so the assertion that they are democratic would be perfectly reasonable to some degree and in certain senses. Examples of countries about which there are challenges to the extent to which the country is democratic (at least from our perspective) have included Cuba, Iran, the People's Republic of China, and the Russian Federation.

Education for Democracy

Unlike "education in democracy," "education for democracy" does not actually require as either a necessary or sufficient condition that the society in which the schooling takes place be a democratic one. This may sound somewhat odd, but the goal of "education for democracy" is the production or maintenance of a democratic social order in a society. While "education in democracy" is intended to be used as a *descriptive* concept, "education for democracy" is *aspirational* in nature. In the United States, it makes sense for us to argue that public schooling involves *both* "education in democracy" (in the sense that schooling takes place in a society that we accept as a democratic one) *and* "education for democracy" (in the sense that one of the key goals of public schooling is to prepare students for life as citizens, and for their roles in meeting the obligations of a democratic society). This is the case, of course, in almost any established democratic society, but it can also be true in settings in which independence or revolution has changed the fundamental nature of the political social order in a society. In a case of the latter sort, part of the job of the public school may be to develop the knowledge, attitudes, and dispositions required for the creation of a democracy.

Democratic Education

If "democracy in education" is descriptive, and "democracy for education" is aspirational, the "democratic education" is best understood to be procedural in nature. Basically this means that in "democratic education" our focus is on the ways in which schooling actually takes place: it includes the administration of the educational institution, the teaching methods used, the curriculum, methods of assessment and evaluation, the identification of the objectives of the educational experience, and the nature of the relationships between the teacher and their students and among the students themselves. There is no single approach to "democratic education," but there are some common themes that usually characterize it. For example, a core feature of "democratic education" is the involvement of students as full and active participants in the decision-making processes about the curriculum, as well as frequently other matters relevant to the operation of the school. School meetings are often an important component of this process, and in many cases students (and sometimes parents), teachers, and staff all have equal votes in the outcome of decisions. Fairly typically, "democratic education" rejects the idea of a set or mandatory curriculum, relying instead on students identifying interests to be explored. The underlying purpose of "democratic education" is the preparation of students for life in a democratic society. Probably the best-known example of "democratic education" in practice is Summerhill, in Suffolk, England, which was founded by A. S. Neill in 1921 (see Neill, 1960). Other schools grounded in the philosophy of "democratic education" include the Sudbury Valley School in Framingham, Massachusetts, founded in 1968, and the Democratic School of Hadera in Israel, founded in 1987.

Critical Pedagogy and the Teacher

In the past few decades, both in the United States and in many other countries there has been an increasing concern among educators about what is called "critical pedagogy," and discussions about critical pedagogy both in K-12 classrooms and in teacher education programs have become ubiquitous. In spite of this ubiquity, though, it is not clear that concerns with critical pedagogy and social justice in educational settings have had the kind of effect or impact outside the classroom that most critical educators had initially hoped. There are a number of reasons for this, not the least of which is that both critical pedagogy and social justice are difficult to define. As Peter McLaren (2003) has observed, neither "constitute[s] a homogenous set of ideas" (pp. 185–186); rather, critical pedagogy and social justice are conceptualized and manifested in a wide variety of ways by many different scholars and educators who, while sharing certain common assumptions and objectives, differ in many other important ways (see Darder, Torres, & Baltodano, 2009; Denzin, 2003; Freire, 2002a, 2002b, 2002c, 2002d; Gay, 1995; Giroux, 1981, 1983, 1988a, 1988b, 1991, 1992a, 1992b, 1994, 1997a, 1997b, 2001a, 2001b, 2003a, 2003b, 2004, 2005, 2008, 2010, 2011; Giroux & McLaren, 1986; Giroux & Simon, 1988; Gruenewald, 2003; Kanpol, 1999; Kincheloe, 2008; McLaren, 1988, 1989, 2002, 2003, 2005, 2015; McLaren & Kincheloe, 2007; Morrow, 2002; Wink, 2000; Young, 1993). Part of the definitional trouble here is that although there does appear to be a relationship between critical pedagogy and social justice, this relationship is neither a necessary nor a sufficient one.

At the heart, critical pedagogy seeks "to empower the powerless and transform existing social inequalities and injustices" (McLaren, 2003, p. 186). It is, as Joan Wink (2000) suggests, "a process that enables teachers and learners to join together in asking fundamental questions about knowledge, justice, and equity in their own classroom, school, family, and community" (p. 71). Furthermore, as Ira Shor (1992) has observed,

[Critical pedagogy refers to] habits of thought, reading, writing, and speaking which go beneath surface meaning, first impressions, dominant myths, official pronouncements, traditional clichés, received wisdom, and mere opinions, to understand the deep meaning, root causes, social context, ideology, and personal consequences of any action, event, object, process, organization, experience, text, subject matter, policy, mass media, or discourse. (p. 129)

Critical pedagogy has its roots in the Frankfurt School (*Frankfurter Schule*), an intellectual movement associated with the *Institut für Sozialforschung* (Institute for Social Research) founded in Germany during the time of the Weimar Republic (1918-1933).[3] Essentially, the intellectuals, academics, activists, and political dissidents who constituted the Frankfurt School were seeking to understand the political milieu of their own age with the goal of transforming social reality. Building on the work of the Frankfurt School, from the late 1960s onwards progressive educators around the world have been developing both the theoretical and practical frameworks needed to apply such perspectives to the field of education. The foundation of much of contemporary critical pedagogy is Paolo Freire's 1968 book *The Pedagogy of the Oppressed*. Freire, a professor at the University of Recife in Brazil, sought in this and other works to develop a philosophy of adult education that would demonstrate solidarity with the poor and oppressed in their struggle to survive by engaging them in a dialogue of greater awareness and analysis. Freire (1973, 1974, 2002a, 2002b, 2002c, 2002d) explored the conservative role and functions of the school in considerable detail. He argued that dominant cultures (for instance, in contemporary American society, the Anglo-American culture) tend to overlook the wants and needs of the dominated cultures with which they co-exist. He suggested that schools, as social institutions involved in the maintenance of the status quo, generally function to impose the values of the dominant culture on dominated groups in society. Basic literacy skills, such as reading and writing, can sometimes thus become for dominated groups acts of memorization and repetition, rather than acts of reflection on meaning and critical translation into the student's own culture. As an alternative to such schooling practices and outcomes, Freire proposed that we engage in what he called *conscientização*.[4] This insight is particularly important in the context of education in the United States. In the past half-century, an extensive body of scholarly literature has emerged dealing with almost every aspect of critical pedagogy and the application of critical pedagogy in different disciplinary fields.

---

[3] There is an extensive body of historical and philosophical research on the history and work of the Frankfurt School. See, for instance, Arato and Gebhardt (1985), Bottomore (2002), Jay (1996), Wheatland (2009), Wiggershaus (1994), and Marcus and Tar (1984).

[4] *Conscientização* is the Portuguese word used by Freire. It is most often translated as "conscientization" (or "critical consciousness") in English, but this is at best a very limited and insufficient translation. Even in Portuguese, the underlying concept of *conscientização* is a complex one. Freire himself once commented, "a conscientização è um tomar posse uma ruptura da realidade," suggesting that it refers to taking a break from reality (see Freire, 2018).

A critical education can be emancipating and transforming, not only for individuals but also for the society writ large – and, in fact, for both the dominant and dominated cultures (see McLaren & Leonard, 1993). Although emancipatory and transformative educational experiences remain relatively uncommon in U.S. public schools, they have received significant support and attention, especially among those who consider themselves to be advocates of critical pedagogy (see, for instance, Giroux, 1991, 1992a, 1992b, 1994, 1997a, 1997b). What critical pedagogy offers, basically, is the recognition that schooling – *all* schooling -- is an intrinsically *political* activity, and that efforts to present it as "objective" or "neutral" are not only misguided but fundamentally misleading and even potentially dangerous. As Peter McLaren (1989) has argued,

> critical pedagogy examines schools both in their historical context and as part of the existing social and political fabric that characterizes the dominant society. Critical pedagogy poses a variety of counterlogics to the positivistic, ahistorical, and depoliticized analysis employed by both liberal and conservative critics of schooling … Fundamentally concerned with the centrality of politics and power in our understanding of how schools work, critical theorists have produced work centering on the political economy of schooling, the state and education, the representation of texts, and the construction of student subjectivity. (p. 159)

The various institutions dedicated to providing education in society can certainly be used to promote democracy and democratic values (see Gutman, 1999), but they can also be (and often are) used to perpetuate an unjust and inequitable status quo. As Henry Giroux has explained, "Central to the development of critical pedagogy is the need to explore how pedagogy functions as a cultural practice to *produce* rather than merely *transmit* knowledge within the asymmetrical relations of power that structure teacher-student relations" (Giroux, 1992a, p. 98).

All education can certainly be analyzed from a critical perspective. As Osborn (2000) has argued,

> the traditions that typically frame research and practice in … education have competed with the realities of growing cultural interdependence and a shift in pressure to assimilate in some areas of public life in the United States. As a result, the politics of cultural control have been either deemphasized or overlooked as most in the field have settled for technicist formulas or inquiry into the nature of … learning that springs from positivistic or interpretivistic paradigms. (pp. 123-124)

Such perspectives on the teaching and learning are invaluable, for they force us to ask fundamental questions not only about *what* we are attempting to accomplish, but also *why* we are trying to achieve our identified ends. It is all too easy for us to rely on platitudes about the role of education for the individual and for the society, just as it is far too easy for us to blame others for the lack of success that education sometimes experiences. However, critical pedagogy not only has implications for understanding our failures but also provides us with some powerful ideas about how education could function as a positive and constructive force in

American education. Critical pedagogy requires that we reexamine the purposes of our instruction, but even more, that we identify the hidden (and often not-so-hidden) biases about social class, race, gender, power, and equity that underlie schooling in our society. From a critical perspective, schooling is not only about teaching and learning but also about social and cultural knowledge, and, perhaps even more, about helping students to develop critical approaches to examining and understanding such knowledge.

Social Justice and Public Education

An essential feature of critical pedagogy is social justice education, and, specifically, the challenge of finding ways to introduce concerns about social justice into the classroom. As Heather Hackman (2005) has argued, "the question of how to teach effectively from a clear social justice perspective that empowers, encourages students to think critically, and *models social change* has been a consistent challenge for progressive educators" (p. 103, emphasis added), and if anything this is an understatement. The gap between theory and practice in education is one that has created on-going problems for teachers, and this has been especially true in the case of critical pedagogy and efforts to promote social justice pedagogy. Moving beyond the classroom to enact social change has been even more elusive. This does not mean that there is no way to reconcile theory and practice in education both in and beyond the classroom – but merely that it is a difficult matter that requires considerable thought. Hackman (2005) has suggested that there are five key components necessary for bridging this gap:

- Tools for content mastery.
- Tools for critical thinking.
- Tools for action and social change.
- Tools for personal reflection.
- Tools for the awareness of multicultural group dynamics. (p. 103)

Underlying all of these components is the classroom teacher's personal reflection on their identity, as well as on that of their students. Reflection on the dynamic of one's own community followed by activism is the final necessary condition for a social justice-oriented curriculum.

Social justice pedagogy is intrinsically linked to the concept of a dialectical stance. As Bill Ayers (1998) explained in the "Foreword" to *Teaching for Social Justice: A Democracy and Education Reader*,

> Teaching for social justice demands a dialectical stance: one eye firmly fixed on the students -- Who are they? What are their hopes, dreams, and aspirations? Their passions and commitments? What skills, abilities, and capacities, does each one bring to the classroom? -- and the other eye looking unblinkingly at the concentric circles of context -- historical flow, cultural surround, economic reality. Teaching for social justice is teaching that arouses students, engages them in a quest to identify obstacles to their full humanity, to their freedom, and then to drive, to move against these obstacles. And so the fundamental message

of the teacher for social justice is: You *can* change the world. (p. xvii, emphasis added)

Patricia Gross (1997) highlights a similar feature in collaborative curriculum design, which is the foundation for learner ownership of the curriculum:

> Joint curriculum design questions predetermined topics and emphases …. [S]tudents and teachers need to study course outlines to establish essentials, suggest options, and find areas of common and individual interest. Students and teachers need to be able to associate course concepts with prior frames of reference and move beyond them into new explorations. When probed, knowledge and the quest for knowledge do not stagnate; they thrive. (p. 66)

Conflict is an inherent component of critical perspectives in education, and this is true regardless of the level at which one teaches or the specific subject matter being taught. Critical pedagogy will inevitably lead to conflict, both internal and external, for both teachers and students. As Power (1998) explained,

> I learned that whenever you are in the classroom -- and especially when you a white, middle-class teacher teaching a multiracial, multilevel group -- you must think through the meanings of democracy, authority, and control. The contradictions inherent in the ideals of equality and liberty, respect for individual differences and the ethos of the group, the need for leadership and the need to share power pose as serious a challenge within a classroom as they do in the larger society. (pp. 106-107)

Paolo Freire (1973) likewise contended that:

> The radical, committed to human liberation, does not become a prisoner of a "circle of certainty" within which reality is also imprisoned. On the contrary, the more radical the person is, the more fully [they] can better transform it. This individual *is not afraid to confront*, to listen, to see the world unveiled. This person is not afraid *to meet the people or to enter into dialogue* with them. This person does not consider [themselves] the proprietor of history or of all people, or the liberator of the oppressed; but [they do] commit [themselves], within history, to fight at their side. (p. 21, emphasis added)

Confrontation and conflict are an essential and necessary part of challenging the status quo. Both teachers and learners will feel a sense of discomfort as a result of this. As Angel Lin (2004) and others have suggested, members of dominant groups will likely see themselves as under attack – their privileged status has generally gone unrecognized, and it comes as a significant shock that they owe their status, resources, and so on to factors that were largely unearned and undeserved.

It is important to note here that the commitments to critical pedagogy and social justice that are presupposed in this chapter are by no means universally accepted. Educational institutions are, by their very nature, most often profoundly conservative, and certainly not all educators are progressive in their values, beliefs, and practices. This is by no means a recent phenomenon or challenge, though – resistance to change (and especially to change related to issues of social justice) has been common throughout our educational history. Such resistance has been especially fierce in debates about both social justice education and critical pedagogy, and can only be expected to remain so. Nevertheless, we believe that the evidence is simply overwhelming that much of traditional public education in the United States has been, and continues to be, grounded in and supportive of the oppression of many groups of students. Lee Anne Bell (2016) has suggested that this oppression consists of a number of overlapping strands, including the fact that oppression is:

- Pervasive.
- Cumulative.
- Durable and mutating.
- Grounded in group-based categories.
- Restrictive.
- Intersecting.
- Internalized.
- Normalizing.
- Hierarchical. (pp. 5-16)

The critiques of critical pedagogy and social justice education (as well as similar and related critiques of multicultural and anti-racist education) typically argue that these are political and ideological efforts, which ought not be reflected or manifested in public education. What this argument overlooks, though, is that, as we have already argued, *all* education is *profoundly* political and ideological in nature. The question is not *whether* education is political, but rather, what its political orientation should be. Joe Kincheloe (2008) has argued that, "whether one is teaching in Bangladesh or Bensonhurst, Senegal or Shreveport, East Timor or West New York, education is a political activity" (p. 8). Further, as Sandy Grande (2007) has argued about critical pedagogy,

> Critical pedagogy is first and foremost an approach to schooling (i.e., teaching, policy making, curriculum production) that emphasizes the political nature of education. As such, critical pedagogy aims to understand, reveal, and disrupt the mechanisms of oppression imposed by the established order, suturing the processes and aims of education to emancipatory goals. (p. 317)

The cognizance of the political and ideological nature of education is necessary to understand the fundamental nature and institutions in which children are educated. To appreciate schools and schooling – including the teaching and learning processes – we need to grasp the complex nexus of the social, cultural, economic, political, and historical contexts within and beyond the classroom in which they exist. These are the highest ideals to which critical pedagogy and social justice-oriented education call us.

Questions for Reflection and Discussion

1. In the beginning of this chapter, the authors draw a distinction between "political" matters and "partisan" matters. Can you explain this distinction in your own words? To what extent can you identify examples of each of these concepts in public education in the United States?

2. This chapter begins with a quote from Martin Bormann, who said that, "Every educated person is a future enemy." What did he mean by this? What are the implications of this quotation for education in a democratic society?

3. Do you agree or disagree with the authors when they argue that while, in general, public school educators should not be partisan in their professional activities, there are some *moral* obligations that we share as professions? What reasons can you offer for your position?

4. Consider the distinctions among "education in democracy," "education for democracy," and "democratic education." Which of these do you believe are appropriate for the public schools to engage in? Which (if any) are not? Why?

5. How would you explain the concept of "critical pedagogy" in your own words? What do you believe the implications of this concept are for classroom practice?

References

Arato, A., & Gebhardt, E. (Eds.). (1985). *The essential Frankfurt School reader.* New York, NY: Continuum.

Ayers, W. (1998). Popular education: Teaching for social justice. In W. Ayers, J. Hunt, & T. Quinn (Eds.), *Teaching for social justice: A democracy and education reader* (pp. xvii-xxv). New York, NY: Teachers College Press.

Bell, L. (2016). Theoretical foundations social justice education. In M. Adams & L. Bell, with D. Goodman & K. Joshi (Eds.), *Teaching for diversity and social justice* (3rd ed.) (pp. 3-26). New York, NY: Routledge.

Bottomore, T. (2002). *The Frankfurt School and its critics.* London, UK: Routledge.

Darder, A., Torres, R., & Baltodano, M. (2009). *The critical pedagogy reader.* New York, NY: Routledge/Falmer.

Denzin, N. (2003). *Performance ethnography: Critical pedagogy and the politics of culture.* Thousand Oaks, CA: Sage.

Freire, P. (1973). *Education for critical consciousness.* New York, NY: Seabury.

Freire, P. (1974). *Pedagogy of the oppressed.* New York, NY: Seabury. (Original work published 1968)

Freire, P. (2002a). *Cartas a quien pretende enseñar.* Buenos Aires, Argentina: Siglo XXI Editores Argentina S.A.

Freire, P. (2002b). *Pedagogía de la autonomía.* Buenos Aires, Argentina: Siglo XXI Editores Argentina S.A.

Freire, P. (2002c). *Pedagogía de la esperanza: Un reencuentro con la Pedagogía del oprimido.* Buenos Aires, Argentina: Siglo XXI Editores Argentina S.A.

Freire, P. (2002d). *Pedagogía del oprimido.* Buenos Aires, Argentina: Siglo XXI Editores Argentina S.A. (Original work published 1968)

Freire, P. (2018). *Conscientização.* São Paulo, Brazil: Cortez Editora.

Gay, G. (1995). Mirror images on common issues: Parallels between multicultural education and critical pedagogy. In C. Sleeter & P. McLaren (Eds.), *Multicultural education, critical pedagogy, and the politics of difference* (pp. 155-189). Albany: State University of New York Press.

Giroux, H. (1981). *Ideology, culture, and the process of schooling.* Philadelphia, PA: Temple University Press.

Giroux, H. (1983). *Theory and resistance in education.* London, UK: Heineman.

Giroux, H. (1988a). *Escola crítica e política cultural* (2nd ed.). São Paulo, Brazil: Cortez Editora.

Giroux, H. (1988b). *Schooling and the struggle for public life.* Minneapolis: University of Minnesota Press.

Giroux, H. (Ed.) (1991). *Postmodernism, feminism, and cultural politics: Redrawing educational boundaries.* Albany: State University of New York Press.

Giroux, H. (1992a). *Border crossings: Cultural workers and the politics of education.* New York, NY: Routledge.

Giroux, H. (1992b). Educational leadership and the crisis of democratic government. *Educational Researcher, 21*(4), 4-11.

Giroux, H. (1994). Doing cultural studies: Youth and the challenge of pedagogy. *Harvard Educational Review, 64*(3), 278-308.

Giroux, H. (1997a). *Pedagogy and the politics of hope: Theory, culture and schooling.* Boulder, CO: Westview Press.

Giroux, H. (1997b). Rewriting the discourse of racial identity: Toward a pedagogy and politics of whiteness. *Harvard Educational Review, 67*(2), 285-320.

Giroux, H. (2001a). *Public spaces, private lives: Beyond the culture of cynicism.* Lanham, MD: Rowman & Littlefield.

Giroux, H. (2001b). *Stealing innocence: Corporate culture's war on children.* New York, NY: Palgrave.

Giroux, H. (2003a). *Democracy beyond the culture of fear.* New York, NY: Palgrave Macmillan.

Giroux, H. (2003b). *La escuela y la lucha por la ciudadanía.* Buenos Aires, Argentina: Siglo XXI Editores Argentina S.A.

Giroux, H. (2004). *Terror of neoliberalism: Authoritarianism and the eclipse of democracy.* New York, NY: Routledge.

Giroux, H. (2005). *Estudios culturales, pedagogía crítica y democracia radical.* Madrid, Spain: Editorial Popular.

Giroux, H. (2008). *La universidad secuestrada: El reto de confrontar a la alianza military-académica.* Caracas, Venezuela: Centro Internacional Miranda.

Giroux, H. (2010). Paulo Freire and the crisis of the political. *Power and Education, 2*(3), 335-340.

Giroux, H. (2011). *On critical pedagogy.* New York, NY: Continuum.

Giroux, H., & McLaren, P. (1986). Teacher education and the politics of engagement: The case for democratic schooling. *Harvard Education Review, 56*(3), 213-227.

Giroux, H., & Simon, R. (1988). Schooling, popular culture, and a pedagogy of possibility. *Journal of Education, 170*(1), 9-26.

Grande, S. (2007). Red Lake Woebegone: Pedagogy, decolonization, and the critical project. In P. McLaren & J. Kincheloe (Eds.), *Critical pedagogy: Where are we now?* (pp. 315-336). New York, NY: Peter Lang.

Gross, P. (1997). *Joint curriculum design: Facilitating learner ownership and active participation in secondary classrooms.* New York, NY: Routledge.

Gruenewald, D. (2003). The best of both worlds: A critical pedagogy of place. *Educational Researcher, 32*(4), 3–12.

Gutman, A. (1999). *Democratic education* (rev. ed.). Princeton, NJ: Princeton University Press.

Hackman, H. (2005). Five essential components for social justice education. *Equity and Excellence in Education, 38*(2), 103-109.

Jay, M. (1996). *The dialectical imagination: A history of the Frankfurt School and the Institute of Social Research, 1923-1950.* Berkeley: University of California Press.

Kanpol, B. (1999). *Critical pedagogy: An introduction* (2nd edition). Westport, CT: Bergin & Garvey.

Kincheloe, J. (2008). *Critical pedagogy* (2nd edition). New York, NY: Peter Lang.

Lin, A. (2004). Introducing a critical pedagogical curriculum: A feminist, reflexive account. In B. Norton & K. Toohey (Eds.), *Critical pedagogies and language learning* (pp. 271-290). Cambridge, UK: Cambridge University Press.

Marcus, J., & Tar, Z. (Eds.). (1984). *Foundations of the Frankfurt School of Social Research.* New Brunswick, NJ: Transaction.

McLaren, P. (1988). Culture or canon? Critical pedagogy and the politics of literacy. *Harvard Educational Review, 58*(2), 213-235.

McLaren, P. (1989). *Life in schools: An introduction to critical pedagogy in the foundations of education.* New York, NY: Longman.

McLaren, P. (2002). Critical pedagogy: A look at the major concepts. In A. Darder, M. Baltodano, & R. Torres (Eds.), *The critical pedagogy reader* (pp. 69-96). New York, NY: Routledge.

McLaren, P. (2003). *Life in schools: An introduction to critical pedagogy in the foundations of education* (4th ed.). Boston, MA: Allyn & Bacon.

McLaren, P. (2005). *Capitalists and conquerors: A critical pedagogy against empire.* Lanham, MD: Rowman & Littlefield.

McLaren, P. (2015). *Life in schools: An introduction to critical pedagogy in the foundations of education* (6th ed.). New York, NY: Routledge.

McLaren, P., & Kincheloe, J. (Eds.). (2007). *Critical pedagogy: Where are we now?* New York, NY: Peter Lang.

McLaren, P., & Leonard, P. (Eds.). (1993). *Paulo Freire: A critical encounter.* New York, NY: Routledge.

Morrow, R. (2002). *Reading Freire and Habermas: Critical pedagogy and transformative social change.* New York, NY: Teachers College Press.

Neill, A. S. (1960). *Summerhill: A radical approach to child rearing.* New York, NY: Hart.

Osborn, T. A. (2000). *Critical reflection and the foreign language classroom.* Westport, CT: Bergin & Garvey.

Power, K. (1998). No little I's and no little you's: Language and equality in an adult literacy community. In W. Ayers, J. Hunt, & T. Quinn (Eds.), *Teaching for social justice: A democracy and education reader* (pp. 102-123). New York, NY: Teachers College Press.

Shor, I. (1992). *Empowering education: Critical teaching for social change.* Chicago, IL: University of Chicago Press.

Wheatland, T. (2009). *The Frankfurt School in exile.* Minneapolis: University of Minnesota Press.

Wiggershaus, R. (1994). *The Frankfurt School: Its history, theories, and political significance.* Cambridge, MA: MIT Press.

Wink, J. (2000). *Critical pedagogy: Notes from the real world* (2nd ed.). New York, NY: Longman.

Young, R. (1993). *Teoría crítica de la educación y discurso en la aula.* Barcelona, Spain: Ediciones Paidós, in collaboration with the Centro de Publicaciones del Ministerio de Educación y Ciencia.

Lightning Source UK Ltd.
Milton Keynes UK
UKHW051150021121
393246UK00004B/44